Tales out of School

Tales out of School

HADLEIGH NATIONAL SCHOOL

Chris Worpole

Illustrated by David Hurrell

The Hadleigh&Thundersley
COMMUNITY ARCHIVE

First published in 2014 by
Hadleigh & Thundersley Community Archive
The Old Fire Station
Hadleigh Essex
SS7 2PA

E-mail: hadleighhistory@gmail.com
www.hadleighhistory.org.uk

ISBN 978-0-9575958-0-4
ISBN 978-0-9575958-2-8 (ebook)

British Library Cataloguing in Publication Data
A catalogue record for this book is available from the British Library

Book Design: Ian Hughes, www.mousematdesign.com

Printed in Great Britain by 4edge Limited, Essex

This book is dedicated to all the children

who attended Hadleigh National School

from 1855 to 1924.

Contents

Acknowledgements

I WOULD LIKE TO THANK all the people who have given their time, expertise, knowledge and support.

In particular, I would like to thank David Hurrell who first suggested that I should write a book about Hadleigh's history and offered to illustrate the book. This is not the original book we decided to produce, which was about Hadleigh High Street in Victorian times, but a book on Victorian Hadleigh is still an ongoing project. I must thank David Hurrell, Nick Turner and Graham Cook for their expertise, encouragement and support. Graham, in particular, has worked tirelessly and with incredible patience during the publishing process. I would also like to thank Malcolm Brown who offered invaluable advice whilst reading the final proofs. I would also like to thank other members of the Hadleigh and Thundersley Community Archive editorial team who gave me advice, access to their research and photographs, and proof read the manuscript. In particular, I must thank Bob Delderfield, Sandra Harvey and Val Jackson.

The staff at the Essex Record Office have given me invaluable help during the months I spent researching the book.

Ian Hawks (the grandson of Alfred Hawks) and his daughter Susan, have provided me with additional photographs and resources, and were always willing to answer my questions. Regrettably, Ian never saw the completed book as he died in 2013.

I would also like to thank Kay Moore, the Search Officer for Hadleigh Parish, for researching the children's deaths in 1900 in the burial register for St. James the Less.

Finally, I would like to thank my family and friends for their support and encouragement. In particular, to Steve, Tim and David Palmer for their technical advice on word processing and the creation of charts. Above all, I would like to thank my sister, Gill Palmer, for her generous sharing of her time in proof reading several versions of the manuscript and for compiling the first draft of the index whilst I was ill.

Illustration Acknowledgements

I WOULD LIKE TO THANK the following for permission to use photographs and illustrative material: Bob Delderfield for nos. 6, 28; reproduced by courtesy of the Essex Record Office nos. 1–2, 5, 22–24; Sandra Harvey for nos. 16, 18, 26; Ian Hawks for nos. 17, 27; David Hurrell for the original drawings; reproduced by the kind permission of the Rector and Fellows of Lincoln College, Oxford no. 3; Wikipedia for no. 4; photographs and charts nos. 7–15,19–21, 25 are the author's own.

I have made every reasonable effort to contact the copyright holders of material reproduced in this book. If any unintentional infringement of copyright has occurred, sincere apologies are offered.

List of Illustrations

Preface

As a RETIRED TEACHER I have found the history of this village school fascinating. I particularly enjoyed finding out about the children who attended the school between 1863 and 1901. At times they made me laugh and cry but, ultimately, they demonstrated that children never change.

As I hope the log book sections of this book will be used by primary school children and education students, I have not written the log book entries chronologically. Instead, I have adopted a thematic approach with sections introducing Hadleigh, the school, the log book and the teaching staff; the curriculum, government inspections and discipline; attendance; and a final section on church attendance, treats, visitors, the building and the night school. I intend to write a schools' pack to accompany the log book sections, which may be used by both teachers and children. In the final chapter I have told the history of the school after 1901 until its closure in 1924.

Chris Worpole
2014

Introduction

THIS IS THE SECOND publishing venture of the Hadleigh & Thundersley Community Archive. We run one of six on-line archives formed early in 2010 as a joint initiative of Debbie Peers of the Essex Record Office and Sue Hampson of Essex Libraries, with the financial support of the Heritage Lottery Fund.

The development of the Hadleigh & Thundersley Community Archive has included public presentations at Hadleigh Library, drop-in sessions, participation in local events, hosting Hadleigh History Fair and developing a presence at Hadleigh Old Fire Station – Hadleigh's new community hub. We have also helped build a mobile phone web app, see: www.teamhadleigh.org.uk.

We are delighted to say that local residents have shown great support for our archive, both by coming to organised events and contributing their personal histories to our website, as evidenced at: www.hadleighhistory.org.uk.

Perhaps stimulated by the apparently casual and relentless destruction of old properties and historic assets in our corner of south-east Essex, residents are realising the importance of documenting Hadleigh and Thundersley's constantly changing landscape. With their help, we are making previously unseen historic documents, pictures and postcards, accessible to present and future generations by publishing them on our website.

The Editorial Board
Hadleigh & Thundersley Community Archive

Hadleigh in 1863

WHITE'S DIRECTORY FOR 1863 provides a good description of Hadleigh in 1863:

"Hadleigh is a small village and parish, 1^1/$_2$ mile N.E. of Benfleet Station, and 6^1/$_2$ miles W.S.W of Rochford, containing 442 souls and 2679 acres of land, extending southward to the marshes on the north side of Hadleigh Bay [sic], opposite Canvey Island, in the estuary of the Thames. The village is 1^1/$_2$ mile from the shore, and the surface of the parish rises in bold swells from the marshes, which are overlooked by the venerable ruins of HADLEIGH CASTLE, standing on the brow of a steep hill, commanding a fine prospect over the estuary into Kent. This fortress was built in the reign of Henry III by Hubert de Burgh, Earl of Kent. . . . Though now almost a mass of ruin, overrun with shrubs and brushwood, it exhibits strong traces of ancient grandeur. . . . As Hadleigh is not named in Domesday book, it is supposed to have been included in the extensive park belonging to the Honor of Rayleigh, in which there is still a large tract of thickly covered woodland, on the north side of the

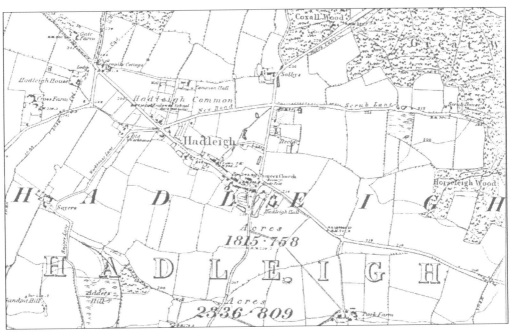

1. The 1st Edition Ordnance Survey Map of 1867

parish. . . . Lady Olivia Bernard Sparrow is now lady of the manor; but part of the soil belongs to the Wood, Woodward [sic], Tyrrell, and other families. The village is pleasantly situated on the London and Southend road, and has a fair for pleasure and pedlary on the 24th of June. It anciently held a market on Wednesday. The Church (St. James) is an ancient structure, distinguished by the peculiarity of the east end of the chancel, which is semi-circular, in the form of a Roman basilica, and separated from the nave by a very heavy arch. It dates from the time of King Stephen, and has recently been thoroughly restored and decorated with several stained glass windows. . . . The Rector and Fellows of Lincoln College, Oxford, are the patrons, and the Rev. Thos. E. Espin, B.D., is the incumbent, and has a new rectory house. In 1820, Mrs. Martha Lovibond gave for the education and clothing of poor children of this parish, £750, now vested in £781. 5s. 3d. three per cent. Consols, in the names of the Rector and the Archdeacon. The dividends are now applied in aid of the National School, built in 1855, and part of the income is given in religious books and clothing. The POST OFFICE is at Miss Benton's. Letters from Rochford, via Ingatestone."

Hadleigh National School

Prior to the National School building opening at Hadleigh in 1855, the education of the village children was mainly limited to the Sunday School set up at the parish church in 1820. White's Directory for 1848 records how this Sunday School was financed: *"In 1820, Mrs. Martha Lovibond gave, for the education and clothing of poor children of this parish £750."* [Worth £31,440 in today's money.] Martha Lovibond was the daughter of Sir Elijah Impey, Chief Justice of Bengal 1774-89. She married George Lovibond Esq. in 1793, and they lived at Hadleigh House.

As early as 1836 it had been suggested that the income from Mrs. Lovibond's trust fund could be used to establish a National School in the village. In October 1811 the National Society for Promoting the Education of the Poor in the Principles of the Established Church was founded, its mission being to ensure that *"the National Religion should be made the foundation of National Education"*. In a letter written in February 1839, Lord John Russell explained that the National Society: *"contend that the schoolmaster should be invariably a churchman; that the Church Catechism should be taught in the school to all the scholars; that all should be required to attend Church on Sundays and that the schools should be in every case under the superintendence of the clergymen of the parish."*

The land for the school was provided by the lady of the manor, Lady Olivia

2. South elevation from architect's plans, 1855

3. Rev. Thomas Espinell Espin   4. George Edmund Street

Sparrow. In December 1853 Lady Olivia Sparrow was awarded former common land when it was enclosed. She donated a plot of former common land on the village's main street for the new school, the site of the present Sandcastles Nursery.

The architect chosen to build the new school building was George Edmund Street, who was later considered by many to be one of the greatest Gothic architects in Europe. (Street's most famous building was to be the Royal Courts of Justice in London.) Between 1844 and 1849 he had been an assistant for the renowned architect George Gilbert Scott. In 1852 he moved to Oxford and this is where the Rev. Espin had probably known of him, as he was also living and working at Oxford. Due to this connection, Hadleigh in 1855 was to have the services of this distinguished architect to build the school, the rectory and restore St. James the Less Church.

Copies of Street's plans, sections and elevations can still be viewed at the Essex Record Office. The interior of the building contained one large school room measuring 39 feet and 10 inches by 16 feet and 6 inches (approximately 12m by 5m). School buildings were designed in this way as the one and only certificated teacher had to be able to observe the entire school.

The school, including fittings, equipment and furniture, cost £450 to build, financed in part by the Lovibond endowment and by local subscriptions. In a letter of September 1855 to Rev. Muirhead Mitchell, Her Majesty's Inspector of Schools, the Rev. Espin had written of the problems in financing the new school: *"Our funds are quite exhausted on the building and sundries, and we must be content with as few fittings as we can possibly get on with. The difficulty of getting money for such purposes in this place, where the property is very much divided amongst small owners, and the interest in the work none, is very great."* Hadleigh National School would have depended for its funds on the fees of the pupils, local donations and government grants.

Government grants had started in a small way in 1833 but, following the recommendation of the Royal Commission on Popular Education in 1861 (known as

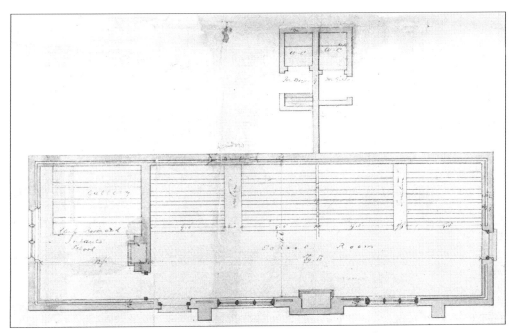

5. Architect's plans of the interior of the school, 1855

the Newcastle Report), the Revised Code of 1862 made payments of annual grants dependent on a school's success in an annual examination in the three Rs, plus a satisfactory level of average attendance. This new system became known as 'payment by results' and it lasted until 1897. It is no wonder that the school log book records the school masters William Kingswood, Henry Yeaxlee and Alfred Hawks giving the children trial examinations before the visits by Her Majesty's Inspector of Schools. In 1878 the school had a deduction of ten per cent in its grant following the inspector's criticism of the keeping of the registers.

The first mistress at the school was Anne Houseley, who was in charge of the school from 1855 until 1861. Born in 1828 at Edensor in Derbyshire, she was working as a school mistress at Neswick Hall in Yorkshire at the time of the 1851 census. Early in 1861 Anne Houseley resigned from her post at Hadleigh, four years later marrying John William Crake, a grammar school teacher. Anne and John had four children, but John died in 1872. In 1878 Anne married the Rev. John Godson, who was still working as a curate. Rev. Godson had been the curate at Hadleigh between 1860 and 1864, and had regularly taught at the National School there. Anne died in 1918, at the age of 90. She had been living at Bromley College in Kent, a charitable institution for the widows of clergymen.

Between 1870 and 1901, state intervention in education increased and this had an effect on Hadleigh National School. There were increasing gaps in the provision of elementary education by the voluntary sector and therefore, in 1870, the Liberal MP W. E. Forster succeeded in persuading Parliament to pass the Elementary

Education Act, which aimed to provide a school place for every child in the country. The voluntary church schools, such as Hadleigh National School, were allowed to exist alongside the new state-managed elementary schools.

The 1870 Act did not introduce either free or compulsory attendance, so Acts of Parliament were passed to remedy this. In 1876 Sandon's Act penalised parents who kept their children away from school, and the first mention of a School Attendance Officer in the Hadleigh school log book was in February 1878. In 1880 Mundella's Act made education compulsory for children between the ages of five and ten, and the parents of Hadleigh were now liable for prosecution at the Petty Sessions at Rochford if they did not send their children to school. On 3 November 1882 Alfred Hawks wrote: *"Mr. Millar* [sic] *was Summoned for neglecting to send his daughter Edith to School and fined 5/-. This has had a good effect on the others."* It was not until 1891 that elementary education was made free, so until then the parents had to pay 1d or 2d per child each week. The school-leaving age was raised to eleven in 1893, and in 1899 to twelve.

A major effect on the school in 1891 was the opening of the Salvation Army Farm Colony, and its consequences for the population of the village. William Booth, the founder of the Salvation Army, had a vision of a radical social experiment. Part of this vision was a farm colony where the poor and destitute of London could be trained in various forms of work, principally farm work and brick making. In March 1891 he had purchased three farms to the south of the village comprising 900 acres. At the end of 1891 there were nearly 200 people living on the colony. The Salvation Army had acquired more land by the end of 1894, with the colonists numbering 435. This led to a corresponding increase in the school population, which had already been causing problems of overcrowding in the National School.

6. Hadleigh National School, c.1910

The school was originally built for 100 children but, in July 1883, there were 122 children on the admissions register. In the inspection report of 1884 the school managers had been warned: *"The* [infants] *room has been crowded during the past year, and, unless the accommodation for Infants is improved, I shall be compelled next year to recommend a reduction of Grant. The enlargement of the room is much to be desired."* But it was to be another eleven years before a new infants room was built on the front of the building, at a cost of £222 12s 0d. The Salvation Army contributed £75 and there were also fundraising events. On 5 July 1895 Alfred Hawks recorded in the log book: *"The School was closed on Wednesday on the event of a Bazaar in aid of the School Building Fund."*

The building of the extension and other alterations were completed during the four weeks of the Summer Vacation in 1895. This increased the capacity of the school to 155 children. On 27 September 1895 the school master, Alfred Hawks, wrote: *"The new room for Infants is now in use and the old Inf.-room used as a Class room for Older Scholars. The alterations are of incalculable value & have given Every Satisfaction."*

The National School Log Book

UNDER THE REVISED CODE of 1862, the master or mistress of a school receiving government grants was obliged by law to keep a log book. Until 1871 this was a daily record of events that occurred, with the contents of these log books varying according to the school. They could include inspectors' visits, weather, school

7. Hadleigh National School log book

closures, sickness and bad behaviour. A major preoccupation of elementary school masters at this time was pupil attendance. In fact, the first comment written in the Hadleigh National School log book, by Miss Cecilia Miller, on 1 January 1863, was: *"Attendance not very good."* The section on attendance in this book is therefore the largest, with chapters recording causes of poor attendance, including sickness, severe weather and working on the local farms.

The Hadleigh National School log book provides very little information about the teaching staff. The log book covers the period 1863 until 1909, when the school was under the direction of one mistress and three masters – Miss Cecilia Miller, Mr. William Batchelor Kingswood, Mr. Henry Yeaxlee and Mr. Alfred Hawks. Although they were supposed to refrain from making personal comments, the early entries often read like a personal diary. One can sense the frustration of Miss Miller in early May 1863 when she wrote: *"Children very tiresome, felt the want of an Assistant in the School."* The next day she gave a girl *"a good caning"* for impudence. That week there was an average of 75.5 children in the school and Miss Miller would have had to rely on monitors and pupil teachers to assist her with the teaching. It is no wonder that there is evidence of her frustration in her log book entries. My favourite entry in the log book was written by Miss Miller on 14 April 1863: *"Mary A. Smith pushed a pencil up her nose, which with some little difficulty was removed."*

This log book is a vital source of information on both education and social conditions in Hadleigh for over forty years. In 1863 Hadleigh was a small farming village with a population of about 440. At the time of the census in 1861 about forty-four per cent of the village workers were agricultural labourers. Wherever possible, when a child's name is written in the log book, I have attempted to find out more about them, including where they lived. The village street referred to in my notes

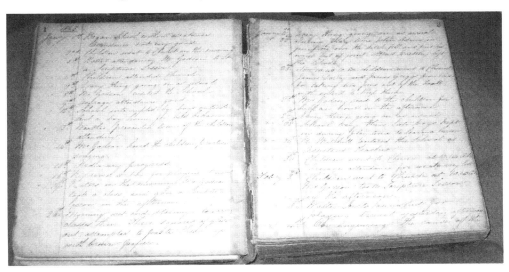

8. The first pages of the log book

was the main street which ran along what is now the High Street, and the London Road between the Salvation Army Temple and Victoria House Corner. The section of the London Road between Morrisons supermarket and St. James the Less was not built until 1924. It has not always been possible to discover more about these children, as most of them came from labouring families, and agricultural labourers often moved between villages looking for work. The children of the local farmers or the rectors would have been educated at home or at private schools.

Pasted into the front of Hadleigh National School's log book is an extract from the Revised Code of 1862:

> *"The principal Teacher must daily make in the Log Book the briefest entry which will suffice to specify either ordinary progress; or whatever other fact concerning the School or its Teacher, such as the dates of withdrawals, commencements of duty, cautions, illness &c., may require to be referred to at a future time, or otherwise deserve to be recorded.*
>
> *"No reflections or opinions of a general character are to be entered in the Log Book.*
>
> *"No entry once made in the Log Book may be removed or altered otherwise than by a subsequent entry.*
>
> *"The Inspector will call for the Log Book at his annual visit, and will report whether it appears to have been properly kept throughout the year."*

When Henry Yeaxlee became the schoolmaster in January 1865 he would often write the comment '*Usual routine*' as his log book entry. But there were some days when unusual things happened in the school. Imagine the excitement of the children when their usually monotonous routine was interrupted! Here are some log book entries which are not included elsewhere:

12 Jan 1863   *School interrupted by boys outside.*
9 Feb 1863   *A dog belonging to Sarah Harvey followed her to School and proved a great nuisance by running in and out all afternoon.*
19 Feb 1863   *George Sewell and Thomas Jermyn came in the School and blacked the faces of several children before 2 o'clock. Sent for Mr. Tyrrell to put a stop to their mischievous tricks.* [George Sewell and Thomas Jermyn were teenage boys employed as agricultural labourers. Mr. Tyrrell, a Hadleigh farmer, was a manager of the National School.]

27 Feb 1863	*During dinner hour Eliza Dolby tumbled into the ditch – put her boots too near the fire and burnt them.*
31 Mar 1863	*William Harvey cried and disturbed the School because he wanted to sit with his sister.*
8 Feb 1864	*Some young fellows shooting across the road shot against the school as the children were coming in.*
7 Apr 1864	*Keys of the Log Book lost at this date and not being found on 9th May lock was picked.*
18 Nov 1869	*Wasted some time in expelling two strange boys from the play-ground.*

9. Examples of daily entries, 1863

On 10 March 1871, Henry Yeaxlee noted in the log book: *"I received the Regulations for 1871."* Under these new regulations, issued as a result of the 1870 Elementary Education Act, the master only had to write an entry in the log book once a week. From this time, the tone and content of the log book entries changed.

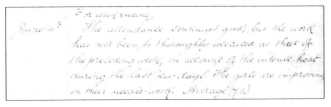

10. Example of weekly entry, 1875

Author's Note

This book is mainly a transcription of the log book entries from 1863 to 1901, with my additional background notes. All the log book entries are written in italics and are reproduced exactly as they were written at the time. This includes spelling, abbreviations, punctuation (or lack of it) and the use of capital letters in the middle of sentences. At times the log book entries do not appear to make sense.

The School Masters and Mistresses

URING THE PERIOD COVERED by the National School log book there was one school
mistress and three school masters – Cecilia Miller, William Batchelor
Kingswood, Henry Yeaxlee and Alfred Hawks. A school house was provided rent-
free on the corner of the village street and Commonhall Lane. Alfred Hawks bought
his own house in Chapel Lane in the 1890s and the school house was rented out by
the school managers. After Alfred Hawks' retirement in 1918, the house was sold.

Miss Cecilia Miller

Miss Cecilia Miller was born at Ramsgate in Kent in about 1839, the daughter of
Charles and Mary Miller. When Cecilia's older sister Mary was baptised on 16
February 1831 Charles Miller was employed as a mason although, on Cecilia's
marriage certificate, he is described as an architect.

There are no records to show whether Cecilia Miller had attended a training
college and was a certificated teacher. She became the mistress of Hadleigh school
in 1861, at about the age of twenty-two, and left in June 1863. Miss Miller was the
first teacher to write in the log book in January 1863.

11. The master's school house (on far right), c.1919

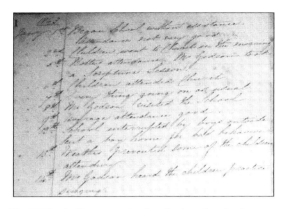

12. Cecilia Miller's first entries in the log book, January 1863

The next reference to her is in the 1871 Census for Deal in Kent. She was living at Prospect Place, the home of her half brother William Malton, with her occupation recorded as retired schoolmistress. Mary Miller, her older sister, was also living in the house. Cecilia Miller was still living at Deal ten years later, with her half-brother William and her sister Mary, but they had now moved to 187 Beach Street, with a view of the sea.

It looked as though Cecilia Miller would remain a spinster but, on 14 November 1882, at the age of forty-three, she married Henry Lamplough, a 69-year-old widower, at St. Andrew Holborn Church, which has the distinction of being Christopher Wren's largest parish church. In the marriage register Cecilia's address was recorded as 12 South Lambeth Road, Lambeth, with the bridegroom living and working as a chemist at 113 Holborn, Saffron Hill. Henry Lamplough had also been living at Deal at the time of the 1881 Census, at 1 Sandown Terrace, Beach Street, so this is probably where Cecilia and Henry met. At the time of the census, Henry's wife Sarah was still alive, but she died soon after, leaving Henry a widower with three surviving adult children.

Henry Lamplough was born in 1813 at Bridlington in Yorkshire, the son of Benjamin and Barbara Lamplough. On Henry's marriage certificate, his father's occupation was recorded as gentleman, but in census returns he was also recorded as a ship owner at Bridlington Quay. Henry's claim to fame was as the inventor of *Lamplough's Effervescing Pyretic Saline*, a patent medicine. With no Victorian equivalent of the Advertising Standards Authority, he was able to claim in an advertisement of February 1873 in the *Chelmsford Chronicle*: *"REMARKABLE, VERY REMARKABLE, Indeed are the effects of Lamplough's Pyretic Saline in Preventing and Curing Bowel Complaints, Smallpox, Fevers, and Skin Diseases."*

Henry Lamplough appears from these surviving records to be a respectable pharmaceutical chemist but, when one delves further into his history, it appears this was not totally the case. On 17 April 1845, at the Court of Excise, Henry had been convicted of selling spirits of wine without licence and fined £2. Seven years later, on 23 April 1852 the *London Gazette* reported that Henry, now of Hamilton Place, had been declared a bankrupt. By the time of the 1891 Census Henry and Cecilia were living at Blaengwrach, a small Welsh village. On 10 November 1891 Henry again appeared in the London Bankruptcy Court, and both Henry and Cecilia now appeared at Neath Bankruptcy Court regarding a business they owned in Wales. Henry and Cecilia moved to Hertfordshire, where Henry died in 1894. Seven years later, in April 1901, Cecilia and her sister were living at Rosslyn House in Richmond Road at Barnet Vale. Cecilia died from cancer and congestion of the lungs in Hadley Road at Barnet Vale, on 5 July 1904, at the age of sixty-four.

William Batchelor Kingswood

The school's first master, William Batchelor Kingswood, commenced his duties on 7 September 1863, at the age of twenty-eight.

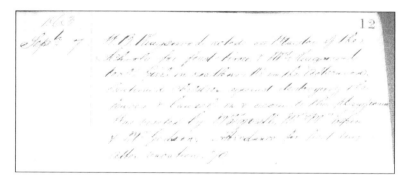

13. William Kingswood's first entry in the log book, 7 September 1863

William was born in 1834, the son of William and Charity Kingswood, at Buxted in Sussex where his father worked as a bricklayer. On 1 January 1857, at the church of St. Mary Magdalene at Hastings in Sussex, he married Miss Sarah Ann Jones from Cranbrook in Kent. Sarah Kingswood, like all the wives of the three Hadleigh masters in the 19th century, would occasionally assist her husband in the school.

The masters of National Schools were often required to undertake 'extraneous duties', and this was the case at Hadleigh. In September 1855 the rector, Rev. Thomas Espin, had given an organ to the church. The vestry minutes for August 1864 contain the following record: *"It was proposed by Mr. Tyrrell, seconded by Mr. Potter, & carried unanimously, that a grant of £5-0-0 be made from the Church Rate annually to the Secretary of the School Committee in consideration of the School master undertaking to play the Organ in Church:- such £5-0-0 to be added to the general fund of the*

School." Thus, William Kingswood, Henry Yeaxlee and Alfred Hawks became the church organist at the parish church, at a salary worth about £215 in today's money.

On 17 January 1865 Mr. Kingswood recorded in the log book that it was his last day at the school. He continued in his career as a schoolmaster, working at East Hoathly National School in Sussex, and at the small village school at Mortimer in Berkshire, where his wife was the mistress. William Batchelor Kingswood died on 10 August 1887 at 15 Wellington Place, Hastings in Sussex. Aged fifty-two, he had been suffering from softening of the brain for ten months and during the last five days had been in a coma caused by renal failure.

Henry Yeaxlee

Henry Yeaxlee was born on 4 August 1843 at Staines in Middlesex, the tenth child of William and Mary Yeaxlee's family of eleven. Like the fathers of most elementary teachers, his father was a skilled artisan, a carver and gilder. Henry was only twenty-one years old when he became the master of the National School on 31 January 1865. His eldest sister Mary Yeaxlee came to live with him in the master's school house. She also worked as a mistress in the school and was often in charge of the school in his absence.

On 31 March 1869 Henry Yeaxlee was married to Miss Lavinia Harvey at St. James the Less Church by the rector, Rev. William Metcalfe. The groom was aged twenty-six, and his bride was the 19-year-old daughter of Stephen and Selina Harvey of Leigh Park Farm. Henry and Lavinia were to celebrate over forty-five years of marriage. The first three of their seven children were born during their time at Hadleigh - Edith Lavinia (b. 1870), Margaret Selina (b. 1871) and Henry Arthur Wellesley (b. 1873) – who were all baptised at St. James the Less by the rector, Rev. William Metcalfe. Lavinia employed Alice, the daughter of the shoemaker William Smith, as a nursemaid.

14. Henry Yeaxlee's last entry in the log book, 19 March 1875

Evidence of the children's appreciation of their master was recorded in the log book on 18 April 1867: "*I have this week been presented with a handsomely-bound Bible as a 'testimonial of affectionate respect', by most of the elder children in the school. This, as far as I know, has been got up, forwarded, and bought by themselves, and it gives me unspeakable pleasure that they thus appreciate my love & care for them.*"

After ten years as the master at the National School, Henry Yeaxlee moved to Tollington Park in Islington, where he found employment as an Assistant School Teacher. The *Chelmsford Chronicle* on 2 April 1875 reported on Henry Yeaxlee's leaving presentation: "*On Saturday, the 26th March, a goodly assembly of ladies and gentlemen met in the schoolroom, their object being to present a mark of esteem to Mr. H. Yeaxlee on his retiring from the post of schoolmaster and organist, which he has occupied in a highly satisfactory manner for the past 10 years. The worthy rector, with Mrs. Metcalfe and Captain Skey arrived with a gilt figured timepiece, under a glass shade, bearing a handsome inscription plate, on which was engraved 'Presented to Mr. H. Yeaxlee, by the parishioners of Hadleigh and his pupils, in token of his ten years' services as schoolmaster of that parish.' In addition to this handsome gift Mr. Yeaxlee also received a highly finished microscope, mounted on a tripod stand, and with extra glasses and adjustments. In an appropriate speech the Rev. W. Metcalfe alluded to Mr. Yeaxlee's valuable services and their sorrow at losing him, concluding by requesting his acceptance of the valuable presents mentioned. Mr. H. Yeaxlee replied in an afecting* [sic] *speech.*"

It was while living at Islington that Lavinia gave birth to Albert Henry (b. 1877), Lucy Ethel (b. 1879) and Archibald Henry (b. 1882). By the time Francis Arnold was born in 1888, the family had moved to 48 Lothian Road, Tottenham. Henry Yeaxlee was still working as a school master, with his daughters Edith and Margaret as assistant teachers, and his son Albert a pupil teacher. His eldest son, known by his middle name Arthur, was working as an optician. By the time of the 1901 Census, Henry and Lavinia had moved house again, living at 83 Woodstock Road, Hornsey. Five of their children were still living with them, and Margaret, Albert and Lucy had followed their father into the teaching profession. Following his retirement, Henry was still living there ten years later as a pensioned teacher, with his wife Lavinia and his 39-year-old daughter Margaret, who was now a head teacher.

Henry Yeaxlee died from heart disease at his house in Acacia Avenue at Eastcote in Middlesex on 2 March 1929, at the age of eighty-five. He had been a widower for several years, as Lavinia died on 22 September 1915, whilst they were living at 15 Windermere Road, Muswell Hill. Although his oldest son Henry was still very young when the family left Hadleigh in 1875, he later returned to the village, calling himself by his middle name Arthur. He opened up a draper's store in the village street (on the site of the present Ancora Restaurant), which later moved to Central Parade (now Latino's Restaurant).

Alfred Hawks

The next school master was Alfred Hawks, who was to remain at the school until December 1918, becoming the longest serving master at the school. Alfred was born on 13 December 1853, the second son of Henry and Eliza Ann Hawks, at Snodland in Kent, where his father Henry worked as a carpenter. In 1871, at the age of seventeen, Alfred was working as a pupil teacher at Snodland. After gaining his teaching certificate at college, Alfred Hawks commenced his duties as the master of Hadleigh National School on 17 May 1875, at the age of twenty-one. (The rector, Rev. William Metcalfe, and his wife Rosa had been in charge of the school since Henry Yeaxlee left two months before.)

15. Alfred Hawks' first entry in the log book, 21 May 1875

During his first Harvest Vacation at the school, Alfred returned to Snodland to marry Miss Sarah Dulton on 12 August 1875 at All Saints with Christ Church. Sarah was also born at Snodland, on 1 August 1856, the daughter of William and Sarah Dulton. Married for sixty-eight years, Alfred and Sarah had ten children – Alice Gertrude (b. 1876), Minnie Florence (b. in 1878), Alfred Augustus (b. 1879), Edith Mary (b. 1881), Kate Beatrice (b. 1884), Margaret and Maud (twins born in 1885 who died less than two weeks later), Frederick Victor (b. 1887), Arthur Leslie (b. 1889) and Doris Mabel (b. 1896). All the children were baptised at St. James the Less.

During the 1890s Alfred and his family moved into Holboro House at 40 Chapel Lane, where they lived until 1940 when Alfred and Sarah Hawks returned to their birthplace, Snodland in Kent. They had spent 65 years in the village of Hadleigh and, in Alfred's obituary in the *Southend Standard*, Mr. Tutt, the headmaster of Hadleigh Council School, commented that: *"Every old inhabitant of Hadleigh and district was known to him and he to them".*

The obituary was entitled *GREAT LOSS TO HADLEIGH* and Alfred was described as a *"familiar and important figure in the parish life of Hadleigh for many years. . . . He became a member of the local Parish Council, then its Chairman and he held this position for a number of years. For a period, he was a member of the Rochford Rural Council and the Rochford Board of Guardians. It might be said that the social life of*

16. Alfred Hawks, c.1906

Hadleigh revolved around Mr. Hawks during his stay in the village. He organised, year after year, glee parties, garden parties and innumerable other parish socials and activities. His services to the church were practically unlimited. Not only did he fill the position of Rector's Warden efficiently for a considerable number of years, but he regularly read the lessons in church and would often play the organ."

From newspaper reports in the *Chelmsford Chronicle*, it is possible to gain further insight into his many leisure interests. In the early 1880s he was captain of the Quoits Club at the *Crown Inn* and was considered *"the backbone of the club"*. Another sporting interest was Hadleigh Cricket Club, with reports of him presiding at the annual general meeting held in the *Castle Inn* in November 1886. As there was no village hall, the schoolroom was often used for concerts and, at one such concert in February 1882, the newspaper reported: *"Mr. Hawks sang several comic songs in a style which caused roars of laughter and he also gave a recitation."*

His obituary also referred to his keen interest in politics: *". . . being an able Chairman at local meetings of the Conservative Party, where he displayed fluency of speech with a fund of good stories to enliven his discourse."* A Freemason of long standing, Alfred Hawks was a member of Trinity Lodge, Rayleigh. He was Worshipful Master of that Lodge in 1906 and, in 1930, he was appointed Past Provincial Assistant Grand Pursuivant in the Essex Provincial Grand Lodge.

Following his move to Snodland in 1940, Alfred continued to interest himself in the life of the parish church, All Saints with Christ, where he was himself christened and married. He read the lessons every Sunday in the church and it was in the churchyard that he was buried, following his death on 14 December 1943, the day after his ninetieth birthday. His obituary concludes: *"At the funeral on Saturday, the Vicar of Snodland conducting the service, paid a striking tribute to the life and influence of the deceased."* His widow Sarah died just over four years later on 19 January 1948.

17. Alfred and Sarah Hawks on their Diamond Wedding Anniversary, 1935

The Teaching Staff

THE ONLY TEACHERS IN the Hadleigh National School who would have attended a teacher training college were the masters, who would have been classed as certificated teachers. The National Society was the first organisation to train teachers and, by 1845, had twenty-two teacher training colleges. Before 1846 each National School would have had only one adult teacher who would be expected to control over a hundred children. This was achieved with the help of monitors, who were the older and brighter children who came to school early to have their lessons before the others arrived. They would then teach these lessons to small groups of children. This is why National Schools, like the one at Hadleigh, were designed with just one large schoolroom, as this one teacher had to be able to observe the entire school. Hadleigh National School continued to use the monitorial system until at least 1900. In July 1895 Alfred Hawks recorded in the log book that there were five monitors, some of whom were his own children who were pupils at the school.

By the mid-1840s this monitorial system was discredited (although it continued

18. The Infant Mistress, Miss Emma Bell, and her class, c.1889

to be used in the Hadleigh National School until the end of the century) and, in 1846, the Committee of Council on Education introduced a system of apprenticeship for pupil teachers. Pupil teachers were able to complete a five-year apprenticeship in teaching and learning within a school from the age of thirteen. The pupil teachers were then allowed to sit the annual Queen's Scholarships examination, to gain entry to a teacher training college, or they could remain in the school as an uncertificated teacher, or assistant teacher. In 1877 the minimum age for apprenticeship was raised to fourteen, with the apprenticeship being reduced to four years.

A study of the Hadleigh census returns provides evidence of the names of some of these pupil teachers and assistant teachers in the Hadleigh National School. In 1861 Mary Lloyd, aged nineteen, was the assistant teacher in charge of the school, with 16-year-old Eliza Pepper a pupil teacher. Ten years later, Ellen Ridgwell, the 15-year-old daughter of the village basket maker was employed at the school as a pupil teacher.

It appears from the log book entries that assistant teachers were mainly employed to teach the infants, who were in a separate room in the school. The first mention of an assistant teacher is on 29 January 1863 when Miss M. Mitchell was appointed. Whether she was the same teacher who was dismissed in January 1864 for *"negligence and want of attention to the children"* is uncertain. In September 1865 Henry Yeaxlee reported that he was: *"Much pleased with the care shown by the Infant School teacher Agnes Ridgwell."* Agnes, aged fourteen, was the daughter of the basket maker, and the sister of Ellen. The log book informs us that the infant teacher left in March 1867, but Henry Yeaxlee does not give her name. However, in February 1872, a bricklayer named Henry Eaton visited the school to complain that his 4-year-old son Arthur was being taught: *"by so young a teacher as was employed (aged 11)."*

On 21 June 1878 Miss Emma Bell became the infant teacher. Born in the village in 1857, Emma Jane Bell was the daughter of Joseph and Ann Bell, who lived in the main village street. At this time her father was employed as an agricultural labourer. Later, Miss Bell would move to South Benfleet with her father and travel to Hadleigh by cart. The Inspection Report of 1882 confirmed that: *"E. Bell is continued under Article 84 of the Code of 1882"*, which probably refers to the fact that she was an uncertified teacher. A former pupil at the school herself, Miss Bell continued to teach at the school until 11 April 1890.

Miss Bell was replaced by Miss Rachel Laura Bragg, who commenced work as the infant teacher on 14 April 1890. Born at Prittlewell in 1863, Rachel was the daughter of John and Rachel Bragg, who lived in the old butcher's shop next to the *Castle Inn*. Her father was employed as a carpenter. Miss Bragg was also recognised under Article 84 by Her Majesty's Inspector in 1890 and praised as being *"careful and painstaking"*. By the following year, there must have been a change in the Code regarding assistant teachers as Mr. E. M. Field, Her Majesty's Inspector, reported that: *"R. L. Bragg is continued under Article 68."*

Miss Bragg left the school on 3 February 1893 and was replaced by Miss Cales (or Coles). By the end of September 1893, Miss Cales had also left the school.

On 2 October 1893 Sarah Hawks, the 37-year-old wife of the master, became the new infant mistress, a position she was to hold until October 1901, when she retired through ill health. Prior to her marriage, Miss Sarah Dulton had worked as a pupil teacher at Snodland in Kent and, having served a four-year apprenticeship, became an assistant teacher. As well as teaching at the school, Sarah Hawks was the mother of seven surviving children and was to give birth to her last baby, Doris Mabel, in March 1896.

In July 1894 Mr. Arthur E. Bernays, Her Majesty's Inspector, reported that *"the teaching staff is still technically insufficient"*, but noted that the master's son and daughter were working in the school without official status. This was probably 16-year-old Alice and 13-year-old Alfred Augustus. In a log book entry in July 1895 Alfred Hawks listed the staff for 1895-6 as: *"Certificated Master. One P. Teacher, Five Monitors, One Candidate on Probation, Infant Teacher Article 68."* The Inspection Report for 1896 indicates that some of the older children were being taught by young teachers. Both Minnie and Alfred Augustus Hawks are named at the end of the report, with Minnie being recognised under Article 68 of the Code, which meant she had completed her teaching apprenticeship and was now classed as an assistant teacher. The inspector recommended that these young teachers should be instructed in teaching methods by the master and, following receipt of the report in October 1896, Alfred Hawks now began *"giving hints to the teachers in the various methods of teaching"*, and observing them in their classes. By 1900 the school employed three assistant teachers – Sarah Hawks, Alice Hawks and Minnie Hawks. When Sarah Hawks resigned in October 1901, it was her other daughter Kate who became the infant mistress.

It was common for the local clergymen to teach Scripture in the National Schools as this was considered the most important subject taught, and it was hoped that it would reform the morals of the working classes. The Hadleigh clergymen were highly educated men who would visit the school regularly, teach lessons and even take charge of the school in the master's absence. Rev. Thomas Espinell Espin, rector of Hadleigh between 1853 and 1868, had graduated from Lincoln College, Oxford with a B.A. in 1846 and an M.A. in 1849, and had been a Fellow of the College, as well as a tutor there. His successor, Rev. William Metcalfe, was the rector of St. James the Less until his death in 1876. A graduate of St. John's College, Cambridge, he was awarded a B.A. in 1854, followed by an M.A. in 1857. Rev. Arthur James Skrimshire, who succeeded Rev. Metcalfe as the rector of Hadleigh in 1876, originally trained as a doctor, graduating from Edinburgh University in 1838, and worked as a physician at Sudbury in Suffolk for several years. In 1854 he undertook a change in career, attending St. Bees Theological College in Cumbria and was ordained as a priest in 1857. Following Rev. Skrimshire's retirement in 1894, Rev. Armine George Metcalfe became the new rector. A graduate of Selwyn College, Cambridge, he often taught in the school when Alfred Hawks was absent.

Until 1868 the parish of Hadleigh was also served by curates. A regular visitor to the school, who taught not only Scripture but also reading, was the Rev. John Godson. Curate of Hadleigh from 1860 to 1864, he studied theology at Queen's College, Birmingham in the late 1850s and was ordained as a priest in 1860. The curate for Hadleigh between 1864 and 1865 was the Rev. Joseph Baines, who also taught regularly at the school. He graduated from Trinity College, Dublin in 1858 and was ordained a priest in 1861. On 31 May 1865 he married Harriet Wood, the daughter of the late Jonathan Wood Senior, a Hadleigh farmer. The day before the wedding the children of the school had made a presentation to him *"to mark their appreciation of his kindness"*. He was succeeded by the Rev. James Walker. Rev. Henry William Smith, the curate from 1866 to 1867, graduated from St. John's College, Cambridge with an M.A. in 1860. He had also run the Collegiate School at Clifton with his wife. Rev. John Yolland, the curate from 1867 to 1868, was a graduate of Queen's College, Oxford, being awarded an M.A. in 1856. No curates were employed after 1868.

Log Book Entries

Miss Cecilia Miller had been appointed mistress in 1861

1 Jan 1863 — *Began School without assistance.*

19 Jan 1863 — *Mr. Godson took a class and gave a Scripture Lesson in the afternoon.* [Rev. John Godson, the curate, visited the school at least once a week, usually to teach the children.]

29 Jan 1863 — *M. Mitchell entered the school as Assistant Teacher.*

6 Feb 1863 — *Miss Mitchell kept at home this afternoon by a sick headache.*

13 Mar 1863 — *Miss Mitchell unable to come to School, suffering with pain in the chest.*

23 Mar 1863 — *Miss Mitchell gone home in consequence of her father's illness.*

15 Apr 1863 — *Miss Raven engaged for a time to assist in the School.* [This was possibly Miss Harriet Raven, a school mistress who was living at Church Hill, Leigh at the time of the 1861 Census.]

| 6 May 1863 | *Children very tiresome, felt the want of an assistant in the School.* |

William Batchelor Kingswood appointed master 7 September 1863

7 Sep 1863	*W. B. Kingswood acted as Master of the School for the first time.*
8 Sep 1863	*Was kept very busy in learning the various lessons and their order of teaching during the whole day.*
17 Sep 1863	*Choir & few larger children attended Divine Service in the morning, the others were under the management of Mrs. Kingswood at their usual Work.*

4 Jan 1864	*Mrs. Kingswood took the infants in the morning and Eliz. Smith in afternoon, the ordinary Teacher having been dismissed through negligence and want of attention to the children.* [Sarah Ann Kingswood was the wife of the master. Elizabeth Smith was the 11-year-old daughter of the village shoemaker William and his wife Mary Ann.]
10 Feb 1864	*Mrs. Kingswood took the school during my absence as usual.* [Master at Ash Wednesday service at church.]
15 Jun 1864	*Had a deal of trouble in quelling a kind of ill feeling which seems to exist in the minds of one or two parents because they <u>have heard</u> their children have been <u>hit</u> by the infant Teacher or have been severely handled by someone else. Tried to convince them of our anxiety for their children's welfare and could scarcely could get a word in "<u>edgeways</u>" but got showered by <u>low abuse</u>, the only thanks an earnest Teacher seems to get.*
31 Aug 1864	*Emily Appleton took the infants in the morning and M. A. Smith in afternoon.* [Emily Appleton was the 11-year-old daughter of William Appleton, an agricultural labourer, and his wife Elizabeth, who lived on the Causeway at Hadleigh. Mary Ann Smith was the 8-year-old daughter of the village shoemaker, William Smith, and his wife Mary.]
22 Sep 1864	*The Teacher of Infants was at school this afternoon after being away ill for a day and a half.*
28 Oct 1864	*Mrs. Kingswood took the whole school today.* [Presumably her husband was absent.]

| 11 Jan 1865 | *Went to church in the morning. Mrs. Kingswood took the School during my absence in Church.* |

Henry Yeaxlee appointed master 23 January 1865

24 Jan 1865   *Went to church this morning and in my absence Miss Yeaxlee took the school.* [Miss Mary Yeaxlee was Henry's older sister.]

2 Feb 1865   *Attended service in the morning with choir, and Miss Yeaxlee took the school in my absence.*

8 Feb 1865   *Went to church this morning with choir, and in my absence Miss Yeaxlee, though suffering from ill health, took the School.*

20 Mar 1865   *Infant School Teacher suffering from severe cough.*

28 Sep 1865   *Obliged to be absent from school this afternoon, in order to attend a Choral Festival at Benfleet.*

8 Nov 1865   *Much pleased with the care shown by the Infant School teacher Agnes Ridgwell.* [Agnes was the 14-year-old daughter of the village basket maker, James Ridgwell, and his wife Catherine. She had been a pupil at the school and would not have been a certificated teacher.]

19 Feb 1866   *Suffering myself from cold and could scarcely speak so as to be heard.*

16 Mar 1866   *Absent myself in the afternoon.*

17 Apr 1866   *Obliged to be absent from school for half the day on account of ill-health. In my absence, a friend visiting me, took the school.*

16 Nov 1866   *Governess absent the last two afternoons from ill health.* [This was probably Henry Yeaxlee's sister, Miss Mary Yeaxlee.]

13 Feb 1867   *Can do but little work in consequence of ill-health.*

25 Feb 1867   *Could do but little work in school to-day in consequence of ill-health.*

15 Mar 1867   *The Governess has been absent on account of ill-health.*

18 Mar 1867   *Governess still unable to attend.*

22 Mar 1867   *The Governess absent this week in consequence of ill-health.*

26 Mar 1867   *The infant school teacher left.*

27 Mar 1867   *The school-work hindered on account of the illness of the teacher.*

28 Mar 1867   *The Governess has returned to school.*

18 Apr 1867   *I have this week been presented with a handsomely-bound Bible as a "testimonial of affectionate respect", by most of the elder children in the school. This, as far as I know, has been got up, forwarded, and bought by themselves, and it gives me unspeakable pleasure that they thus appreciate my love & care for them.*

10 May 1867   *Was absent myself from the School in the afternoon in consequence of a journey.*

24 Sep 1867   *Being unwell I am unable to give the proper attention to my school duty.*

25 Sep 1867	*Obliged to close school at four o'clock this afternoon by reason of ill health.*
26 Sep 1867	*Was obliged to leave school for an hour this afternoon in consequence of ill health.*
1 Oct 1867	*Obliged to leave school for an hour this afternoon, which was under the Governess' care.*
15 Oct 1867	*I can do no work this afternoon having a severe cough.*
28 Nov 1867	*Governess absent this afternoon through ill-health.*

◈

28 Jan 1868	*Governess absent in the afternoon and her place supplied by a friend.*
9 Mar 1868	*Absent myself this afternoon.*
25 Mar 1868	*Not able to do much work myself today feeling rather unwell.*
28 Apr 1868	*The Governess absent this afternoon on account of bad health.*
8 Jun 1868	*School obliged to be closed for a week in consequence of the illness of the Master.*

◈

4 Feb 1869	*The School closed today on account of the Master's unfitness to attend.*
9 Jul 1869	*Rather ill myself – cannot do much work.*
27 Jul 1869	*Absent from school myself in the afternoon, the school conducted by the Governess.* [Probably Henry's new wife Lavinia.]
23 Sep 1869	*Absent from school myself this Afternoon on account of illness.*

◈

19 Jan 1870	*The School has been closed on account of the Master suffering from severe sore-throat and cold.*
25 Jan 1870	*Allowed the Teacher to go home this morning early – by reason of illness.*
15 Jun 1870	*I was absent from school for an hour this afternoon, detained by an organ-tuner.* [Henry Yeaxlee was the church organist.]
21 Jul 1870	*I have scarcely done any real work in school for two or three days, owing to illness.*
30 Nov 1870	*The Governess is absent this afternoon.*

◈

21 Apr 1871	*The Governess has been absent two afternoons on account of illness.*
20 Oct 1871	*The School closed on Friday because of the Master's ill-health.*

◈

9 Feb 1872	*I was this afternoon visited by Mr. Eaton, the father of one of the Infants, who was very dissatisfied that his boy was taught by so young a teacher as was employed (aged 11).* [Mr. Henry Eaton, a

bricklayer, lived in the village street, with his wife Maria and their family. Arthur Eaton was their 4-year-old son.]

26 Jul 1872   *Feeling extremely unwell from heat and fatigue, I closed the school earlier than usual on Thursday Morning.*

~⁊⁊~

2 Jan 1873   *I was obliged to close the school on Friday, as I was suffering from ill-health.*

11 Jul 1873   *The head monitor M. A. Smith has left this week.* [This Mary Ann Smith was the 14-year-old daughter of another shoemaker, Thomas Smith, and his wife Mary. Mary Ann Smith, the daughter of William Smith, may have been her cousin.]

24 Oct 1873   *The School routine has been uninterrupted, except by a half-holiday, given on Thursday as the Master was absent on pressing business.*

~⁊⁊~

30 Jan 1874   *I was obliged to close the school on Friday, being myself unwell.*

10 Jul 1874   *The school was closed this afternoon to allow the Master a half-holiday.*

23 Jul 1874   *Being extremely unwell I was unable to attend school on Tuesday morning.*

20 Nov 1874   *The school was closed on Wednesday afternoon & Thursday morning in consequence of my absence.*

~⁊⁊~

12 Mar 1875   *I have closed the school this afternoon Thursday, the Managers having kindly allowed me a holiday tomorrow.* [Henry Yeaxlee was to leave the school the following Friday after ten years as the master.]

Between 19 March and 17 May 1875, in the absence of a master, the rector ran the school

9 Apr 1875   *Mr. Yeaxlee having left, after ten years teaching in the School; and the new master being unable to come just yet, the School has been carried on by Rev. W. Metcalfe and Mrs. Metcalfe.*

Alfred Hawks appointed master 17 May 1875

21 May 1875   *I, Alfred Hawks, commenced my duties May 17th as Master of this School. I was accompanied by the Revd. W. Metcalfe, at the opening of School on Monday morning.*

15 Oct 1875   *I have myself given more time to the Lower Standards as they naturally become unsound in their work if left entirely to Monitors for any length of time.*

12 Nov 1875	*The School was closed on Tuesday to give the Master a holliday* [sic]*, when the windows were mended.*

⸎

14 Jan 1876	*On Wednesday I was called home and obliged to close the School for the rest of the week. The Rector promised to manage School for me till I returned on the following Wednesday, but on reaching the Station, I heard of his death, consequently the School was closed for a week.* [The master's 13-year-old sister had died and he returned to Snodland in Kent. The rector, Rev. William Metcalfe, died on 17 January from pleuritic effusion. Aged forty-five years, he was buried in the churchyard on 22 January, the funeral being conducted by the rector of North Benfleet.]

⸎

22 Jun 1877	*My teacher has left the School this week and will not be present at the Examination* [The HMI Inspection on 26 June].
27 Jul 1877	*The School was closed on Wednesday to give the Master a holliday* [sic].
21 Sep 1877	*On Wednesday afternoon the School was taken by the Mistress to give the Master a holliday* [sic].

⸎

7 Jun 1878	*Dismissed the children at 4 this afternoon, as the Master is suffering from ill-health.*
17 Jun 1878	[Her Majesty's Inspector on his visit commented on the workload of the master Alfred Hawks and recommended the appointment of an Assistant Teacher.]
21 Jun 1878	*On Wednesday Emma Bell commenced teaching in the Infant room.*

⸎

18 Apr 1879	*I left School early this Afternoon to catch the train, leaving Mrs. Hawks in charge.*
30 May 1879	*Miss Bell has been ill this week and unable to attend.*
13 Jun 1879	*Mrs. Hawks took charge of the School on Tuesday as I was unable to attend from ill-health.*
18 Jul 1879	*The School was conducted by Mrs. Hawks yesterday afternoon.*

⸎

6 Feb 1880	*I was unable to attend School on Thursday and Friday owing to ill-health. The School was conducted by Miss Bell and Miss Groomes. Registers were called by Mrs. Hawks.* [Miss Groomes was a friend of the rector, Rev. A. Skrimshire, and his wife.]

⸎

4 Feb 1881	*I was unable to attend on Friday from ill-health. Consequently Miss Bell took charge.*

⁓

19 May 1882	*Miss Bell has been unable to attend School since Wednesday on account of ill health.*
21 Jul 1882	*I was absent yesterday from ill-health.*

⁓

20 Apr 1883	*I was absent on Friday through ill-health.*

⁓

15 Feb 1884	*Miss Bell has been absent two days owing to the death of a brother.*
25 Jul 1884	*Miss Bell is absent to-day from ill-health.*

⁓

1 May 1885	*Owing to an outbreak of Smallpox in Benfleet, the Managers have asked Miss Bell, who resides there, not to attend the School for a time, which will affect the progress of the Infants.*
8 May 1885	*Miss Bell is still absent.*
15 May 1885	*Miss Bell returned to her duties on Monday.*
20 Nov 1885	*The School has been conducted by Miss Bell this week owing to the indisposition of the Master.* [The previous month, Margaret and Maud, the newly-born daughters of Alfred and Sarah Hawks had died and been buried by the rector on 17 October.]

⁓

15 Jan 1886	*Miss Bell has not been able to attend School since Monday having caught a violent cold.*
26 Feb 1886	*I was unable to attend School three days this week owing to illness.*

⁓

24 Feb 1888	*Miss Bell met with an accident on Tuesday on her way home – she was thrown from a cart and is likely to be laid up some time.*
2 Mar 1888	*Miss Bell returned to her duties on Wednesday.*
6 Jul 1888	*Miss Bell is sick and not able to attend School.*
13 Jul 1888	*Miss Bell returned to her duties on Thursday.*

⁓

26 Jul 1889	*The School has been conducted by Miss Bell this week owing to the indisposition of Master.* [As well as running a school of 100 pupils with only one other teacher, Alfred Hawks was the father of six children.]

⁓

9 Jan 1890	*The School was closed on Thursday morning owing to illness of teachers.*
17 Jan 1890	*Miss Bell is still unable to attend.*

11 Apr 1890	*Miss Bell left the School today and was presented with Writing desk, Bag and Purse of money by the parents, children and friends.* [Miss Bell continued teaching and, on 2 March 1908, at the age of forty-eight, she married Charles Butcher, a railway signalman, at the Park Road Wesleyan Chapel at Southend. She died in 1928, aged 68.]
9 May 1890	*Miss Bragg the new Infant Teacher commenced work on Monday April 14.*
30 May 1890	*Miss Bragg is doing good work with the Infants.*

24 Apr 1891	*The School was left in charge of Miss Bragg to-day Friday the master being absent.*
20 Nov 1891	*Miss Bragg is absent this week through indisposition.*

26 Feb 1892	*Miss Bragg has not been able to come since Tuesday owing to ill-health.*
4 Mar 1892	*Miss Bragg is still unable to attend school.*
17 Jun 1892	*I was absent this afternoon owing to the illness of my father.* [Henry Hawks, a carpenter, died at Snodland in Kent, aged 67.]

3 Feb 1893	*Miss Bragg left and Miss Cales appointed.* [The name of the new teacher could be Coles.]
10 Mar 1893	*Both the Infant teacher and the monitor for this room are sick and unable to attend School, consequently I have had great difficulty in keeping up the regular routine of the school.*
17 Mar 1893	*The monitor is still indisposed and the Infants mistress was also obliged to go home at noon.*
24 Mar 1893	*I have the whole school to teach single-handed, consequently the work is becoming seriously affected.*
15 Apr 1893	*Miss Cales resumed her duties on Monday but the monitor for this room has not yet returned.*
13 Oct 1893	*Mrs. Hawks commenced her duties in the Infant room on Monday October 2.* [Sarah Hawks was the wife of the master. Aged thirty-seven, Sarah was the mother of seven children, aged between three and seventeen.]

2 Feb 1894	*The Infant mistress was indisposed three days and unable to attend.*
20 Jul 1894	*I was absent on Thursday and examined Leigh Board School for the distribution of prizes £10 in money annually given by Mr. Millar Q.C.* [Frederick Charles James Miller Q.C. lived at Leigh House. £10

would be worth nearly £600 in today's money, a very generous prize fund.]

2 Nov 1894   *I was absent yesterday afternoon and the Rector came & assisted in the School.* [This was the new rector, Rev. Armine George Metcalfe, who had only been in the village a few weeks.]

8 Mar 1895   *With the exception of one monitor all the teachers have been down with Influenza and the School has been conducted by the Rector.*

26 Jul 1895   *Staff 1895-6 Certificated Master. One P. Teacher, Five Monitors, One Candidate on Probation, Infant Teacher Article 68.*

21 Feb 1896   *The Rector has taken charge of the School three days this week, owing to indisposition of the Master.*

13 Mar 1896   *The Infant Mistress being indisposed, the Infant Class will be taken by the Monitor from the big room for the next four or five weeks. She is just 18 years old (Minnie F. Hawks).* [Mrs. Sarah Hawks was the Infant Mistress at this time and was expecting her tenth child. Doris Mabel was born on 15 March 1896. Minnie Florence was Alfred and Sarah's second eldest child, born on 21 February 1877.]

23 Oct 1896   [The Inspection Report lists A. A. Hawks as teaching Arithmetic, Grammar, Geography, History and Music. Alfred Augustus was Alfred and Sarah's third child and eldest son. He would have been aged about seventeen at this time.]

30 Oct 1896   *I have spent a great deal of time this week in supervising the lower Classes and giving hints to the teachers in the various <u>methods</u> of teaching.*

20 Nov 1896   [I have given] *lessons on teaching to all the teachers.*

4 Dec 1896   *The Rector took charge of School on Wednesday Afternoon to allow the Mistress to visit a good School at Southend.*

3 Feb 1897   *I have spent a good deal of time again this week with the teachers at their different classes.*

12 Mar 1897   *I have again spent much of my time this week in criticising the teachers at their work and was pleased to find such an improvement since any last hints on <u>method</u> to them.*

22 Dec 1897   *A Grant of £25.10.0. has been made under the Voluntary Schools Aid Grant in respect of the current financial year for the purpose of increasing Salaries and effecting rep*airs. [This grant would be worth about £1,455 in today's money.]

⚘

2 Sep 1898	*I am glad to say the teachers are working very hard to make up for the lost time and progress is perceptible even in the short space of 3 weeks.* [The school was closed for eleven weeks due to an outbreak of measles, and also for the Summer Vacation.]
23 Sep 1898	*Mrs. Hawks was indisposed all the week.* [Sarah Hawks was now forty-two years old and, as well as teaching the infants' class, she had a home to run and a family to look after. Two of her children, Frederick and Arthur, would have been at school, whilst Doris was still only two.]
21 Oct 1898	*I have devoted a considerable time to the Pupil Teacher's class and am glad to find a marked improvement especially in Writing & Arithmetic.* [The Inspector's Report for 1898, which had just been received, criticised the Pupil Teacher's instruction.]
18 Nov 1898	*I have spent a great deal of time with the teachers at their various classes.*
2 Dec 1898	*I examined the Pupil Teacher's Class to-day and was very pleased indeed in the progress made.*

⚘

24 Feb 1899	*Mrs. Hawks has been indisposed during the week and unable to attend school.*
3 Mar 1899	*A Grant of £30.10.0. has been made under the Voluntary Schools Aid Grant for the purpose of maintaining increased Salary £13, increasing staff £2.10.0. and equipment & repairs £15.* [This grant would be worth about £1,740 in today's money.]
17 Mar 1899	*The Master has been indisposed since Tuesday and unable to attend School.*
24 Mar 1899	*The Master still unable to attend School and the Rector has taken charge of the School.*
15 Sep 1899	*Miss A. Hawks was appointed 11/9/99 as Art. 68 Subject to approval by the Inspector in the place of the late P. Teacher.* [Alice Gertrude, at nearly 23 years, was the eldest of the Hawks children. Article 68 meant that she was employed as an Assistant Teacher like her mother and younger sister Minnie. Unfortunately, the name of the Pupil Teacher is not known, although Alfred Augustus, the eldest son, had been teaching in the school in 1896.]
29 Sep 1899	*Since the holiday a good number of Children have been admitted and the teachers are working with great energy.*

15 Dec 1899	*There is quite an Epidemic of Influenza among the children and nearly all the teachers have been indisposed.*

~

26 Jan 1900	*A Grant of £27.0.0. has been made under the Voluntary Schools Aid Grant for the purpose of maintaining increased Salary £13, increasing Staff £2.0.0. and equipment & repairs £12.* [This grant would be worth about £1,540 in today's money.]
9 Mar 1900	*The Rector is taking charge of the School this afternoon.*
23 Nov 1900	*The School has suffered slightly from the absence of one of the Teachers during the last fortnight.*

A Typical School Day

WHAT WAS A TYPICAL school day like at the village school? Let us go back in time to April 1861 and visit the Ridgwell family in their small cottage on the village street. Next to the *Crown Inn* is a group of cottages, where Hadleigh library stands today. The photograph shows this row of cottages about sixty years later. The first cottage is the shop of John Giggins, a baker and grocer. Next door is the home of James and Catherine Ridgwell and their eight children. James, aged thirty-eight, is the village basket and sieve maker. Born at Bocking in Essex, he married Catherine Thorington on 14 November 1842 at St. Peter's Church, Thundersley. Catherine's illegitimate son Walter was only a baby then and he now helps his stepfather in the basket-making business, along with his half-brother James.

Let us imagine it is about 8 o'clock on Monday 8 April 1861. Catherine has a busy day ahead of her, as Monday is traditionally washing day and she also earns extra money making straw bonnets. Fortunately, she is helped in the house by her 13-year-old daughter Mary Ann. The three men have had their breakfast and are now at work, making the baskets from willow grown nearby. Catherine and Mary Ann now have just an hour to get Lewis, Agnes, Alfred and Ellen ready for school. The cottage has no bathroom so the children have to wash in a bowl of water. Victorian schools are very strict about cleanliness believing it is 'next to godliness'.

19. The row of cottages in the High Street where the Ridgwells lived, c. 1920s

If the children come to school with dirty faces, fingers and nails they are sent home. The children do not wear school uniform, but dress in simple plain clothes – a plain dress and a white pinafore for the girls, and trousers, shirt and jacket for the boys. On their feet they wear sturdy lace-up boots which have been bought from one of the village shoemakers. Next they sit down to breakfast of bread, which is still warm from the baker's shop next door. While Mary Ann checks that the children have their school pence (school is not free and each child has to pay twopence (2d) a week), Catherine feeds and dresses baby Alice.

The school day begins at 9 o'clock and it is important not to be late or the children will receive a scolding from the mistress, Miss Mary Lloyd. Most people in Victorian times had no way of telling the time. Only wealthy people owned clocks and watches, but others had to guess the time by daylight and by the sun and moon. So it is not surprising that children arrive at school at different times - some early and some late. The four Ridgwell children are lucky that their walk to school takes less than five minutes, some of their fellow pupils live at Daws Heath and have to walk over a mile to school.

Here comes Miss Lloyd into the school yard, ringing the bell to announce the beginning of the school day. Mary Harriet Lloyd is only nineteen and was a pupil teacher for Miss Houseley, the former mistress of the school. Born at Hadleigh in 1841, Mary Lloyd was baptised at St. James the Less on 5 September 1841 by the curate, Rev. Henry Whittington. Her father George has lived in the village for many years and used to own the baker's shop next to the Ridgwells. He and his wife Mary, with their daughters Mary and Matilda, now live on the green, between the wheelwright's shop and the *Crown Inn.*

When the school bell rings, the children line up according to height; one line for boys and one for girls. The boys enter the schoolroom first and stand to attention, in silence, by their desks. The boys clasp their hands behind their backs and the girls clasp theirs in front. After saying good morning to the teacher, the boys bow and the girls curtsey, and then they sit down. Miss Lloyd then calls the register, with the children answering, "Yes, Miss". Next the children are inspected to ensure they are properly dressed and that their hands are clean.

The school day begins with a prayer and a hymn – today the children sing *All Things Bright and Beautiful.* As pupils at a church school, the children are expected to attend church on Sunday and learn the Lord's Prayer. Religious education is the most important part of the curriculum at a National School and the children will have a daily lesson in Scripture. The village curate, Rev. John Godson, regularly visits the school to take these lessons, ensuring that the children receive the correct religious instruction.

Ellen and Alfred are in the infants' classroom at the far end of the school. The children sit at desks made of wood and iron and are taught by the pupil teacher, Eliza Pepper, who is the 16-year-old daughter of the village hurdle maker. She is aided by monitors who are older children at the school. Ellen, aged five, is not the youngest child in the infants' class as Mary Pleasant is only two. The classroom is very bare with little to stimulate the children, or distract them from their work. Thirty years later, the school is still being criticised by the inspector for not having pictures on the wall.

Lewis, aged twelve, and Agnes, aged nine, are taught in the large schoolroom, with the other children who are aged over seven years. The children are divided into Standards, according to their abilities, not their age. A pupil cannot leave a Standard and move on to another until he or she has passed the examination during the annual inspection. As can be seen from the original plan (see page 5), the large school room accommodates four Standards. To ensure the children are not too distracted by the other classes, curtains separate each pupil area.

Like all Victorian schools, the National School at Hadleigh concentrates on teaching the 'three Rs': Reading, wRiting and aRithmetic. The teachers and monitors teach using the 'chalk and talk' method. The teacher chalks some words or sums on the blackboard and then talks about them. The children then copy what is written there on to their school slates. These are boards made from a piece of quarry slate set in a wooden frame. A slate pencil (not chalk) is used to form the letters. The slate pencils are sharpened on the school wall. In the infants' class, Ellen and Alfred only use slates, which are much cheaper than paper, and can be wiped clean and used again and again. Often the children use their own spit and the cuff of their sleeve! This is the origin of the phrase 'to wipe the slate clean'. Another Victorian teaching method is to make the children recite things 'parrot fashion' until they are word perfect. The lessons usually last half an hour which means that Miss Lloyd can move from Standard to Standard during the morning, while the pupil teachers and monitors teach the other children.

In their reading lesson the older children will each be handed a book called a reader. Each child has to read out loud to the class and the other children follow the story in their books. Children aged about nine, like Agnes, read from a book of moral stories, with titles like *Harriet and the Matches*. Lewis, who at twelve years old will be leaving school soon to join his father and brothers in the family basket-making business, reads from the Bible. The National Society considers reading the second most important subject after religion, as the children would not be able to read the Book of Common Prayer and the Bible unless they had learnt to read.

When the reading lesson ends, the children then begin the writing lesson, which is concerned not with writing sentences and composition, but with handwriting and spelling. The infants' class use sand trays to learn their letters. These are wooden trays filled with sand. The teacher writes a letter of the alphabet on the blackboard and the children practise writing the letter by drawing in the sand with their fingers. Afterwards they smooth out the sand and copy the next letter from the blackboard. The older infant children, like Alfred, have progressed to writing on slates.

In Standard I the children are still using slates, but are now writing down dictated sentences in order to practise their spelling. In Standard II they are learning to use pen and ink by writing in copybooks. The copybook is ruled with lines and at the top of each page is printed a sentence, which is to be copied on each line to the bottom of the page. Usually the sentence is a proverb like 'Think before you speak'. The aim of the lesson is to fill the page with lines of almost identical, neat 'copperplate' writing. The proverb is used so that the mind of the pupil is improved whilst copying out the sentence. The children use dip pens which have hard, steel nibs that are dipped into the inkwells. All the children are made to write with their right hand; if they use their left hand they are punished by a rap on their knuckles with a ruler. Children are also punished for spilling ink which 'blotted their copybooks', a phrase still used today for a misdemeanour. As the children move up the Standards the dictation becomes more difficult.

The children now begin the arithmetic lesson, which concentrates on the four rules of number – addition, subtraction, multiplication and division. In the infants' class Alfred and Ellen will learn to name the numbers, starting with 0 to 10, when the teacher points to them on the blackboard. Using only their slates, they will practise writing these same numbers and will learn to count. The older infants will progress to simple addition and subtraction sums. The children will use an abacus to help them.

By Standard I the children will write, from dictation, the numbers up to 20, and also name them. As mental arithmetic is considered important, they will begin to orally add and subtract numbers up to 20. In Standard II the children will be adding and subtracting more difficult sums, still using their slates. They now learn their multiplication tables by chanting them and are expected to learn them up to their 12 times table. This is because Britain's currency at this time is based on the number 12. Known as 'pounds, shillings and pence', there were 12 pence (12d) in one shilling (1/-) and 20 shillings (20/-) in one pound (£1).

Lewis is now using compound rules to calculate weights and measures. He uses imperial weights and measures, such as pounds and ounces, and inches, feet and yards. Today the older children have been given a problem to solve by the teacher: *"How many furlongs, rods, yards, feet and inches will reach round the earth, supposing it to be 25,020 miles?"* (The answer is 25,020 miles = 200,160 furlongs = 8,006,400 rods = 44,035,200 yards = 132,105,600 feet = 1,585,267,200 inches. No wonder they needed an abacus!)

The final lesson of the morning is Scripture. Today the village curate, Rev. John Godson, is visiting the school to test the older children on the catechism, which is a manual for the instruction of those preparing to be brought before the bishop for confirmation. It was in the form of questions followed by answers which had to be memorised.

The morning lessons finish at midday with a prayer and the children now have two hours free from lessons. There are no school dinners in Victorian times so most of the children go home for a meal. This is why the lunchtime is so long, to give the children time to walk home and then return for afternoon school at 2 o'clock. Lewis, Agnes, Alfred and Ellen are hungry after working hard all morning and run home for their lunch. It is too far for some of the Daws Heath children to walk home so they bring sandwiches to eat in the school yard. Today the four children of James and Mary Pleasant, who live in Daws Heath Road, are staying at school. William and George Pleasant, aged eight and seven, quickly gobble down their sandwiches and then begin a game of football with their friends. Edmund is only four and prefers to play chase with his friends. The boys have been told by their mother to look after their sister, 2-year-old Mary, but they are too busy having fun to remember this.

All too soon it is 2 o'clock and Miss Lloyd is ringing the bell for afternoon school, which lasts until 5 o'clock. Afternoon lessons are often the same as those in the morning – more reading, writing and arithmetic. The children also recite poems. Today Lewis is asked to stand up by his teacher and recite from *Horatius* by Thomas Macaulay:

> *"Then out spake brave Horatius,*
> *The Captain of the Gate:*
> *To every man upon this earth*
> *Death cometh soon or late.*
> *And how can man die better*
> *Than facing fearful odds,*
> *For the ashes of his fathers,*
> *And the temples of his gods?"*

Let us hope the class do not have to recite all 590 lines of the poem!

In the infants' class Alfred and Ellen are having a less boring time in their singing lesson. Agnes is spending her afternoon with the sewing mistress. The girls are taught how to sew linen and make garments, important skills they will need if they become domestic servants when they leave school. All the children have a drill lesson to improve their fitness. They have to march into the school yard in silence and in order. The lesson will involve marching, running, jumping and stretching.

The Ridgwell children are relieved when 5 o'clock comes and they can go home. A final prayer is said, the children say *"Good afternoon, Miss"* to their teachers and lead out of the school room in silence. The life of a Victorian school child is hard and the children are very tired as they walk home. Discipline is very strict in the school and if the children break the rules they will be rapped across the knuckles with a ruler or made to stand in the corner with a dunce's cap on.

Miss Lloyd is also tired as she walks home to eat her supper. Sadly, in October 1861, she caught diphtheria from one of her pupils and, after four days illness, died on 29 October, aged twenty years. On 5 November Mary Lloyd was buried in the parish churchyard, her funeral service conducted by the curate, Rev. John Godson.

Don't Blot Your Copybook

THE NEWCASTLE COMMISSION'S REPORT in 1861 on elementary education recommended that public money could be saved if payment of the annual grant to schools was made dependent on a school's success in achieving standards of literacy and numeracy in its pupils. Such success would be tested annually by Her Majesty's Inspectors. The Committee of Council on Education therefore introduced the Revised Code of 1862. Classes in elementary schools were named Standards I to VI, roughly corresponding to ages seven to twelve. The curriculum became mainly restricted to the three Rs, with the addition of needlework, plus religious instruction in church schools.

The Revised Code stated: *"Every scholar for whom grants are claimed must be examined according to one of the following standards:"*

	Standard I	Standard II	Standard III
Reading	Narrative in monosyllables.	One of the Narratives next in order after monosyllables in an elementary reading book used in the school.	A short paragraph from an elementary book used in the school.
Writing	Form on black-board or slate, from dictation, letters, capital and small manuscript.	Copy in manuscript character a line of print.	A sentence from the same paragraph, slowly read once, and then dictated in single words.
Arithmetic	Form on black-board or slate, from dictation, figures up to 20; name at sight figures up to 20; add and subtract figures up to 10, orally, from examples on black-board.	A sum in simple addition or subtraction, and the multiplication table.	A sum in any simple rule as far as short division (inclusive).
Reading	Standard IV A short paragraph from a more advanced reading book used in the school.	Standard V A few lines of poetry from a reading book used in the first class of the school.	Standard VI A short ordinary paragraph in a newspaper, or other modern narrative.
Writing	A sentence slowly dictated once by a few words at a time, from the same book, but not from the paragraph read.	A sentence slowly dictated once, by a few words at a time, from a reading book used in the first class of the school.	Another short ordinary paragraph in a newspaper, or other modern narrative, slowly dictated once by a few words at a time.
Arithmetic	A sum in compound rules (money).	A sum in compound rules (common weights and measures).	A sum in practice or bills of parcels.

After criticisms regarding the restrictive curriculum, the Education Department expanded the curriculum of elementary schools in the 1870s through special grants, for not more than two 'specific' subjects, for individual pupils in Standards IV to VI, and 'class' subjects for the whole school above Standard I.

In November 1875 Alfred Hawks introduced English grammar and geography into the Hadleigh school's curriculum. However, in 1876, the parents were not so enamoured of the new subjects *"saying it would be a great deal better if we taught them to read and write".* One parent, when his child was sent home with a slate on which was written the geography facts which had to be learnt, threatened to break the slate if this occurred again! As well as a prescribed curriculum, the government also imposed timetables on the schools. History did not appear to be a priority at the Hadleigh school, and the only record of it in the log book was in the 1896 inspection report, which records that Alfred Hawks' eldest son was teaching history.

In July 1880, Alfred Hawks commented: *"I have given several Object Lessons and find they answer admirably."* Object lessons were introduced by the Victorians in order to teach children to observe, to take careful notice of their surroundings and to give them the language to describe their observations accurately. The teacher would show the children an object, or a picture, and then ask the children leading questions taken from a textbook. From 1884 Alfred Hawks recorded the list of object lessons required by HMI, and the choice of objects is often quite bizarre. In this way the children received instruction in scientific subjects.

The influence of Her Majesty's Inspectors on the structure of the lessons was immense, as a system of 'payment by results' had been introduced by the Revised Code in 1862. This led to the children being given 'trial examinations' to prepare them for the annual inspection. These were first introduced in 1863 by William Kingswood, and continued by both Henry Yeaxlee and Alfred Hawks. It is fascinating to read the comments by the masters on these examinations in the log book and then compare their evaluations with those of the inspector at the next inspection visit!

Log Book Entries

Miss Cecilia Miller had been appointed mistress in 1861

19 Jan 1863	*Mr. Godson took a class.* [The curate visited the school at least once a week, usually to teach the children.]
26 Jan 1863	*Mr. Godson read to the children for half an hour in the afternoon.*
16 Feb 1863	*Mr. Godson read to the children in the afternoon.*
19 Mar 1863	*Told James Keyes he should have no play for a week if he were not more industrious.*
26 Mar 1863	*Elizabeth Webb showed sulkiness over her Exercise – kept her in to learn what she ought to have written.* [12-year-old Elizabeth was the daughter of an agricultural labourer, Charles Webb, and his wife Sarah. They lived in the village street.]
24 Apr 1863	*Mr. Godson gave a Reading lesson.*
27 May 1863	*Complained of slow progress made by 1st Class in Reading – not able to devote sufficient time to them.*

Between 6 July and 27 July 1863, there was no official master or mistress.
It is unclear who taught the children

6 Jul 1863	*Visited by Mr. Godson who gave a reading lesson in the morning.*

William Batchelor Kingswood appointed master 7 September 1863

11 Sep 1863	*Gave the First and Second classes (boys) extra time in arithmetic in afternoon: only 1 out of 14 being able to put down 37 and add 4, from dictation.*
15 Sep 1863	*Took extra time in morning and afternoon in teaching First and Second classes to form their small and capital letters.*
22 Sep 1863	*Gave children home lessons for the first time today.*
2 Oct 1863	*Devoted a great deal of time with the First and Second classes of Boys in their writing in copy books.*
13 Oct 1863	[Kept in] *Walter Hills for neglecting to learn his home lesson.* [Walter, aged about eight, was the stepson of Thomas Smith, a shoemaker, and his wife Mary.]
14 Oct 1863	*Found the 1st Class Boys exceedingly stupid in Arithmetic, not being*

able to work the simplest sums in either simple or compound (Arithmetic) Subtraction.

10 Nov 1863   *Several of the third class began [to] write in Copy Book for the first time.*

11 Feb 1864   *Kept several in for negligence in lessons.*

12 May 1864   *The Children wrote their quarterly letters to their Parents which were seen by the Rev. Baines.* [These quarterly letters informed the parents of the dates of the holidays. Rev. Joseph Baines had replaced Rev. Godson as curate.]

26 May 1864   *The Rev. Baines took Standard IV in arithmetic.*

1 Jun 1864   *Mr. Baines took Standards III and IV in Arithmetic from 11 to 12.*

30 Jun 1864   *Rev. Joseph Baines took Standards III and IV in Arithmetic.*

1 Jul 1864   *Gave the children extra time in Numeration.*

6 Jul 1864   *Rev. Baines took Standards III and IV in Dictation.*

14 Sep 1864   *Gave Standard IV a preliminary examination in Dictation and Arithmetic on Paper in the Afternoon.*

28 Sep 1864   *Rev. Espin examined children in the afternoon.* [Rev. Espin was the rector.]

3 Oct 1864   *Rev. Baines examined Standard II in afternoon.*

11 Oct 1864   *Rev. Baines took Standard II in several subjects this morning.*

14 Oct 1864   *Gave the whole of the Standards an examination the first of a series intended as a trial to be held every Friday morning.*

18 Oct 1864   *Rev. Baines took Standard II this morning.*

19 Oct 1864   *Examined the Infants in afternoon.*

21 Oct 1864   *Made the weekly examination of all the classes in the morning and find the plan to answer.*

25 Oct 1864   *Rev. Baines took classes in morning.*

2 Nov 1864   *Rev. Baines took part of school in morning.*

30 Nov 1864   *Rev. Baines taught in the morning.*

14 Dec 1864   *Rev. Baines took school for an hour in morning.*

20 Dec 1864   *Rev. Baines examined school in morning.*

10 Jan 1865   *Rev. Baines took part of school in morning.*

19 Jan 1865   *Rev. Baines took Standards II, III & IV this morning.*

Henry Yeaxlee appointed master 23 January 1865

24 Jan 1865   *Revd. J. Baines called this morning and took Standards III, IV & V in Arithmetic.*

31 Jan 1865   *Revd. J. Baines took Standards III & IV this morning in Arithmetic.*

7 Feb 1865   *Revd. J. Baines called this morning and took Standards III & IV in Arithmetic.*

17 Mar 1865   *Revd. J. Baines called in the afternoon and addressed the children, thus kindly relieving me. Examined the 3rd Class in reading, and found that through the efforts of their teacher, at least six of them could read first-class books.*

3 May 1865   *School visited by Revd. J. Baines who gave lessons to First and Second Classes.*

24 May 1865   *Mr. Thompson called and took Standards V & IV.*

19 Jun 1865   *Took the Infant School myself.*

23 Jun 1865   *I have given much time to the Infants myself this week.*

4 Jul 1865   [Visited] *in the afternoon by the Revd. T. E. Espin who inspected the reading of Standards III & IV.* [This is the first recorded visit by the rector since Mr. Yeaxlee became the master.]

19 Sep 1865   *Visited by Revd. Walker, who expressed a desire to aid in the teaching.* [Rev. James Walker was the new curate.]

27 Oct 1865   *First monthly examination of Classes 1 & II for prizes.*

10 Nov 1865   *Monthly examination. Prizes to M. A. Smith and Alice Smith.* [Mary Ann and Alice were the daughters of the village shoemaker William and his wife Mary Ann. They were aged nine and seven.]

17 Nov 1865   *I feel more and more the want of a paid monitor.* [Elementary schools at this time used the monitorial system.]

20 Nov 1865   *A great deal of time taken up in making Church decorations which it seems was the custom before me.*

⚜

23 Feb 1866   *Examination Day. Mary Ann Smith first in Class I. Alice Smith in Class II.*

9 Mar 1866   *Examination rather unsatisfactory.*

13 Apr 1866   *Examination for prizes, the 1st worked hard.*

18 May 1866   *Examination Day. Good papers.*

8 Jun 1866   *Examination Day. First and third classes did very well.*

15 Jun 1866   *Examination papers very good.*

13 Jul 1866   *Examination Day.* [The weekly examination was held even though the attendance was extremely poor because of smallpox in the village.]

26 Oct 1866   *Gave the children a final examination.* [This was before the annual inspection the following week.]

30 Oct 1866   *Visited by Revd. Smith who gave the standards an examination.* [The curate had given his usual lesson the day before.]

17 Dec 1866	*First day of Examination for Prizes.*
18 Dec 1866	*Second day – for Arithmetic.*

𝓂

10 Jan 1867	*Visited by Revd. T. Espin who gave away prizes (presented by himself, Sir Charles Nicholson and Mr. S. Harvey) to the most proficient in Standards VI, V, IV & III.* [Mr. Stephen Harvey of Leigh Park Farm was later to become Henry Yeaxlee's father-in-law.]
7 Jun 1867	*Usual examination.* [There were two examinations in June and two in July.]
2 Aug 1867	*Examined the first Standard this morning – gave a prize to James Gilman.* [James was the 6-year-old son of John and Susan Gillman. His father was an agricultural labourer and rented a cottage near to the *Crown Inn.*]
3 Oct 1867	*Gave the children a little extra time.*
4 Oct 1867	*First Class examination.* [They were examined the following week as well.]
25 Oct 1867	*Gave first and second Classes a long examination this morning.* [He repeated this on 1 and 25 November.]
8 Nov 1867	*Gave Standards VI, V, IV an examination.*
6 Dec 1867	*Gave the first and second Classes a preparatory examination.*
16 Dec 1867	*First Day of the Christmas Examination – Scripture and Catechism.*
17 Dec 1867	*Second Day – Grammar and Reading examined by Rev. J. Yolland.*
18 Dec 1867	*Third Day – Composition.*
19 Dec 1867	*Fourth Day – Arithmetic.*

𝓂

6 Jan 1868	*Mr. Espin paid his farewell visit in the afternoon to give the prizes earned by the Christmas examinations.*
17 Jan 1868	*Examination Day.*
5 Feb 1868	*Gave the third class an examination to test the merits of the teacher. I find them moderately good.*
6 Feb 1868	*Examined the 4th Class for the same purpose as yesterday, with a like result.*
14 Feb 1868	*Gave the first & second Classes a long paper-examination.*
21 Feb 1868	Gave the 4th Class an examination for prizes.
5 Mar 1868	*Gave the first class an examination for the morning.*
18 Mar 1868	*Gave the VIth Standard an examination. I find the Reading faulty.*
31 Mar 1868	*Gave I & II Classes their Quarterly Examination.*
1 Apr 1868	*Prizes to Emma Harvey, S. Anderson, A. Ridgwell.* [Emma was the 7-year-old daughter of George and Mary Harvey. George farmed 18

acres in Daws Heath Road. Alice was the same age, the daughter of James and Catherine Ridgwell, who lived in a cottage near the *Crown Inn*. James was the village basket maker, while Catherine worked as a dressmaker and bonnet maker.]

3 Apr 1868	*Examination for Prizes – M. A. Smith, Sarah Anderson.* [Mary Ann Smith was either the daughter of William Smith or Thomas Smith, both shoemakers.]
19 Jun 1868	*Examination Day.*
3 Jul 1868	*Examination day for First & Second Classes.*
4 Sep 1868	*Gave the higher Standards a morning examination.*
11 Sep 1868	*Occupied the whole morning in examining the 1st & 2nd Classes.*
24 Sep 1868	*Gave Standard I an examination.*
1 Oct 1868	*Began the Quarterly examination this morning.*
2 Oct 1868	*Was obliged to take a part of the afternoon to finish the Examination.*
9 Oct 1868	*Gave the first & second Classes an examination.*
30 Oct 1868	*Examination in the afternoon.*
6 Nov 1868	*Gave the 1st Class a paper-examination this morning.* [This was the first of five such examinations given before Christmas.]
7 Dec 1868	*Received some prizes this afternoon for the children from Lady Nicholson.*

⁓⁓⁓

15 Jan 1869	*Revd. W. Metcalfe came this morning to distribute the Christmas prizes.*
15 Dec 1869	*Gave the 1st Class their Scripture Examination.*
16 Dec 1869	*Continued the Scripture & Arithmetic Examination for the Christmas prizes.*

⁓⁓⁓

16 Mar 1870	*Visited this morning by the Revd. W. & Mrs. Metcalfe who distributed the remaining Christmas prizes.*
17 Jun 1870	*Gave the under classes an examination this morning and found them satisfactory.*

⁓⁓⁓

23 Jan 1871	*Examination for the Prizes.* [Examinations continued for three days.]
16 Feb 1871	*Gave the First & Second Classes extra-time in Writing and Arithmetic this Morning.*
17 Mar 1871	*This morning (Friday) the Rector and Mrs. Metcalfe visited the School to give the Christmas Prizes.*

15 Apr 1871	*I have given the upper Classes Home Lessons this week, and I find them successful.*
28 Apr 1871	*I have examined Classes 3 & 4 this morning, and find them rather deficient: I want more teaching power, and I find the parents to be the great hindrance to their children's education.*
29 Sep 1871	*I gave the upper classes a trial examination this morning, & I find Class II very much the worse for their six weeks absence from School.*
13 Oct 1871	*I have departed from the usual school routine this week, by giving occasional trial examinations.* [This was in preparation for the visit by HMI on 18 October.]
27 Oct 1871	*The school-work has not proceeded very much this week, the Master being very unwell.*

⚶

4 Oct 1872	*I have given Classes I & II some trial examination papers, and this has in a small degree interfered with the ordinary routine – but the time allotted to secular instruction has not been interfered with.* [This was in preparation for the visit by HMI on 10 October.]

⚶

17 Jan 1873	*On Friday Morning the Rector visited the School to distribute prizes given by himself to the First Class.*
24 Jan 1873	*I have this morning thoroughly examined the Third and Fourth Classes and I do not find their progress so satisfactory as I anticipated.*
30 Jan 1873	*I gave Classes III & IV another thorough examination and I find the Teachers are working with considerable vigour.*
16 May 1873	*I have commenced a series of Friday Morning examinations, and I do not find the children so forward as I anticipated.*
8 Sep 1873	*I have recommenced the weekly examinations.*
26 Sep 1873	*I have given paper examinations.*
2 Oct 1873	*I have repeated the paper examinations.*
3 Oct 1873	*I have broken through the ordinary routine by giving frequent paper examinations.* [This was in preparation for the annual visit by HMI on 10 October.]
10 Oct 1873	*I have given several paper examinations this week.*

⚶

23 Jan 1874	*I have given greater attention to the working of the lower classes than I generally can afford the time to do.*
4 Sep 1874	*I am preparing a series of paper examinations for the next month.*
18 Sep 1874	*The usual routine has been interfered with by trial examinations to Classes I & II.*

25 Sep 1874	*The morning work has been slightly deranged by the trial paper examinations.*
16 Oct 1874	*The routine of work has been slightly broken into by paper examinations.*
30 Oct 1874	*This week has been a time of shaking the newly-raised children into their place.*

⌘

Between 19 March and 17 May 1875, in the absence of a master, the rector ran the school

16 Apr 1875	*The usual routine of Study has been carried on.*
23 Apr 1875	*Children have gone through the usual work steadily.*
30 Apr 1875	*First class have decidedly improved in Arithmetic; viz. Long Division of Money; in which they had been imperfectly instructed.*

Alfred Hawks appointed master 17 May 1875

11 Jun 1875	*The work as represented on new Time Table, has been strictly carried out.*
18 Jun 1875	*I have commenced the trial examinations, which prove to be of great benefit to the children.*
25 Jun 1875	*I have devoted the greater part of my time to individual teaching, as several children are very backward.*
16 Jul 1875	*Children have improved in the execution of the weekly Examination Papers.*
23 Jul 1875	*I find from the trial-examinations the children are still favourably advancing in their studies.*
17 Sep 1875	*I have given the children two examinations this week, and have been somewhat disappointed in their work, no doubt arising from the lazy mood, which their holliday* [sic] *has brought them into.*
24 Sep 1875	*A good portion of time this week has been devoted to individual teaching.*
1 Oct 1875	*The children appear to be succeeding very fairly in the Exam. Papers with the exception of one or two in the II Standard.*
15 Oct 1875	*I have myself given more time to the Lower Standards as they naturally become unsound in their work if left entirely to Monitors for any length of time.*
22 Oct 1875	*Usual Routine has been interfered with by trial-examination papers.*
19 Nov 1875	*I have commenced the Geography and Grammar lessons being required*

for the next Examinations, which will be held in June. [The school would be awarded extra grants for teaching these 'specific' subjects.]

⟋⟍

11 Feb 1876   *I have this week devoted a considerable time to the teaching of the four rules in Arithmetic to the upper Standards.*

18 Feb 1876   *I have again been devoting a great portion of my time to the backward children, there being 3 boys in the III Standard who appear to be almost void of Common Sense. I have inflicted punishment – but after continually testing them and finding it a failure I cannot but* pity *their ignorance, hoping they may in due time turn out to be bright youths.*

17 Mar 1876   *I have devoted a great portion of my time to the upper Standard as they appear to be decreasing instead of increasing in their Arithmetic.*

24 Mar 1876   *The School continues to be in very fair order of working, the children showing signs of some good marks of improvement.*

7 Apr 1876   *The children appear to increase in their interest of their work.*

28 Apr 1876   *I have had a great disturbance with the parents respecting the children learning Geography – calling it a pack of rubish* [sic]*, and on sending Geography home by a child to learn, the parent threatened to break the slate if it came home with such rubish* [sic] *on again. This, of course, only occurs among the ignorant.*

5 May 1876   *A great disturbance still prevails among the parents concerning the Geography, which I find a very great difficulty to meet.*

12 May 1876   *I find the children are not very forward for the coming Examination from a trial-exam. which I gave them on Tuesday.*

16 Jun 1876   *I still find a very great difficulty in teaching Grammar & Geography: the parents seem to be determined their children shall not learn, saying it would be a great deal better if we taught them to* read *and* write.

23 Jun 1876   *I find Jethro Nunn (Standard V) who has been away from the village a considerable time, does not know his poetry and is also very backward in Geography. The Analysis required by the New Code for Standard V I have not attempted, as I find the time is insufficient.* [Jethro Elisha Nunn, the son of John and Amy Nunn, was born at Hadleigh in 1865. The son of an agricultural labourer, his knowledge of geography later improved, as he became a first mate in the Merchant Service and presumably travelled further than Essex.]

30 Jun 1876   *I have been preparing a list of books for the Standards this year, as we are short of them, especially for the lower Standards.*

28 Jul 1876	*I have commenced teaching the children letter-writing and find it answers admirably, it creates a nice feeling between teacher and taught, and certainly improves them in General Knowledge.*
22 Sep 1876	*The studies are carried on very pleasantly the children seemed to have gained in acuteness from the late Vacation.*
29 Sep 1876	*The School is now in very good working order, and has the prospect of passing a good Examination next year. The School was visited this afternoon by the Revd. A. J. Skrimshire who asked a few questions on Geography, and obtained very satisfactory answers.*
17 Nov 1876	*The Arithmetic in the upper Standard appears to be making very slow progress.*

✑

26 Jan 1877	*The children are working very satisfactorily for the next Examination* [HMI Inspection]; *and appear to have more confidence in themselves than they had previous to the last Examination.*
2 Mar 1877	*I have devoted more time to dictation in the upper Standards as I found it was getting behind.*
9 Mar 1877	*On Tuesday and Thursday the School was visited by the Rector, who examined the children's Geography.*
16 Mar 1877	*I find the children in Standard III are still very backward in their Long Division sums.*
20 Apr 1877	*I have devoted a considerable time to Standard one as they appear to be somewhat backward in their reading.*
18 May 1877	*I have had a little difficulty again with the Home Lessons.*
15 Jun 1877	*The children are working well for the Examination.*
21 Sep 1877	*I have got some new cards for the Infants and to be making good progress with them.* [A recommendation of the HMI report in June was that the infants required reading sheets.]
16 Nov 1877	*The children are executing their studies with great energy.*

✑

8 Feb 1878	*The School has been visited by the Rector this week who congratulated the children on their good style of writing.*
12 Apr 1878	*The routine has been slightly interfered with by the trial examinations.*
19 Apr 1878	*The children are working well for the Examination.* [The HMI Inspection was on 4 June.] *I have devoted a little more time to the lower Standard again this week and find them progressing satisfactorily.*
31 May 1878	*I have devoted a great deal of time this week to the lower children.*
19 Jul 1878	*The children, who were thoroughly discouraged at the last*

Examination, are working with remarkable energy and determination. [The HMI Inspector visited on 4 and 17 June and was critical of the school.]

26 Jul 1878   *The children have learned their Home Lessons during the past week very satisfactorily.*

27 Sep 1878   *Maps and other necessaries have been supplied by the Managers.*

11 Oct 1878   *The upper Standards are working at the "Arithmetical Test Cards" with great energy.*

20 Dec 1878   *I have given some trial examinations to the upper Standards this week and find they are progressing favourably.* [This was after a measles epidemic in the previous two months led to low attendance and closure of the school.]

7 Feb 1879   *I have devoted more time to the Lower Standards this week, and have found them very backward.*

22 Mar 1879   *The children are learning their Home Lessons remarkably well.*

4 Apr 1879   *I have given several trial examinations this week and find the children steadily progressing.* [This was probably in preparation for the HMI Inspection on 18 June.]

6 Jun 1879   *I have given some trial examinations this week.*

7 Nov 1879   *I have given a trial Examination this week to the upper Standards.*

2 Jan 1880   *Given trial examination papers this week and find the children rather backward.*

30 Apr 1880   *I have given the Children some trial-examinations this week and find them very satisfactory. Arithmetic in Standard II rather weak.*

7 May 1880   *The children are working very hard for the Examination, and are taking great pains with their Home Lessons.* [The children were examined on 1 June by HMI Assistant.]

21 May 1880   *I have devoted a great deal of time to Standard II this week as they were backward in Arithmetic.* [Her Majesty's Inspector agreed, reporting: "Arithmetic on the whole very fair, I should like the Children to show more ability in applying rules."]

9 Jul 1880   *I have given several Object Lessons and find they answer admirably.*

12 Nov 1880   *I am working to a Time table drawn up in accordance with approved scheme.*

18 Feb 1881   *I have given several trial-examinations this week and find the children satisfactorily improving.*

25 Feb 1881	*I have devoted the greater part of the week to the teaching of Standard I.*
1 Apr 1881	*I am still devoting the greater part of my time to the teaching of Standards I & II as they require a great deal of help in their Arithmetic.*
27 May 1881	*Had some new Arithmetic Test Cards on Wednesday; most of the Children worked the Sums very satisfactorily.*
24 Jun 1881	*We have a new set of Geographical Readers for the upper classes this week.*
21 Oct 1881	*Examined the upper Standard in Geography and was satisfied with the result.*
25 Nov 1881	*Examined the Children on Thursday and was tolerably well satisfied with the result – found Standard 1 weak in Arith. I have therefore devolved more time to that subject.*
16 Dec 1881	*I have devoted the greater part of my time this week to Standard III especially for Arithmetic.*

᷈⁓

13 Jan 1882	*Gave the Children a trial Examination – Arithmetic is rather weak in the Upper Classes.*
10 Feb 1882	*I have devoted more time than usual to Arithmetic and find the Children in the upper Standards are decidedly more forward than they were last year at this time. I attribute it to the much more regular Attendance; owing to the favourable weather.*
6 Apr 1882	*I have devoted more time to Standard II this week especially in dictation.*
21 Apr 1882	*Gave the children a trial Examination and find the Upper Standards improving, especially in Arithmetic in which they were rather weak last year.*
28 Apr 1882	*Have devoted a great deal of time this week to the lower Standards.*
30 Jun 1882	*Yesterday afternoon the Rector called and gave me permission to get what books &c. that was* [sic] *required for the coming year.*
15 Dec 1882	*I gave a trial examination on Wednesday 1st Standard did very well upper Standard still very weak.*

᷈⁓

9 Feb 1883	*I have devoted the greater part of my time this week to Standard I.*
11 May 1883	*Gave a trial Examination on Wednesday and found Standard II improved in Geography.*
23 Nov 1883	*I have devoted the greater part of time this week to Standard I.*
21 Dec 1883	*Received a note from Mr. Healing approving of the poetry selection.* [Mr. Thomas Healing was the Inspector's Assistant who had inspected the school in June.]

⌇

18 Jan 1884	*I have spent more time this week with Lower Standards. Standard II shows great weakness in Arithmetic from a trial examination given on Wednesday.*
1 Feb 1884	*I have to-day examined the Infants and found them very backward. The results of the trial examinations in the Standards are much more satisfactory this week.*
21 Mar 1884	*Gave the upper Standards a trial examination and found the Arithmetic weak in Standard III.*
25 Apr 1884	*I gave the Upper Standards a trial-examination in Arithmetic and the result was very satisfactory.*
16 May 1884	*Gave the Children a trial Examination on Tuesday, found the Upper Standards greatly improved in Arithmetic. Standard I has improved in Writing and Reading.*
25 Jul 1884	*In the place where Geography is shown as being taught by the Time Table, Spelling will be substituted.*
1 Aug 1884	[With the inspection report, Alfred Hawks had also received a list of object lessons for Infants.]
	Object Lessons for Infants 1885:
	Cow, Horse, Sheep, Builder, Gold, Silver, Iron, Cotton, Wool, Silk, Leather, Paper, Straw, Fowls, Sponge, Bread Meals, Glass, Bricks, Water, Chalk, Swallow, Lark, Coal, Fishes, Sugar, Tea, School, Grass, Basketmaking.
24 Oct 1884	*I have paid Special Attention to the teaching of Arithmetic to Standard III this week.*
28 Nov 1884	*I have devoted extra time to the Upper Standards this week.*

⌇

9 Jan 1885	*Gave the whole School a trial-examination on Wednesday.*
13 Feb 1885	*Examined the children on Friday and was fairly well satisfied with the results.*
8 May 1885	*Gave the children a trial Examination on Thursday and found Standard I greatly improved in their Arithmetic.*
26 Jun 1885	*Poetry repeated on the day of Examination*
	Standard IV, V, VI The Deserted Village [by Oliver Goldsmith]
	III The battle of Blenheim [by Robert Southey]
	II The Village Blacksmith [by Henry Wadsworth Longfellow]
	I The blind boy [by Colley Cibber].

⌇

14 May 1886	*I gave the children a trial Examination on Thursday and found Standard IV had made good progress in their Arithmetic.*

18 Jun 1886	*I gave the Children a trial-examination on Wednesday.*

∽๛∾

10 Jun 1887	*I have given several trial-examinations and been fairly satisfied with the results. Standard V have not done so well as they might.*
8 Jul 1887	*The Children have had several trial-examinations this week.*

∽๛∾

20 Apr 1888	*I have given the children several Examinations during the week and find the results are very satisfactory.*
30 Nov 1888	*The children are working most satisfactorily.*

∽๛∾

24 May 1889	*I have given two trial-examinations this week.*
12 Jul 1889	*The work for next Examination has already been commenced with earnestness.* [The next HMI inspection was due in a year!]
15 Nov 1889	*I have devoted the greater part of my time this week to the Upper Standards.*

∽๛∾

6 Jun 1890	*I have given a trial examination and find the children very well up to their work.*
31 Oct 1890	*The children appear to be making very fair progress, and are taking great interest in their work.*

∽๛∾

6 Mar 1891	*The children throughout the School are working hard.*
5 Jun 1891	*Gave the children trial-examination on Wednesday.*
17 Jul 1891	*Infants are drilled between ordinary lessons.* [Her Majesty's Inspector had recommended more attention to physical exercise, and this was the reason for the extra drill.]
17 Jul 1891	<u>*Object Lessons for Infants 1891-92*</u> *A book, Farm-yard, House, Sheep, Butterfly, Horse, Hen, Trees, Primrose, Potato, Soap, Sponge, Milk, Butter, Sugar, Meat, Coal, Post Office, Seasons, Money, Slate, Umbrella, Table, Wild Flowers, Leather, Carpenter's Shop, Blacksmith's Shop, Elephant, Basket.*
13 Nov 1891	*The boys are now making a little progress in drawing.* [This may have been a new subject on the curriculum.]

∽๛∾

11 Mar 1892	*The general routine of the school is now carried on with re-doubled earnestness, although the work of the year is, of course, very backward.* [This was due to the closure of the school for six weeks due to a diphtheria outbreak.]
8 Apr 1892	*Gave trial-examination on Wednesday.*

27 May 1892	*I have given a trial examination in all subjects this week. The Arithmetic has been very successful especially in problems.*
24 Jun 1892	*The Drawing examination took place this morning.*
8 Jul 1892	*Gave the children their last trial-examination on Wednesday.*
29 Jul 1892	*The result of the Drawing Examination has just come and reports the work to be "Excellent".*

～ఞ～

| 16 Jun 1893 | *Gave a trial Examination on Wednesday.* |
| 3 Jul 1893 | [This entry regarding the curriculum was written in the log book on the day of the annual inspection.] |

Poetry for 1893-94

St. I & II	*Evening Song* [name of poet illegible]
	The Visit *J. Taylor*
III	*Llewellyn & his dog* *Spencer*
IV-VI	*Horatius & selection from Griffiths & Farran: Poetry for the young*
V-VI	*The funeral of William the Conqueror* [name of poet illegible]

English   *Schedule II*

List of Object Lessons 1893-94
A Steel Pen, Cotton, Wool, A Bell, The Qualities of a Butterfly, Tea, A boat, Gold, Paper, The Cat, Dog, Lion, Robin, Cow, An Orange, An India rubber ball, A Kite, Gloves, The Policeman, A Straw Hat, A yard measure, Ink, Rain, Rice, The Stinging Nettle, An Apple, A Grocer's Shop
Form and Colour

| 27 Oct 1893 | *Most of the Recommendations of H. M. Inspector have already been attended to especially with regard to books.* |

～ఞ～

22 Jun 1894	*The School was examined in Drawing on Monday by Lieu. Col. Gower and a half holiday given.*
20 Jul 1894	*I have given two trial examinations this week.*
2 Aug 1894	*All Lessons on the Time Table marked 3.15 to 4 are extended to 4.10 allowing 10 mins. recreation from 3.15 to 3.25.*
	Object Lessons for the Year Ending June 30th 1895
	A penny, A Farm Yard, A Potato, The Tiger, The Frog, Sugar, Sponge, The Shoemaker, The Primrose, Tea, Wild Flowers, A Basket, The

Camel, A Bell, A Blacksmith, Winter, The Lion, Salt, The Sea-shore, The Cat, Qualities of Water, Wool, A Candle, An Umbrella, Clothing, The Hen, Milk, Birds' feathers, Iron, Coal.
Form and Colour

Poetry for 1895

I & II	*What the tiny drop said*	[name of poet illegible]
III	*England's* [word illegible]	*(Bernard Barton)*
	Bird in the Cage	*(Bowles)*
IV-VI	*The Church of Brou*	
	The Castle	*(M. Arnold)*
VI	*(in addition) The Church*	

11 Jan 1895	*Gave trial-examination on Monday – children appear to be making very good progress.*
11 Apr 1895	*Gave trial-examination on Wednesday.*
21 Jun 1895	*The Drawing Examination was held on Tuesday.*
16 Jul 1895	[Written in the log book and initialled by Her Majesty's Inspector, Mr. Arthur E. Bernays.]
	Maps of the county as well as of England and Scotland will now be required together with a supply of charts to illustrate the geographical definitions, there is no globe. It is essential, too, that there shd. be a set of Geography Readers for the 3rd Standard.
16 Jul 1895	[This entry regarding the curriculum was written in the log book on the day of the annual inspection.]

Poetry for 1895-6

Stand. I & II	*Summer Song (Mary Howitt)*
III	*Llewellyn & his dog (Spencer)*
IV.V.VI	*Loss of the Birkenhead (Francis Hastings Doyle)*
	Barbara [rest of entry is illegible]
Stand. VI	*Twilight Calm (Christina Rossetti)*
P. Teacher	*How they brought the good news from Ghent to Aix (Robert Browning)*

Class Subjects for 1895-6.
English – Schedule II

<u>*Geography*</u>

Stand. I & II	*Definitions & Meanings & use of a Map*
Stand. III	*England*
Stand. IV & V & VI	*British Isles*
Maps V & VI	*Essex, Ireland, Scotland.*

<u>*List of Object Lessons 1895-96*</u>

A Book, Insects, Salt, Cork, A Bottle, Common Vegetables, Cow, The Sheep, Birds, Elephant, Bread, Clothing, Railway Station, Basket, Butter Making, The Frog, Wheat, An Apple, Spring, Money, Water, Ink, Cotton, Coffee, Tea, Trees, The Lion, The Nettle, Rice, Slate. Form & Colour.

11 Oct 1895	*I have devoted a great deal of time to Stand. IV especially the Arithmetic. The children are much interested in their Geography, although it is somewhat difficult for them being a new Subject.* [There had been an attempt to introduce this as a 'specific' subject in 1875.]
18 Oct 1895	*Commenced map training to Stand. V.VI.VII.*
25 Oct 1895	*The children appear to be very much interested in their new subject (Geography) although great difficulty is experienced in remembering the somewhat difficult names. I have introduced a little composition in Standard IV taking a paragraph from the lesson read and find it fairly mastered.*
1 Nov 1895	*Most of the subjects appear to be making headway. I have thoroughly inspected the work of each class.*
22 Nov 1895	*I have examined the School throughout and glad to find good progress especially in the Reading of lower Standards which in the early part of the year was very weak.*
13 Dec 1895	*I have examined the Upper Classes in Geography this week and was fairly satisfied with result. Composition is making some headway.*
19 Dec 1895	*The 4th Standard has now finished their poetry. Grammar in the Upper Standards is making very slow progress.*

⁂

3 Jan 1896	*Most of the Standards have now finished their rules in Arithmetic and the next fortnight will be spent in exercises of those rules before working any problems. Nearly all the work will be on paper. The Map-drawing in St. V & VI is making some progress. During the past week I have confined myself to one sentence in parsing for St. IV & upwards and the result has been most satisfactory.*

17 Jan 1896	*I find the plan of teaching English in connection with reading answered extremely well.*
24 Jan 1896	*Next week I propose giving lessons on Arithmetic problems and Mental Arithmetic.*
31 Jan 1896	*I have given the School a thorough Examination this week and find the work sounder in most Subjects than I have known before. My plan throughout the past six months has been not to attempt too much at once not* [sic] *to thoroughly clear the way as we go.* *During the coming month of February nearly all the Arithmetic Lessons will be devoted to the teaching of problems thus giving the children an opportunity of practically applying the rules which they have been learning.*
14 Feb 1896	*The Composition of Standard V does not make satisfactory progress.*
28 Feb 1896	*We have nearly mastered the Map drawing to Stand. V & upwards. Essex only remains.*
27 Mar 1896	*I am glad to say several dull & backward children have been making better progress.*
17 Apr 1896	*Most of the work for the year has been covered – there only remains Sq. measure in Arithmetic for Stand. IV and the drawing of Map of Essex.*
1 May 1896	*On Monday next I hope to give the School a trial Examination.*
8 May 1896	*The trial-examination on Monday gave general satisfaction although of course there are faults yet, but I am much pleased to see the increased interest taken by the children in all the work.*
19 Jun 1896	*To-day I have given an extra lesson on Drawing thus departing slightly from the usual routine.*
26 Jun 1896	*On Thursday the School was examined in Drawing when all the boys were present.*
24 Jul 1896	<u>*Object Lessons for Infants 1896-97*</u> *A book, Farm-yard, Camel. Glass tumbler, Inside of a house, An India-rubber ball, The Sheep, Butterfly, Milk, Potatoe* [sic]*, Sponge, Post Office, Rice, Cork, The qualities of water, Salt, Winter, Grocer's Shop, The Cow, Wheat, Blacksmith's Shop, A Bell, A Slate, Elephant, Ice, Wild Flowers, Coal, The Sea-shore, The Robin, Bread.* <u>*English for 1896-7*</u> *Schedule II throughout the School* <u>*Geography*</u> *for Stand. IV upwards as per Code for St. IV with Maps of the St. Lawrence, England & Ireland*

Poetry

Stand. I & II	[entry illegible]	*(Mr. Alexander)*
III	*Wreck of the Hesperus*	
IV.V.VI	*I am minstrel of all I survey*	
	Boudicca	
VI	*The Solitary Reaper*	*(Wordsworth)*
	[entry illegible]	
Pupil teacher	*Horatius*	*(Macaulay)*

Alteration in Time Table

In place of Geography on the Time Table Object Lessons will be taken for Standards I, II & III while for the Upper Standards it will remain as it is. Drill for 11.30 to 12 on Wednesday.

18 Sep 1896   *We have now commenced the new work for the year.*

9 Oct 1896   *The work is now making good progress.*

16 Oct 1896   *The Object Lessons in the Lower Standards appear to be of great interest to the children.*

Object Lessons for Stand. I, II & III

I & II   Water, Porous Bodies, Clay, Hard & Soft Bodies, Plastic Bodies (putty), Sugar, Coal (uses), Coal (the mine), Coal (properties), India Rubber, Cat, Dog, Sheep, Pig, Parts of a plant, the Root, Stem, Leaves, Liquids & Solids, [the next two entries are illegible], *Soluble Substances, Flowers, The Cat's Big Cousins, Sand, (Water & Land Geographically), Iron, Cast Iron, Wrought Iron.*

III   Land, Water (Geographically), Dog, Cat, Lion, Elephant, Ox, Sheep, Whale, Fishes, Insect, Tea Plant, Sugar Cane, Wheat, Potatoe [sic]*, Apple Tree, Palm Tree, Oak Tree, Ind. Rubber, Mahogany, Gold, Silver, Copper, Iron, Tin, Zinc, Lead, Marble, Glass, Leather.*

6 Nov 1896   *The lower Standards are certainly making progress in their work. Object lessons are very successful.*

13 Nov 1896   *We have been giving a considerable time to Mental Arithmetic this week – and the sums have benefited a good deal.*

20 Nov 1896   *I have given the School a thorough trial-examination.*

29 Jan 1897   *I have thoroughly examined the whole of the School especially Standards I to III inclusive. The work in nearly every case is certainly more thorough – more attention has been paid to such matters as the proper formation of figures and letters as also the*

	Reading is more finished & I was glad to find the teachers had insisted upon slower and consequently a more <u>thorough</u> system of Reading.
12 Feb 1897	*Grammar is receiving special attention this week and is to be continued as I find it a bit weak.*
26 Feb 1897	*I have given the School a searching examination throughout and find a little weakness in the Reading of Stand. I. The Arithmetic is making rapid progress.*
12 Mar 1897	*The object lessons are quite enjoyed by teachers and scholars.*
2 Apr 1897	*I am giving trial examinations and am pleased to say the aspects pointed out to the teachers have been well attended to.*
23 Apr 1897	*We are giving repeated Examinations throughout the School. Grammar which was weak is certainly making good progress.*
21 May 1897	*Several trial-examinations have been given this week.*
28 May 1897	*The results of trial-examinations have been satisfactory.*
11 Jun 1897	*I have examined the whole of the School this week. The Arithmetic came out remarkably well especially the problems. The style of Writing has much improved.*
2 Jul 1897	*Drawing Examination 30th June.*
10 Sep 1897	*I am pleased to say the children take very pleasantly to their work.*
8 Oct 1897	*<u>Object Lessons for Sts. I & II 1897-98</u>*

A Sponge, Blackbird, Candle, Fire, Skylark, A Letter, The Song Thrush, Robin, A Tree, Garden, Chair, Penny, Money, Tea, Rat, Cup & Saucer, The Seasons, Farmer, Farm-yard, Beast of Burden, Blacksmith, Horse, Cat, Cat Tribe, The Dog, Dog Tribe, Butter, Cheese, Bread, A Kettle.

<u>Standard III</u>
Land & Water, Iron, What is this?, Parts of a plant, Knife, Fork, How plants grow from seeds, Buttons, Roots of Plants, Pin, What is water?, Needle, How crockery is made, Matches, Flowers & blossoms, Coal, Gas, Balloons, Dry fruits, Life-boat, Wool, Poisonous plants, The Lighthouse, Cotton, Dew, The Sea, An Ocean Steamer, The leaves of plants, What is a plant?, Air & water compared, Fruits & Seeds.

<u>Infants</u>
A Brick, Cork, Cow, Elephant, Railway Station, Dog, Spring, Ink, Tea, The Nettle, Insects, A bottle, Sheep, Bread, Basket making, Wheat, Money, Cotton, Trees, Salt, Rice, Vegetables, Birds, Clothing, Butter, An Apple, Water, Coffee, The Lion, Blacksmith's Shop.

Geography Sts. IV-VII
British N. America, Australia & England.
Maps: Basin of St. Lawrence, England, Scotland.

Poetry

IV.V.VI	*The Church of Brou*	*(M. Arnold)*
III	*Lucy Grey*	
I & II	*The Use of Flowers*	*(Howitt)*
	The Violas	*(Taylor)*
P. Teacher	*Song of the last minstrel*	

22 Oct 1897	*The Classes are now all in good working order. I have examined the lower Sts. & [am] well pleased with the progress.*
10 Dec 1897	*I have given a trial examination this week and find some of the subjects very sound, especially the Object Lessons in the three Standards.*
4 Mar 1898	*Examined the School throughout.*
18 Mar 1898	*I have had several examinations this week on Slates and find considerable progress has been made since the Inspector's Visit.*
1 Apr 1898	*Examined the whole school and am glad to say I found a marked improvement.*
22 Apr 1898	*Admitted several fresh Children who appear to have had no previous instruction notwithstanding their advanced age – This has a very bad effect on the infant Class where I am obliged to place them and makes the work of the Teacher extremely arduous.*
6 May 1898	*I have examined the whole School this week and was much pleased with the general improvements in the lower Standards. Stand. IV and upwards did not show quite so much progress in Arith. & Writing.*
20 May 1898	*I am glad to say the trial-examinations have been very satisfactory although of course faults still exist.*
26 Aug 1898	*We have admitted a good number of children and in several cases children even at the age of 7 do not know their letters. This is a great drawback to the work in Standard I.*
9 Sep 1898	*The work is going on with great energy.*
23 Sep 1898	*I examined the School this morning for the first time & in most places it was satisfactory.*
21 Oct 1898	*The Class Subjects for the Year Ending 1899 are:*

English and Geography throughout the School.
<u>*Geogr. for Stand. IV & upwards*</u>
The British Isles.

<u>*Poetry*</u>
Stand. IV	*Horatius*
III	*The Bridge (Longfellow)*
II	*Compassion*
I	*The Children's Hour*

The Geography now takes the place of <u>Object Lessons</u> as shown on the Time Table but is taught by Obj. Lesson in the Lower Standards.

<u>*Stand. III*</u>
Countries, Mountains, Coastline, Capes (Seas, Bays & Gulfs), Towns, Lakes, Exports, Imports, Manufactures, Coal Fields, Ports, Railways, Islands, Boundaries, Fisheries, Plains, Hills, Minerals, Rivers.

<u>*Stand. II*</u>
Cardinal Points, Plains & Hills, Mountains & Valleys, Springs & Lakes, A River (Thames), How rivers are fed, The Mouth of a river, The Ocean & Seas, Capes, Islands & Straits, Peninsulas, Bays & Gulfs, The Map [the remainder of the entry is illegible.]

<u>*Stand. I*</u>
Cardinal Points, The Sun, Plans, Use of Maps

16 Dec 1898	*I have spent a good deal of time with the lower Classes.*

20 Jan 1899	*Examined the whole of the School and was fairly satisfied with the result.*
27 Jan 1899	*I am glad to say the Mental work in Arithmetic has much improved.*
3 Feb 1899	*Had an examination throughout the School in Mental Arithmetic and was much pleased with the progress.*
10 Feb 1899	*I am glad to say the mental work in Arith. is making good headway.*
3 Mar 1899	*A great deal of the Arithmetic lessons have mental* [work] *especially in the lower Standards.*
19 May 1899	*I have thoroughly examined each class this week and was much pleased with most of the work.*
2 Jun 1899	*I propose giving the final examination on Monday next to the upper Standards.*

7 Jul 1899	[The school year closed as usual on 30 June.] *I have re-arranged classes for the coming year. All the children in the Infants qualified by age have been placed in Stand. I.*
14 Jul 1899	<u>*Objects for Infants 1899-1900*</u> *Bricks, Cork, The Cow, Elephant, Railway Station, Dog, Ink, Tea, Spring, The Nettle, The Frog, Sheep, A Bottle, Bread, Basket making, Wheat, Money, Slate, Rice, Cotton, Trees, Vegetables, Butterfly, Sea-shore, Butter, Apples, Water, Coffee, The Lion, Blacksmith's Shop.*

<u>*Poetry*</u>

IV.V.VI	*Resignation*
	Lighthouse
III	*I am Monarch*
I & II	*What the raindrop said*

<u>*Class Subjects*</u>
English throughout the school Sch. II
Geography throughout the school
Sts. IV.V.VI Europe

8 Sep 1899	*The Scholars have settled down to the usual Routine of work.* [After the Summer Vacation]
3 Nov 1899	*The Attendance has been good and consequently the work has made greater progress.*
10 Nov 1899	*Gave the children a trial examination and was much pleased with some of the classes.*
12 Jan 1900	*I find the bad attendance before Christmas has greatly affected the work. Examined the upper Standards to-day.*
26 Jan 1900	*The work is now progressing very favourably.*
2 Feb 1900	*I have devoted more time to lower Standards.*
2 Mar 1900	*To-day is the end of the second term of School work. I intend giving an Examination on Monday.*
9 Mar 1900	*I am glad to find much improvement in the problems in Arithmetic which I believe is brought about by giving more attention to Mental exercises.*
23 Mar 1900	*The problem work in Arithmetic is making great headway.*
6 Apr 1900	*I have devoted a great deal of my time to the teacher's* [sic] *Classes and am much pleased with the work.*

12 Apr 1900	*I have examined the whole School this week in Oral work and feel quite confident that this part of the School work has much improved.*
25 May 1900	*I have again spent a good deal of time at the Teacher's* [sic] *Classes.*
1 Jun 1900	*Examined the School on Wednesday.*
8 June 1900	*A great deal of time has been devoted to Oral teaching.*
29 Jun 1900	*The classes have been re-arranged throughout the School and the new work commenced in earnest.* [The school year ended on 30 June and Her Majesty's Inspector had visited on 20 June.]
7 Sep 1900	*The work has been carried on in accordance with the New Code.*
14 Sep 1900	*The children are settling down to their new work.*
5 Oct 1900	*The children appear to be making headway in all the Standards.*
23 Nov 1900	*I have spent a good deal of time among the lower Standards and find the work generally satisfactory.*

All Scripture is Breathed out by God and Profitable for Teaching

(2 Timothy Chapter 3 Verse 16)

UNDER THE REVISED CODE of 1862, Scripture was not an obligatory subject for elementary schools, but in church schools, like Hadleigh National School, it was considered the most important part of the curriculum. Often the village curates would visit the school and teach Scripture lessons. In the 1860s the Reverends John Godson, Joseph Baines, James Walker, Henry William Smith and John Yolland were frequent visitors for this purpose. The learning of the catechism, which was a manual for the instruction of those preparing to be brought before the bishop for confirmation, was also important. It was in the form of questions followed by answers to be memorised. The principal elements of the Anglican faith were included, such as the Apostles' Creed, the Ten Commandments and the Lord's Prayer. The 1870 Elementary Education Act introduced a 'conscience clause', which allowed parents to withdraw their children from religious instruction. As a church school, Hadleigh National School was inspected by the Diocesan Inspector, who was usually a local clergyman.

Log Book Entries

Miss Cecilia Miller had been appointed mistress in 1861

5 Jan 1863	*Mr. Godson took a Scripture Lesson.* [Rev. John Godson was the curate for Hadleigh from 1860 to 1864.]
19 Jan 1863	*Mr. Godson gave a Scripture lesson in the afternoon.*
2 Feb 1863	*Mr. Godson took a Scripture Lesson in the afternoon.*
23 Feb 1863	*Mr. Godson took a Scripture Lesson.*
2 Mar 1863	*Mr. Godson came and led prayers.*
3 Mar 1863	*Mr. Godson took a Scripture Lesson.*
30 Mar 1863	*Mr. Godson took a Scripture Lesson.*
20 Apr 1863	*Mr. Godson took a Scripture Lesson.* [The curate visited every week after this to teach Scripture.]
18 May 1863	*Mr. Godson examined 1st and 2nd classes in Scripture History.*
28 May 1863	*Questioned all the classes in Scripture History in the afternoon and found them rather deficient and inattentive.*

Between 6 July and 27 July 1863, there was no official master or mistress.
It is unclear who taught the children

6 Jul 1863	*Visited by Mr. Godson who gave a Scripture* [lesson] *in the afternoon.* [He continued teaching Scripture every week in July.]
15 Jul 1863	*Mr. Godson examined the children in the Church Catechism – found them rather deficient.*
16 Jul 1863	*Spent some time myself in teaching them that subject.*

William Batchelor Kingswood appointed master 7 September 1863

14 Sep 1863	*Mr. Godson gave a Scripture lesson to first Class in the morning.* [He taught this class twice more in September.]
25 Sep 1863	*Gave the whole school a lesson on the Church Catechism from 9.15 to 10.15 a.m.*
6 Oct 1863	*Mr. Godson took first Class in Scripture in morning.* [He taught this class twice more in October.]
17 Nov 1863	*Mr. Godson took 1st Class in Scripture in morning.*
8 Dec 1863	*Mr. Godson took his class.* [He taught this class twice more in December.]

8 Jun 1864	*Rev. Baines took Standards III and IV in Scripture.* [Rev. Baines was curate from 1864 to 1865.]
24 Jun 1864	*Rev. Baines took Standards III and IV in Scripture.*
12 Jul 1864	*Rev. Baines took Standards III and IV in Scripture.*

Henry Yeaxlee appointed master 23 January 1865

24 Jan 1865	*Revd. J. Baines called this morning and took Standards III, IV & V in Scripture.*
31 Jan 1865	*Revd. J. Baines took Standards III & IV this morning in Scripture.* [He gave two further lessons in February.]
2 Mar 1865	*Revd. J. Baines took Standards III & IV this morning in Scripture.* [He gave four further lessons in March.]
4 Apr 1865	*The Revd. J. Baines makes his usual visit.*
28 Apr 1865	*School visited by Revd. J. Baines who gave his ordinary lessons.*
10 Oct 1865	*Visited by Revd. Walker who took Standards III, IV & V in Scripture.* [Rev. James Walker replaced Rev. Baines as curate.]
24 Oct 1865	*Visited by Revd. Walker who gave a Scripture lesson to Standards III, IV & V.*

◊

6 Feb 1866	*Again visited by Revd. Walker, who took Standards IV & V in Church Catechism.*
20 Feb 1866	*Visited by Revd. J. Walker who gave Standards IV & V catechism teaching.* [He continued with the lessons for the next two weeks.]
15 Oct 1866	*Revd. Smith came in the morning and gave the 1st and 2nd Classes a lesson.* [Rev. Henry William Smith was the new curate.]
29 Oct 1866	*Revd. Smith gave his usual lesson this morning.*
26 Nov 1866	*Visited by Revd. W. Smith who gave the first class their usual Scripture lesson.*
3 Dec 1866	*Revd. W. Smith gave his lesson in the morning..*

◊

11 Feb 1867	*Visited by Revd. W. Smith who gave his usual Scripture lesson.* [He visited once a month up to 13 May, when he gave his last Scripture lesson.]
11 Apr 1867	*Gave 1st Class an extra Scripture lesson.*
23 Oct 1867	*Visited in the afternoon by the Rev. J. Yolland who gave his usual lesson.* [Rev. John Yolland was the new curate.]
4 Dec 1867	*Rev. J. Yolland gave his usual lesson.*

◊

15 Dec 1869	*Gave the 1st Class their Scripture Examination.*
16 Dec 1869	*Continued the Scripture Examination.*

✐

16 Jun 1871   *On Thursday the School was visited by the Diocesan Inspector Revd. A. B. Chalker & examined in Scripture and Catechism. Children were allowed a half-holiday in the Afternoon.* [Rev. Alfred Ball Chalker was the rector of North Benfleet.]

✐

19 Jan 1872   *Having thoroughly considered the requirements of the Diocesan Inspection, I find that it is impossible to meet them properly, unless I neglect some of the work for the Government Inspection.*

12 Jul 1872   *On Thursday the School was inspected in Religious Subjects by the Revd. Canon Chalker, assisted by the Revd. W. Metcalfe.*

✐

20 Jun 1873   *The registers were not marked for one day in this week; there having been a Diocesan Inspection in the morning and the usual holiday in the Afternoon.*

✐

5 Jun 1874   *I have received a message from one of the parents this week asking that her child may be excused learning the Catechism.* [Use of the 'conscience clause'.]

26 Jun 1874   *Yesterday (Thursday) the Religious Subjects' Examination was taken by the Revd. A. Chalker. The Attendance was poor. The school was closed in the afternoon as usual.*

Alfred Hawks appointed master 17 May 1875

9 Jul 1875   *On Monday the Religious Subjects Examination was conducted by The Revd. Canon Chalker Rector of North-Benfleet.*

✐

4 Aug 1876   *The School was inspected on Monday in the Religious Subjects by Canon Chalker, when the Rector was present.*

✐

21 Jun 1878   *This afternoon the School was inspected in the Religious Subjects.*

✐

25 Jul 1879   *The Revd. Maude inspected the School in religious Knowledge on Tuesday morning and a half-holliday* [sic] *was given in the Afternoon.* [Rev. Charles Frewen Maude was the rector of Woodham Mortimer in Essex.]

ᕯᕯ

23 Jul 1880	*The School was inspected to-day in the Religious Subjects by the Revd. Maude and a half-holliday* [sic] *given in the Afternoon.*

ᕯᕯ

7 Jul 1882	*The Diocesan Inspector not being able to come to-day, the Examination was Conducted by the Rector and a holiday given in the afternoon.*

ᕯᕯ

6 Jul 1883	*The Children were examined on Wednesday in Religious Knowledge by the Diocesan Inspector Rev. Maude, a holliday* [sic] *was given in the Afternoon.*

ᕯᕯ

2 Jul 1886	*The School was examined on Monday Afternoon by the Revd. Kempe* [sic] *in Religious Knowledge who has given a most satisfactory Report.* [Rev. Godfrey Kemp was the rector of Rawreth.]

ᕯᕯ

24 Jun 1887	*Yesterday the School was examined in Religious Subjects by the Rev. Kempe* [sic].

ᕯᕯ

18 May 1888	*The School was inspected in Religious Knowledge on Tuesday afternoon.*

ᕯᕯ

29 Jul 1892	*The Scripture Examination was held on Tuesday and a half-holidy* [sic] *given on Wednesday afternoon.*

ᕯᕯ

14 Jul 1893	*The School was inspected on Thursday in Religious Knowledge by the Rev. G. Kemp.*

ᕯᕯ

8 Jun 1894	*The School was inspected in Religious Knowledge this afternoon.*
16 Nov 1894	*The Rector called on Tuesday & gave a Scripture lesson to the upper classes.* [This was the new rector, Rev. Armine George Metcalfe, who had only been in the village for six weeks.]

ᕯᕯ

21 Jun 1895	*The Scripture Examination was held on Monday Afternoo*n.

ᕯᕯ

15 May 1896	*The School was examined in Religious Knowledge to-day.*

ᕯᕯ

14 May 1897	*The examination in Religious Knowledge took place on Thursday afternoon when 150 Children were present.*

19 Nov 1897   *During the past week the Children have been to Church at the end of the morning session consequently the time shown on the Time Table for Religious Instruction has been taken from the beginning and placed at the end.*

⚜

13 May 1898   *The School was examined by the Diocesan Inspector on Religious Knowledge on Tuesday Afternoon.*

⚜

9 Jun 1899   *The School was inspected in Religious Knowledge on Wednesday afternoon.*

⚜

18 May 1900   *The School was examined in Religious Knowledge on Monday by the Rev. G. Kempe when the Attendance was very good.*

A Stitch in Time

UNDER THE REVISED CODE of 1862, needlework for the girls was an important and obligatory part of the curriculum. It provided some of the skills needed for working as a servant, such as the cutting out and sewing of garments, as well as mending. For working class girls at this time, 'going into service' was usually the only occupation available to them. Up to the First World War, more girls and women were employed in domestic service than in any other occupation. In the village of Hadleigh, they would either work for the local gentry, in houses such as Hadleigh House, Hadleigh Hall, Solby's House and the rectory, or they would have to find employment in London. At the time of the 1861 Census, there were thirteen females in domestic service in the village. In the 1860s and 1870s the task of teaching needlework was usually assigned to the master's wife or the infant mistress. From the late 1860s Lady Nicholson of Hadleigh House would award prizes of cloaks at Christmas to the two girls producing the best needlework.

The importance of the subject is demonstrated by its inclusion in the HMI inspection reports from 1875, which at first praised the level of work. In January 1879 Miss Agnes Groomes first helped with the needlework while the infant mistress was indisposed. Miss Groomes lived at the rectory with the Rev. Skrimshire and his wife, and was the 37-year-old daughter of Rev. John Groomes, the vicar of Shalford in Essex, who had died in 1872. The responsibility for teaching needlework in the period 1880 to 1886 appears to have been given to Miss Groomes, with Her Majesty's Inspectors commenting favourably on how well the subject was taught.

By 1887 Miss Emma Bell, the infant mistress, was leaving her class for three afternoons each week to teach needlework to the older girls. In the inspection report that year, Her Majesty's Inspector, Mr. Edward Maclaine Field, criticised this decision: *"Needlework is I regret to say not satisfactorily taught and I cannot recommend payment of the grant . . . provision should be made for supplying Miss Bell's place on Needlework afternoons with a more efficient teacher than at present and the attainment should improve."* Mr. Field was still critical of the attainment the following year, but recommended payment of the grant. In 1891 he again criticised the teaching of the subject by Miss Rachel Laura Bragg, the new infant mistress: *"Exercises such as patches and button-holes are done in a manner which show that they are not taught by right methods. The subject comes out on the whole only tolerably and the teacher should study a good manual."* Ironically, ten years before this, Rachel Bragg had been earning her living as a dressmaker, according to the 1881 Census.

The teaching of needlework by the infant mistress again became an issue in 1893 with Her Majesty's Inspector, Mr. Arthur E. Bernays, recommending that Mrs. Sarah Hawks (the master's wife, who was now the infant mistress) ought not to be responsible. He repeated his criticism the following year: *"Attention is directed to Article 85 (d) of Code. [I] recommend that the Infants' Mistress be no longer allowed to teach Needlework to the elder girls."* The school managers responded to this by appointing Alice Gertrude Hawks, the master's 19-year-old daughter, as the sewing mistress.

Log Book Entries

William Batchelor Kingswood appointed master 7 September 1863

7 Sep 1863   *Mrs. Kingswood took girls in needlework in the Afternoon. [Mrs. Sarah Kingswood, the wife of the newly appointed Master.]*

6 Nov 1863   *Girls did needlework in morning.*

21 Dec 1863   *The Girls did their needlework in the morning.*

8 Jun 1864   *Girls did Needlework as usual in the morning.*

Henry Yeaxlee appointed Master 23 January 1865

23 Jan 1865   *Girls brought very little needlework in the afternoon and were employed at their usual lessons.*

1 Apr 1866   *The new Sewing-mistress took the girls in the afternoon for the first time.*

3 Apr 1867   *In consequence of a Confirmation at South Benfleet the girls took needlework in the morning.*

17 Aug 1868   *The new Sewing Mistress came in the Afternoon.*

7 Jan 1869   *The sewing girls presented the Governess with a New Year's Gift.*

8 Dec 1869   *Visited in the afternoon by Lady Nicholson to inspect the sewing.*

24 Oct 1870   *Visited by Mrs. Metcalfe and friend who inspected the needlework.*

7 Jun 1872   *The sewing mistress was absent on Thursday afternoon because of illness in her family.*

29 Nov 1872   *The sewing-mistress has been absent during part of the week.*

13 Dec 1872   *The girls have devoted more time than usual to needlework in the afternoons.*

17 Jan 1873   *The children . . . received the prizes for needlework which had been sent by Lady Nicholson: and also each received a piece of cake, which was also given by the same lady.*

2 May 1873   *The Mistress having been absent this week the sewing-instruction has been omitted and it will be resumed on Monday next.*

17 Oct 1873	*The Sewing-class has not been taken this week: owing to the illness of the mistress.*

❧

23 Oct 1874 *Needle-work from Lady Nicholson has been received.*

11 Dec 1874 *I have received a note this week from Lady Nicholson in which she states her intention to refuse giving any cloaks as prizes to those girls who have been doing work for her for several weeks. She had previously promised in a note to send two cloaks to the two best, and she now withdraws from the obligation by asserting that the work is very ill done. It is but common justice to my children for whom I feel more consideration than Lady Nicholson can be supposed to have, to state that, the allegation is wholly without foundation, and that from personal observation, I know the work to have been equal, and in part superior to that which was worked by some of the same girls last year, and with which Lady N. was extremely pleased. Although I can surmise a reason for Lady Nicholson's adverse decision, I do not feel at liberty to mention it.*

❧

8 Jan 1875 *During the vacation some of the elder girls have worked more needlework for Lady Nicholson, and two of them have received presents from her.*

Alfred Hawks appointed master 17 May 1875

4 Jun 1875 *The girls are improving in their needle-work.*

15 Oct 1875 *Lady Nicholson has again promised cloaks to the two best needle-girls, finding the work is improving.*

❧

13 Oct 1876 *There has been no sewing this week, the mistress being unable to attend.*

❧

20 Apr 1877 *The Governess has been provided with the material on which the girls are to be taught cutting out, sewing etc. to be examined by the Inspector.*

27 Apr 1877 *There has been no needlework this week the Mistress not being at home.*

❧

1 Mar 1878 *The girls have had no sewing this week owing to the illness of the mistress.*

22 Mar 1878 *During the indisposition of the Mistress the sewing has been conducted by a Mrs. Trigg.* [Lucy Trigg was in her late forties and married to

James, a gardener. They lived at Rectory Cottage in Rectory Road.]

~

31 Jan 1879	*The Sewing has been conducted by Miss Groomes, a friend from the Rectory, owing to the indisposition of the Mistress.*
23 May 1879	*Miss Groomes from the Rectory is taking the Girls this Afternoon.*
14 Nov 1879	*Miss Bell has been conducting the Sewing, owing to the indisposition of the Mistress.*

~

23 Apr 1880	*Miss Groomes continues to take the Sewing.*

~

4 Mar 1881	*Miss Groomes is conducting the Sewing again.*
6 May 1881	*Miss Groomes is still conducting the sewing.*
23 Sep 1881	*Miss Groomes has re-commenced Sewing again.*

~

17 Mar 1882	*Miss Bell has conducted the Sewing this week as Miss Groomes has been unable to attend.*

~

29 Feb 1884	*Miss Groomes is conducting the Sewing lessons.*

~

22 Apr 1886	*Miss Groomes has been unable to attend to the Needlework this week having a bad cold.*

~

23 May 1890	*Miss Groomes came on Thursday and gave Miss Bragg some assistance with the sewing.*

~

26 Oct 1894	*On Tuesday and Thursday all the girls are taught sewing together from Standard I & upwards.*

~

16 Jul 1895	[Written in the log book and initialled by Mr. Arthur E. Bernays, the HMI.] *A sewing frame ought to be provided.*
11 Oct 1895	*Miss A. Hawks has been appointed Sewing Mistress to the older children.* [19-year-old Alice was the first of the master's children to commence work at the school.]

Sing, Sing, Sing, Sing...Everybody start to Sing

ALTHOUGH MUSIC WAS A part of the Victorian school curriculum, it was confined to singing traditional songs and hymns. The children would also have to learn all five verses of the National Anthem. The masters of the school were expected to play the organ at St. James the Less Church and, until 1867, a school choir would often attend mid-week church services with the master. Henry Yeaxlee and Alfred Hawks also sang at concerts in their leisure time, so this would have been a subject they would have enjoyed teaching. In the mid-1860s the school even employed a music teacher, Mr. David Bellingham. The singing lessons were inspected by the local clergymen, ladies of the village and Her Majesty's Inspector. HMI instructed the master as to which songs should be performed during the annual inspection, with these lists often recorded in the log book. In 1885 Mr. Healing, Her Majesty's Inspector, suggested that: *"a few more modern & sprightly songs should be taught".*

Log Book Entries

Miss Cecilia Miller had been appointed mistress in 1861

14 Jan 1863   *Mr. Godson heard the children practise singing.* [Rev. John Godson was the curate.]

William Batchelor Kingswood appointed master 7 September 1863

10 Sep 1863   *Practised singing the National Anthem.*

17 Sep 1863   *Choir attended Divine Service in the morning.*

6 Nov 1863   *Attended service with the choir.*

5 Feb 1864   *Taught the children a new tune "Hurrah for Merry England".*

10 Feb 1864   *Start with Singers to the Church in morning.* [Ash Wednesday]

24 Feb 1864   *The Singers went to Church this morning.*

22 Jun 1864   *Singing class at Church in the morning from 11 to 12.*

21 Sep 1864   *Several of first and other classes went to Church to sing at ½ to 11.*

Henry Yeaxlee appointed master 23 January 1865

2 Feb 1865   *Feast of Purification, attended service in the morning with choir.*

8 Feb 1865   *Went to church this morning with choir.*

31 May 1865   *Went to church this morning with the choir on the occasion of the marriage of the Revd. J. Baines.*

19 Jul 1865   *Went to church this morning with choir.*

20 Sep 1865   *Went to church this morning with choir.*

27 Sep 1865   *Went to church this morning with choir.*

29 Sep 1865   *Went to church this morning with choir being Michaelmas Day.*

24 Jan 1866   *Went to church this morning with choir.*

25 Apr 1866   *Mr. Bellingham, a musician from London, gave the children a singing lesson in the afternoon.* [David Charles Bellingham was born at Battersea in about 1836. By the time of the 1871 Census he had moved to 3 High Street, Prittlewell.]

24 May 1866   *Visited by Mr. D. C. Bellingham who gave the children a singing lesson.* [Mr. Bellingham continued to visit the school once a month to teach the children.]

7 Aug 1866	*Went to church with some of the choir.*
8 Nov 1866	*Visit by the Choirmaster.* [Mr. Bellingham now began weekly visits to the school.]
11 Dec 1866	*Visited by Choirmaster Mr. D. C. Bellingham who inspected the school singing.*

❧

15 Jan 1867	*Visited by the Choirmaster.*
24 Jan 1867	*Visited in the Afternoon by Mr. D. C. Bellingham.*
6 Feb 1867	*Went to church this morning with choir.* [Also for the next two Wednesdays.]
21 Feb 1867	*Visited by the Choirmaster.*
2 Apr 1867	*Visited by the Choirmaster.* [This was the last visit recorded in the log book.]
1 May 1867	*Went to church this morning with choir.*
11 Jun 1867	*St. Barnabas' Day. Went to church in morning with choir.*
9 Oct 1867	*Went to church this morning with Choir.*
18 Oct 1867	*Went to church in morning with choir.*
13 Nov 1867	*Went to church in the morning with choir.* [Also for the next three Wednesdays.]

❧

10 Nov 1871	*I have devoted more than usual time this week to Music teaching.*
17 Nov 1871	*I have again given special attention to music.*
24 Nov 1871	*More attention to Music teaching.*

❧

| 13 Sep 1872 | *I have devoted more time than usual to Music teaching, taking the time from the Scripture Time.* |
| 8 Nov 1872 | *The school was visited and the singing lesson inspected by Mrs. Metcalfe & Miss Cumming.* [Mrs. Metcalfe was the rector's wife. Miss Ellen Cumming was the 29-year-old daughter of Richard Cumming, a former carpet manufacturer, who had retired to Hadleigh from Notting Hill. The family lived in the house next to the blacksmith's in the main village street.] |

❧

| 27 Jun 1873 | *The school was visited on Monday Afternoon by Miss E. Cumming and a lady friend, who inspected the singing.* |
| 28 Nov 1873 | *The School was visited on Wednesday Afternoon by the Revd. W. Metcalfe, who inspected the singing.* |

Alfred Hawks appointed master 17 May 1875

2 Jul 1875   *The School was visited on Thursday by Mrs. Metcalfe, who inspected the Singing.*

29 Oct 1875   *The School was examined on Tuesday. List of Songs for Examination: Blue Bells of Scotland; The Spider and Fly; The first grief; All among the Barley; Woodman spare that tree; The Cuckoo; The Sparrow; Hymns of the Fisherman's Children; Dear* [next word illegible]*; Glorious Apollo; Home Sweet Home.*

22 Sep 1876   *The Rev. A. J. Skrimshire visited the School on Wednesday morning, and made some new arrangements about the Choir.*

21 Jun 1883   *List of Songs for 1883. The Prince of Wales, Sparkling Rill, On the heather, Little birds, King Christmas, Harvest time, Gaily our boat, National Anthem.* [This entry was written on the day of the annual inspection.]

26 Jun 1885   *List of Songs. The Spider and the Fly, To Farm, Keep in time, Hardy Norsemen, Summer time, Raise from hands, Rainy day, National Anthem.* [This entry was written on the day of the annual inspection.]

2 Jul 1889   *Songs for 1889*
                 Eight hundred years ago
                 Raise your hands
                 Harvest Song
                 Bright-eyed May
                 The Mill
                 Infants
                 Children of the city
                 The sparkling rill
                 Smiling May.

2 Aug 1894   *Songs for 1894*
                 Spring
                 Merry May
                 Distant Bells
                 Evening Bells
                 The Flowers.

16 Jul 1895   *Songs for past year*
Love at Home
Harvest morn [or Harvest moon]
Last Rose of Summer
Harvest Home
The Flowers
Infants
The Clock
Robin & Pussy
Boys & Girls.

14 Jul 1899   *Songs for 1899-1900*
Rule Britannia, Bright-eyed May, The Spider, Hurrah for England, Ring the bell watchman.

An Inspector Calls

Victorian schools were visited by the government's school inspectors at least once every year. Known as HMI, this title was short for 'Her Majesty's Inspector'. From 1 August 1863 funding for elementary schools depended in part on the outcomes of pupil examinations conducted by the school inspectors. This came to be known as 'payment by results'. The Newcastle Commission had recommended in 1861 that a grant should be paid in respect of every child who passed an examination in reading, writing and arithmetic. This provision was introduced by the Revised Code of 1862. Over the following years the conditions of the Revised Code were gradually relaxed. For example, the examinations were taken by a sample of children only. The system of payment by results remained in place for about thirty years, until the early 1890s.

As outlined in a previous chapter on the school curriculum, in order to expand the restricted curriculum, additional grants were awarded in 1871, 1875 and 1880 for 'specific' or 'class' subjects, and these were also examined by the inspectors.

The Revised Code of 1862 also required that: *"The summary of the Inspector's Report, when communicated by the Committee of Council to the Managers, must be copied into the Log Book."* This was to be done by the Secretary of the Managers, who was also required to sign the entry. As can be seen from the log book entries of Hadleigh National School, this requirement was not always strictly adhered to, with the rector of the village often allowing the master to copy the report into the log book. At times, the reports do not make sense, but whether this was due to the inspector, or the person who copied the report into the log book, is unclear.

Consequently, the annual examination by HMI was extremely stressful for both the teaching staff and the children, and the masters at Hadleigh National School introduced a system of trial examinations.

Log Book Entries

William Batchelor Kingswood appointed master 7 September 1863

23 Oct 1863   *Greater part of the Afternoon was occupied in getting the Statistics for the Government Reports.*

28 Oct 1863   *Government Inspection by Her Majesty's Inspector The Rev. Mitchell. Mr. Godson and Mr. Tyrrell were also present. There were 83 children present and a dull wet morning.* [Rev. Godson was the curate and Mr. Tyrrell was a local farmer. They were both school managers.]

5 Oct 1864   [Visit by Rev. M. Mitchell, H.M. Inspector for Schools.]

Henry Yeaxlee appointed master 23 January 1865

3 Oct 1865   *Some time occupied in preparing Government reports.*

4 Oct 1865   [Written and signed by Mr. Nevill Gream, H.M. Inspector for Schools.]

School inspected. Mr. Henry Yeaxlee certificated teacher of the 2nd class.

<u>*Copy of Report*</u>

This is a very fairly conducted country school, more teaching power is required to make it an efficient school. The Master is working conscientiously. [The managers gave the children a half-holiday. Mr. Nevill Gream lived in Chelmsford, Essex, and was Inspector of Schools for Essex 1865-78.]

〰

31 Oct 1866   [Written and signed by Mr. Nevill Gream, H.M. Inspector for Schools.]
Mr. Henry Yeaxlee certificated teacher of the 4th class.

1 Nov 1866   <u>*Copy of Report*</u>
This is a well-conducted school. The instruction is well-imparted. [The children were given the usual half-holiday.]

〰

7 Oct 1867   [Written and signed by Mr. Nevill Gream, H.M. Inspector for Schools.]
Mr. Henry Yeaxlee certificated teacher of the 4th class.
[James Tyrrell, a school manager, copied the report into the log book and signed it. The children were given their usual half-holiday.]
<u>*Copy of Report*</u>
The order in the school continues good. The instruction has suffered from the recent harvest which has engaged the labour of children, and from the indisposition of the master.

31 Oct 1867   *Received government report.*

〰

14 Oct 1868   [Written and signed by Mr. Nevill Gream, H.M. Inspector for Schools]
Mr. Henry Yeaxlee Certificated teacher of the 4th class. School examined 99 present. Gave the usual half-holiday.
[James Tyrrell, a school manager, copied the report into the log book and signed it.]
This school is nicely conducted. The order is good & the Instruction is improved since last year. The Scripture is very well taught.

〰

14 Oct 1869   [Written and signed by Mr. Nevill Gream, H.M. Inspector for Schools]
Mr. Henry Yeaxlee Certificated teacher of the 4th class.
[The rector copied the report into the log book and it was signed by himself and Mr. Tyrrell.]
The Instruction in this school is well imparted, and the order nicely maintained. Gave the children a half-holiday.

〰

13 Oct 1870 [Written and signed by Mr. Nevill Gream, H.M. Inspector for Schools]
Mr. Henry Yeaxlee certificated teacher of the 4th class.
[The rector copied the report into the log book and it was signed by himself and Mr. Tyrrell.]
This school is in good order and efficiently instructed. The writing is particularly good. [The children were given a half-holiday.]

18 Oct 1871 [Written and signed by Mr. Nevill Gream, H.M. Inspector for Schools]
Mr. Henry Yeaxlee certificated teacher of the 2nd class.
[The rector copied the report into the log book and signed it.]
This school is kept in excellent order, and well instructed.

20 Oct 1871 *The school examined on Wednesday morning. The Revd. W. Metcalfe present. Usual half-holiday.*

10 Oct 1872 [Written and signed by Mr. Alexander Finch, the H.M. Inspector's Assistant, who lived at Colchester in Essex.]
Mr. Henry Yeaxlee, Certificated teacher of the 2nd class.
[Mr. Tyrrell copied the report into the log book and signed it.]
This School continues to bear testimony to the excellent teaching and training of the children by the Master.

10 Oct 1872 *The School examined to-day 91 present. I have by Mr. Metcalfe's direction given the usual examination holiday to-morrow.*

10 Oct 1873 [Written and signed by Mr. Nevill Gream, H.M. Inspector for Schools]
Mr. Henry Yeaxlee certificated teacher of the 1st class.
[The rector copied the report into the log book and it was signed by himself and Mr. Tyrrell.]
The School is in good order and the Instruction generally is well imparted. The Arithmetic in the higher Standards requires attention.

10 Oct 1873 *The school was closed this afternoon.*

16 Oct 1874 [Written and signed by Mr. Nevill Gream, H.M. Inspector for Schools]
Mr. Henry Yeaxlee certificated teacher of the 1st class.

16 Oct 1874 *The school was examined to-day. It was closed in the afternoon, the children having their usual half-holiday.*

[Mr. Tyrrell copied the report into the log book and signed it.]
This is a very praiseworthy specimen of a country school. The Reading and Writing are very good, and the Discipline admirable.

13 Nov 1874   *The school was visited on Thursday morning by Mr. Tyrrell, who came to give notice of the arrival of the report.*

Alfred Hawks appointed master 17 May 1875

29 Oct 1875   *The School was examined on Tuesday.* [26 October]

12 Nov 1875   [Mr. Tyrrell copied the report into the log book and signed it.]
Copy of Report
This School is still kept in very good order, and notwithstanding the change of Teacher, the instruction continues to be very satisfactory. The needlework is very well taught. The Grant is only saved from a deduction under Article 32(c) by the operation of Article 33.
Alfred Hawks Certificated Teacher of the 2nd Class.

26 May 1876   *The School was visited this morning by Mr. Tyrrell who informed me of the date fixed for Examination.* [The school was now inspected in June or July, instead of October.]

30 Jun 1876   *The Examination was held on Monday and a holliday* [sic] *was given on Tuesday.* [HMI inspected the school on 26 June.]

28 Jul 1876   [The rector, Rev. Arthur James Skrimshire, copied the report into the log book and signed it.]
Copy of Report 1876
The School is in good order and the instruction is efficiently imparted. The sewing has also much improved. The fence at the back of the School should be repaired.
Alfred Hawks Certificated Teacher of the 2nd Class.

28 Jul 1876   [Written by Alfred Hawks]
The School has the appearance of marked improvement since the Examination, the children are working with double energy after receiving such an encouraging report, having had only the 8 months for their work, and I think I have every confidence in my children that they will persevere to make a much higher percentage at the next Examination.

22 Jun 1877   *My teacher has left the School this week and will not be present at the Examination.*

29 Jun 1877   *The School was inspected on Monday at 10 o'clock and a holliday* [sic] *given in the afternoon.*

[Rev. Arthur James Skrimshire copied the report into the log book and signed it.]

Copy of Report 1877

This School is in good order and the instruction appears to be imparted with care and efficiency as far as the small teaching power will go, but the Infants are below the mark and a paid Monitor should be engaged as the School is too large for one Teacher. Sheets for the Infants to read from are required, and a good map for the principal room.

None of the Scholars for whom Honour Certificates were claimed satisfy the requirements of the Regulations of the 9th February 1877. Mr. Hawks will shortly receive his Certificate.

4 Jun 1878   [This entry was written in the log book by the HMI Inspector, whose name appears to be G. A. Help.]

Visited the School. I have no confidence in the Registers. The manner in which they have been kept points either to gross ignorance or can be [word illegible] *on the part of the Teacher. No register of Attendance has been kept from the 1st of the month* [word illegible] *consequently the attendances of the children have been lost. The meetings of the school for June 3rd and 4th must be reckoned.*

17 Jun 1878   [The HMI Inspector returned for a follow-up visit.]

2 Aug 1878   [Rev. Arthur James Skrimshire copied the report into the log book and signed it.]

Copy of Report 1878

The order and general efficiency are fair. The spelling of the third and fourth Standards are very defective. The Geography was unsatisfactory and it is with hesitation that I commend a grant for Grammar. The attainments of the Infants are very moderate and their intelligence has not been cultivated. The teacher has been somewhat overtasked during the past year. The manner in which the Registers have been kept I consider most discredible. The needlework is good. A printed copy of the Regs. required under the 7th Section of the Elementary Educ. Act 1870 should be procured and maps of England and Europe are needed. [Word illegible] *feel compelled to order a deduction of one tenth to be made from the grant for faults of Registration (Article 32b). An Assistant Teacher (Article 79) should be appointed at once or a Pupil*

Teacher transferred from some other School if the average Attendance during the current year is to exceed 60.

⸺

20 Jun 1879   *The School was inspected on Wednesday by H.M. Inspector.*
[Rev. Arthur James Skrimshire copied the report into the log book and signed it.]
Copy of Report 1879
The order is good: the results of Examination show a decided improvement in the instruction. I should like to find more intelligence in the Reading and Geography. First Standard is weak in Arithmetic, the notation being imperfect. The writing is now good. The Registers must be kept with still greater care. The attainments of the Infants are very fair, their intelligence should be developed by means of lessons on animals, and common things. Picture cards should be provided for them. A map of Essex is needed.
The Scholar numbered 44 on the Exam. Schedule is disqualified under Article 19 (B).

⸺

4 Jun 1880   *The Children were examined on Tuesday by HMI Assistant.*
15 Jun 1880   [This entry was written in the log book by the HMI Inspector, whose signature is illegible.]
Visited the school and found the work going on with all due order. Checked the Registers & found them correct & apparently well kept.
2 Jul 1880   [Rev. Arthur James Skrimshire copied the report into the log book and signed it.]
Copy of Report 1880
The order and general efficiency are creditable. Reading is very fairly fluent and fairly intelligent. Writing and Spelling are good. Arithmetic on the whole very fair, I should like the Children to show more ability in applying rules. Geography is imperfect, and I recommend a Grant under Article 19 (c) for Grammar with much hesitation, the work of the fourth and fifth Standards being very poor. The attainments of the Infants are now good. The first class of Infants should have suitable reading books.
Alfred Hawks Certificated Teacher of the 2nd Class.

⸺

10 Jun 1881   *The Children were examined on Wednesday afternoon when 93 children were present.*
[Rev. Arthur James Skrimshire copied the report into the log book

and signed it.]

Copy of Report 1881

The order is fairly good: the general efficiency very fair. The first and second standards did well in Examination, but the Spelling and Arithmetic of the Third, Fourth and Fifth Standards show weakness. (Arithmetic is especially weak as regard the ability to apply rules.) Reading is well taught in the lower, and very fair in point of intelligence in the upper Classes. The Attainments of the Infants are satisfactory. (Singing needs more attention.) Writing being good. The prepared Specimens of Needlework shown one are excellent: the work done at my visit is satisfactory.

Alfred Hawks Certificated Master of the 2nd Class.

| 30 Jun 1882 | *The school was inspected by A. Finch HMI's Assistant on Tuesday and the Inspector and his Assistant called again on Wednesday morning.* |

[Rev. Arthur James Skrimshire copied the report into the log book and signed it.]

Copy of Report 1882

Order and tone are good, and the general efficiency is very fair. The results of Examinations show improvement in the Instruction in several points. I should, however, like to find more intelligence in the Reading, Arithmetic and Geography of the first Class.

The Attainments of the Infants are good. The Needlework is very credible.

E. Bell is continued under Article 84 of the Code of 1882.

| 25 May 1883 | *Visited on Monday by the Rector and Mr. Tyrrell who informed me of the day of Inspection.* |

| 21 Jun 1883 | *The School was inspected by Mr. Healing to-day when there were 122 present: a holliday* [sic] *was given on Friday.* [Mr. Thomas Healing of Kentish Town was an Inspector's Assistant.] |

Copy of Report 1883:

The school increases in numbers, Order is well maintained, and the Instruction in many points is very fairly efficient. The Reading has some fluency, more more [sic] *expression and a proper observance of the stops should be arrived at. The Handwriting of the first Standard is bold though the letters are sometimes joined improperly, but the writing on paper is, on the whole, far too small. A bolder and less crowded hand will produce better results in Spelling. Arithmetic is weak in the first Standard but in the other Standards show signs of careful teaching. The parsing of the fourth and fifth Standards must be much more complete, and the answering in geography much more general before the class Subject can be pronounced satisfactory. The Sewing is very credible. Another easel and blackboard would be found useful. The use of an official Cash Book would render the accounts more easy to keep and examine. To earn next year the mark awarded this year under Art. 109 (b) there must [be] fewer failures in Spelling and Arith. and improvement in the points noticed. The Infants are very fairly taught especially in Reading & Writing. In Mental Arithmetic, variety of Exercises is needed; and the children trained to take proper use of hard wk. questions. All the details of Inf. drill need great attention, including suitable Physical exercises, the proper distribution & collection of books, marching and the orderly changing of places. Improvements in these points will be looked for.*

13 Jun 1884	*Several of the Children who were to have been presented at the Examination have left the village.*
27 Jun 1884	*The School was inspected to-day by H.M. Inspector and Assistant and the School closed in the afternoon.*
1 Aug 1884	[Rev. Arthur James Skrimshire copied the report into the log book and signed it.]

Copy of Report 1884

The order is very fairly good. The general efficiency is fair. I should like to find the instruction more thorough in several respects. Reading is improved. Handwriting is improved. Spelling is very unequal that of the fourth and fifth Standards is very weak. Arithmetic is unequal the second Standard is weak in notation, the second and third Standards show little ability in applying rules, and the fourth Standard show weakness in reduction and the application of rules to practical examples. The Knowledge of Grammar is very fair and Recitation, except in the third Standard, was good. The Geography is very far from creditable. I am surprised that children so improperly taught should have been presented to me for Examination. Needlework is well taught. Singing is very fair. A blind is required for the East window. There must be three sets of Readers for the fourth and fifth Standards and Copy books are required for the Upper

Classes. The Admission Register must be kept in accordance with the requirements of the Department. The Register in use is not suited to these requirements. The Infants have been very well taught except in Number, in which the children six years of age should be more advanced. A series of lessons on creatures and common things (to be illustrated by pictures) should be gone through systematically three or four times in the year. The ventilation of this room must be improved. The room has been crowded during the past year, and, unless the accommodation for Infants is improved, I shall be compelled next year to recommend a reduction of Grant. The enlargement of the room is much to be desired.

E. Bell is continued under Article 84.

12 Jun 1885 — *There is a good deal of sickness in the village and it is doubtful whether several of the children for Examination will be present on the 24th.*

19 Jun 1885 — *Albert Brett who was to have been presented in Standard I left the village on Saturday.*

23 Jun 1885 — *Visited this afternoon by Mr. Finch HMI's Assistant, who checked the Registers and found them correct.*

26 Jun 1885 — *The School was inspected on Wednesday by Mr. Healing HM Sub Inspector.*

Copy of Report 1885

The School is in good order, and in some respects appears to be taught with considerable vigour, and some success. The Reading is in general fluent very and free from monotony in many cases pleasingly expressive. To a large extent this may be said, too, of the Recitation. Intelligence is shown in the explanation of words and phrases in the upper Classes, but to too small an extent in the lower. The writing on Slates is very good and the papers are in a bold and legible hand. The Copy books are neat; and the spelling very fair. Mental Arithmetic should receive greater Attention; the answering should be more prompt and general & Tables be more perfectly learned. The Arithmetic of the Upper half of the School is disappointing in the large number of unsatisfactory passes (few Scholars in the fourth & fifth Standards have done more than two sums) and in the little power shown to apply the rules to practical problems. The parsing is very weak in the 4th Standard.

The Needlework is creditable. The Infants are well instructed in

Handwriting and Number. The Reading should show more fluency. Considerable intelligence is shown in the Knowledge of Common things. More Attention is needed to the Class Drill to make the Scholars less awkward in class movements. The Sewing is good & the Singing very fair: a few more modern & sprightly songs should be taught.

E. Bell is continued under Art. 84.

---

11 Jun 1886   *Visited on Wednesday by the Rector who gave notice of the Examination.*

18 Jun 1886   *HMI Rankine Esq. visited the School this morning.* [Mr. Adam Rankine of Woodford in Essex.]

9 Jul 1886   *The School examined by HMI Rankine Esq. on Saturday July 10th.*

23 Jul 1886   [The report was copied into the log book by Alfred Hawks.]

                <u>*Copy of Report 1886*</u>

                <u>*Mixed School*</u> *This school is conducted with ability and intelligence. The general character of the work is very good.*

                <u>*Infants' Class*</u> *The Infants continue to be very carefully taught. Some instructive amusements might with advantage be provided.*

---

13 Jul 1887   *Inspected the School.* [Written and signed by H.M. Inspector for Schools, Mr. Edward Maclaine Field of Ingatestone.]

15 Jul 1887   *School inspected on Wednesday and closed Thursday afternoon and Friday. The Registers were examined on Thursday by HM Inspector and Mr. Healing.*

10 Feb 1888   [The report for 1887 was not copied into the log book by Alfred Hawks until seven months later. Parts of the report do not make sense.]

                <u>*Copy of Report 1887*</u>

                <u>*Mixed School*</u>

                The general order of the School is creditable, but there was a good deal of talking and other communication between children during the Examination. The work is somewhat uneven. Although reading except in the second Standard to fluent answers to questions on the text ought to be much better. The written Arithmetic of the first and second Standards is good but the papers of the Upper Standards and oral Arithmetic generally are decidedly weak. Composition is also below a fair mark. English passes fairly but the quality of the answers in Grammar in the fourth & fifth Standards should be better. Needlework is I regret to say not satisfactorily taught and I cannot recommend payment of the grant under Article 109 (c). A supply of books is required for the first and second Standards. One Blackboard in indifferent condition is obviously inadequate for the needs of Five Standards & a Class of Infants.

Infant Class

The Infants are bright-looking and in fairly good order, and they are kindly managed. But I think that their attainments have probably suffered from the new arrangement whereby Miss Bell leaves the Class for three afternoons in the week to teach Needlework to the older girls. Their Reading and writing are fair but their Arithmetic is only tolerable. They learn no Recitation and do not seem to get a sufficient amount of Physical Exercise.

I recommend payment of the higher grant under Article 106(a) and of merit grant on the Second Scale for the year. But for these recommendations to be repeated provision should be made for supplying Miss Bell's place on Needlework afternoons with a more efficient teacher than at present and the attainment should improve. The children should not be allowed to rely upon mechanical aids in Arithmetic and they should learn to answer questions in class by show of hands.

2 Jul 1888	*Inspected the School.* [Written and signed by H.M. Inspector for Schools, Mr. E. M. Field.]
13 Jul 1888	*Copy of Report 1888*

The school has much improved since last year. The defects of order which were then noticed have been corrected and the work is sounder and better throughout. Reading, Handwriting and Spelling pass fairly well and Grammar well. But more Attention to style in Recitation and much better answers on the matter are needed. In some Standards very little comprehension of the Reading books was shown and oral Arithmetic and problem work are still poor, though in other respects this subject has been much better taught.

In needlework exercises there are still considerable faults and the garments indicate want of system, but I am able now to recommend payment of the grant.

I recommend payment of the full Grant for English and of a higher Merit Grant than was paid last year, but improvements in the points above noticed will be looked for. Mr. Hawks needs assistance of some kind with the elder children, whom he teaches alone.

The Infants are very fairly instructed in Elementary Work, but their other subjects especially physical exercises, need development. Their room should be made more cheerful by the addition of some good sized pictures.

E. Bell is continued under Article 84.

᷇

2 Jul 1889   *Inspected the School.* [Written and signed by H.M. Inspector for Schools, Mr. E. M. Field.]

5 Jul 1889   *The school was examined on Tuesday and a half-holiday given.* [The report was not copied into the log book until nearly a year later, on 20 June 1890.]

Copy of Report 1889

The school is creditably organised and disciplined and there are some good points in the work, but, on the whole, the improvement of the last year has not been maintained. Reading is weak in the first Standard (which is generally ill-prepared in oral work) and the general results in this subject are not above fair. Answers on the matter of the books problem-work and Mental Arithmetic are poor. Composition is also indifferent in the fifth Standard; but spelling and Arithmetic (except as regards problems and the whole work of the fifth Standard) come out very fairly. Recitation is mostly well said and understood, and Grammar passes with some success. Needlework is fair except in the second Standard.

The Infants are under very fair discipline but they have considerably fallen off in attainments and are by no means well trained in matters of class drill. Reading is the most unsatisfactory subject, but none of the elementary work has been properly taught, nor is the object teaching at all effective. Payment of the grant under Article 106 (b) is doubtfully recommended and another year much greater proficiency will be expected. The Class might be more carefully supervised by the Head Teacher. The Registers should be tested by the Managers at least once a quarter at irregular intervals.

E. Bell is continued under Article 84. [In April 1890 Miss Bell left the school.]

᷇

9 May 1890   [The school had been closed for three weeks by a measles epidemic.] *A few have been left so weak as to be quite unfit for Examination and must consequently appear on the Exception Schedule.*

13 Jun 1890	*Two Children which* [sic] *were to have been Examined have not yet returned to School owing to sickness.*
11 Jul 1890	*The Rector called and checked the Registers on Wednesday and thoroughly tested the statements made on the Exception Schedule relative to children for Exceptional Treatment.*
21 Jul 1890	*Inspected the School.* [Written and signed by H.M. Inspector for Schools, Mr. E. M. Field.]
25 Jul 1890	*The School was inspected on Monday and a half-holiday given.*
19 Jun 1891	[Again the report was not copied into the log book until nearly a year later.]

<u>*Copy of Report 1890*</u>

There is marked improvement in the work both of the elder scholars and of Infants since last year. The Reading and Spelling of the elder scholars pass well throughout, and Arithmetic is very accurate, though not, except in the fifth and sixth Standards, intelligent as tested by success in problems and the oral examination but this is the only weak point in the results of the year. The passes are mostly well earned and all the written work is well put down upon paper. English and Needlework both pass with fairly good success.

The Infants were in indifferent condition last year, and the present teacher, who is careful and painstaking, has been here only three months. The improvement which has taken place not only in the actual details of instruction, which give promise of really good work in future, but in the discipline, spirit and general intelligence of the class is much to her credit.

R. Bragg is recognised under Article 84. [The new infant teacher]

2 Jul 1891	*Inspected the School.* [Written and signed by H.M. Inspector for Schools, Mr. E. M. Field.]
22 Jul 1891	[The report was copied into the log book by Alfred Hawks, but signed by Rev. A. J. Skrimshire.]

<u>*Copy of Report 1891*</u>

<u>*Mixed School*</u>

The school is in good order and a considerable proportion of the work done in examination is also good. Careful and clear Recitation, fluent Reading is very fair style, neat and accurate paper work and generally good results in English are its chief merits. There is less success to answers to questions on the matter of Reading books. The second, fifth and sixth standards are weak in problem work and

Mental Arithmetic is decidedly poor. In Needlework the upper Standards must improve. Exercises such as patches and button-holes are done in a manner which show that they are not taught by right methods. The subject comes out on the whole only tolerably and the teacher should study a good manual. Accommodation for hats and cloaks is required.

Infant Class

The management of the Infants is careful and painstaking, though not yet in all aspects skilful. More system in object teaching, better oral Arithmetic and better Reading in the second class are required. There should also be more attention to physical exercises. A good deal of the elementary work comes out fairly well and in recognition of the improvement produced by the present Teacher I am able to recommend payment of the grant under Article 98 (b) on the second scale. The gallery requires alteration. The Registers must be tested by the Managers at least once a quarter at irregular intervals as required by paragraph 6 of the circular on Registration (appendix II of the Revised Instructions to HM Inspectors). Attention is required to Article 85 (d).

R. L. Bragg is continued under Article 68.

A. Hawks (Certified teacher First Class).

12 Jul 1892	*Inspected the School.* [Written and signed by H.M. Inspector for Schools, Mr. E. M. Field.]
5 May 1893	[The report was not copied into the log book by Alfred Hawks until ten months after the inspection. It was later signed by Captain James S. Trotter of Hadleigh House.]

Report 1892

Mixed School

I am glad to report that the work of the school has again improved and is now in great part of really high quality. The children read and recite remarkably well and, with the exception that some of the problem work is not very successful, they show most creditable accuracy. and neatness in their written exercises. Singing by note passes well and needlework has improved. English is fairly good and the only subject in which there is any general weakness is Mental Arithmetic. Order is very satisfactory. These results are all the more creditable as work was interrupted for many weeks by an epidemic in the winter.

Infant Class

The alteration of the gallery has much improved the Infants accommodation. Miss Bragg has evidently been taking much pains with her work and I think only needs experience to succeed well. At present there are faults: The Arithmetic shows the lack of systematic and well graduated teaching: the object lessons are not so given as to command the interest of the younger children while the older children who show some knowledge and intelligence answer indiscriminately and without show of hands. There is great improvement in Physical Exercises, but the more special branches of Infants' Instruction could of course be further developed with advantage. The children are well behaved but they should be made a little smarter in matters of Class Drill.

Miss Bragg is continued under Article 68.

A. Hawks Certified Teacher 1st Class.

3 Jul 1893   *School inspected. The last report shd. be signed by the Correspondent.* [Written and signed by H.M. Inspector for Schools, Mr. Arthur E. Bernays.]

13 Oct 1893   [The report was copied into the log book by Alfred Hawks and signed by Rev. A. J. Skrimshire.]

Copy of Report 1893

The older scholars have passed a very fair examination. though spelling is a weak point above the second Standard which together with the first has not acquired much proficiency in Reading, but the instruction of the Infants is not yet such as it should be, especially as regards word-building, drill, object lessons and manual occupation. Nor is the discipline satisfactory in the lower part of the school, many of the children being very inattentive. The Master has, however, been singlehanded for two months and even now his staff is clearly inadequate. English has been taught with fair success, but the full grant for singing is barely earned, and it is desirable that the girls should learn to mend garments as well as make them. A fresh set of books is required for the grouped standards, the forms for the junior classes are inconveniently placed, more cupboard accommodation should be provided in the main room, the ball frame needs altering as suggested, one of the blackboards ought to be ruled, there are very few pictures or other apparatus for teaching the Infants, and flap desks should be affixed to the gallery seats, the

backs of which are not of satisfactory height. The walls also have a bare appearance, the ventilation is imperfect and the offices [outside toilets] must be reconstructed in the manner advised.
Miss Cales is recognised under Article 68 of the Code.
Alfred Hawks Certificated Teacher 1st Class.

∞

9 Mar 1894   *Most of the articles mentioned in the Report have now been provided.*

24 Jul 1894   *School inspected.* [Written and signed by H.M. Inspector for Schools, Mr. Arthur E. Bernays.]

25 Jan 1895   [The report was copied into the log book by Alfred Hawks on 25 January 1895 and signed by the rector, Rev. Armine G. Metcalfe.]

Copy of Report 1894

Although the teaching staff is still technically insufficient, the Master's son and daughter being both without status, I am glad to record a very great improvement in the work of the Upper school. In fact the instruction and discipline are now so good a character that the maximum grants have been recommended. In English, however, the knowledge shown by the first class is not yet so exact as it should be. The Managers are to be congratulated upon the improvement of the premises, but the rooms are very much overcrowded, the Average Attendance of the Infants having exceeded the accommodation. Apex ventilation, also, continues to be needed, an additional desk is required and there ought to be a lavatory, or a couple of fixed wall-basins.

Infants' Class

The Infants have shared in the general progress of the School, and though in the elementary course they are not yet so proficient as could be wished, in spite of the fact that ten of the children are over seven years of age, there is evidence of careful and systematic teaching and I have, therefore, recommended a higher grant than would in ordinary circumstances have been earned. There is one space, however, for marching and other exercises, and the Mistress ought not be responsible for the Needlework of the elder girls. This subject is reported to be fair . . . dotted calico must not be used for examination specimens. The supply of pictures is still inadequate the gallery remains unaltered and there are no boxes of objects for the collective lessons. The special attention of the Managers is requested to the enclosed form 69. Apex Ventilation should be

provided and the Infants' class-room should be enlarged it being below the minimum size allowed by Rule 7(a) of Schedule VII of the Code; the Infants teacher should also devote the whole time to them. The staff should be at once strengthened so as to meet the requirements of Article 73 which are not at present satisfied (Article 108).
S. Hawks is recognised under Article 68.
Alfred Hawks (Certified Master 1st Class)

16 Jul 1895	*School inspected.* [Written and signed by H.M. Inspector for Schools, Mr. Arthur E. Bernays.]
19 Jul 1895	*The Examination was held on Tuesday and the Attendance has fallen off a bit towards the end of the week.*
15 Nov 1895	[The report was copied into the log book by Alfred Hawks and signed by Rev. Armine G. Metcalfe.]

Copy of Report 1895

Mixed School

The School has passed a very fair examination in the primary subjects; Handwriting and Composition being creditably taught, but there is some want of fluency in the Reading. Arithmetic is a weak point in the second and fifth Standards particularly in the former, the spelling of the fourth Standard is very inaccurate, the Problems are not well worked and none of the classes are skilful in Mental calculations. Nor has the teaching of English been sufficiently thorough and the discipline is by no means equal to that of the last year though some allowance must be made for the overcrowding of the desks on the day of my visit. Needlework has received careful attention (though the Infants' Mistress ought not to be responsible for it) but the garments shown by the girls should not be left unfinished.

Infant Class

The Infants' Class has had some disadvantage this year: the chief being the crowded state of the little Class-room. The same grant under Art. 98 cannot again be recommended unless in the new Class-room [to be built in the Summer Vacation 1895] *there is more suitable Infant training and general progress in Needlework and the Elementary Subjects. The children in the upper division acquit themselves fairly well; but the remaining divisions greatly need more effective Drill and instruction. The best points are the Objects Teaching, the Recitation and some of the Occupations.*

The Registers must be tested by the Managers at least once a quarter, at irregular intervals as required by paragraph 6 of Appendix II of Instructions to Inspectors.

Attention is directed to Article 85 (d) of Code. H. M. Inspector recommends that the Infants' Mistress be no longer allowed to teach Needlework to the Elder Girls. I am to enquire whether the Managers can make some other arrangement. The School would be very much improved by the addition of a room.

S. Hawks is recognised under Article 33 of the Code.

Alfred Hawks Certificated Teacher 1st Class.

4 Jun 1896	*First visit under Art. 84b.* [Written and signed by H.M. Inspector for Schools, Mr. Thomas Healing.]
5 Jun 1896	*Sub-Inspector Thos. Healing paid a surprise Visit yesterday & gave some useful hints.*
10 Jul 1896	*The School was visited by H.M. Sub-Inspector Mr. Muchard on Wednesday who remained the whole of the morning. A holiday was given in the Afternoon.*
23 Oct 1896	[The report was copied into the log book by Alfred Hawks and signed by Rev. Armine G. Metcalfe.]

<u>Copy of Report 1896</u>

<u>Mixed School</u>

The premises have been greatly improved by the erection of a new Infants' Classroom on which the Managers are to be congratulated. With the increased accommodation the order has improved and it may be expected that the quality of the instruction will soon rise to its former level.

The first class is well taught by the Head Master, the other classes are in the care of young teachers who work diligently but require to be instructed in method especially in giving oral lessons.

Much of the Recitation was very good, the Singing from the Staff Notation was good and the needlework fairly good. The Oral Arithmetic should be strengthened.

<u>Infants' Class</u>

The Infants are now taught in a new and well furnished room. They are fairly well instructed in Reading and Writing, Objects and Recitation but the Arithmetic and Needlework are somewhat below the level usually reached in a good Infants' School. The oral teaching, too, should be much quietly carried on and the movement of the children should be more methodical and free from unnecessary noise. Improvements in these respects will be looked for in these respects next year if the same variable grant is to be recommended. A Pupil Teacher must not be allowed to serve in School for more than 25 hrs. a week as specified in paragraph 1 of the Memorandum of Agreement.

H. M. Inspector remarks that the Offices [outside toilets] *might be kept cleaner.*

M. Hawks is recognised under Art. 68 of the Code subject to her furnishing a satisfactory Medical Certificate on the Enclosed Form (Form 42).

S. Hawks is continued under that Article.

A. A. Hawks: Arithmetic, Grammar, Geography, History, Music
Alfred Hawks (Certified Master 1st Class)

19 Mar 1897   *First visit under Art. 84b.* [Written and signed by H.M. Inspector for Schools, Mr. Frederick Dugard, who was living at Woodford.]

18 Jun 1897   *Visited the School.* [Written and signed by H.M. Inspector for Schools, Mr. Frederick Dugard.]

10 Sep 1897   [The report was copied in the log book by Alfred Hawks and signed by Rev. Armine G. Metcalfe.]

<u>*Copy of Report 1897*</u>

<u>*Mixed School*</u>

The School is conducted with much brightness and ability. and the instruction has improved in several respects. The expressive recitation of the first class and the intelligent Reading above the second st. are very praiseworthy. The Oral answering in the Class Subjects was generally good and the written exercises creditably accurate. With increased attention to the Handwriting and Oral Arithmetic of the lower Sts., and the more orderly movements of classes, the higher Principal Grant should be soon obtained. The Scholars are well behaved and earnest in their work.

<u>*Infant Class*</u>

The Infants Class is pleasantly ordered. The elementary teaching is of good quality and the Oral Lessons are fairly good.

S. Hawks is continued under Article 68 of the Code.

M. F. Hawks is recognised under Art. 68 subject to her furnishing a satisfactory Medical Certificate on the Enclosed Form.

Alfred Hawks Certificated Master 1st Class

~~~

2 Feb 1898	*Visited the School.* [Written and signed by H.M. Inspector for Schools, Mr. Frederick Dugard.]
4 Feb 1898	*The Attendance was fairly good yesterday when H. M. Inspector visited the School.* [The incorrect date has been written in the log book either by the Inspector or Alfred Hawks.]
11 Feb 1898	*Several improvements suggested by the Inspector have been carried out.*
21 Oct 1898	<u>*Copy of Report 1898*</u>

<u>*Mixed School*</u>

At my visit without notice five months before the end of the school year the school was in good order and the instruction was proceeding satisfactorily except in the class under the Pupil Teacher. In the standards more immediately under the Master's care there was much animation and intelligence in the Reading and class subjects. Simple mental and written calculations, however, required attention throughout the school. The offices [toilets] *were not in a satisfactory condition.*

<u>*Infants' Class*</u>

The infants are taught with much care and kindness and they do well in their mechanical exercises. The Reading of the highest division was somewhat weak; some easier reading sheets should be used. Special care should be taken to keep the offices in a satisfactory condition.

M. Hawks is recognised under Article 68 of the Code.

Alfred Hawks (Certificated Master 1st Class).

21 Dec 1898	*First visit of Inspector Art. 84b.* [Written and signed by H.M. Inspector for Schools, Mr. William Mulhall of Ilford in Essex.]

~~~

16 Jun 1899	*School inspected.* [Written and signed by H.M. Inspector for Schools, Mr. Frederick Dugard.]
20 Oct 1899	<u>*Copy of Report 1899*</u>

<u>*Mixed School*</u>

The scholars are well behaved and attentive and a cheerful tone prevails. The instruction is somewhat unequal; in the highest section and the 2nd Stand. much of the elementary work is of good quality; the teaching of Arithmetic is however too mechanical generally, and the Reading in some of the Standards falls below the level usually reached in a good school. Drawing, Needlework and Singing are fairly good and the Drill moderate. The general knowledge shown in the class Subjects was not strong at either visit and Geography is only fairly taught. A higher degree of intelligence will be looked for in the current year.

Infants' Class

The numbers present in the Infants' Class exceed those for which the Teacher is qualified. Reading is still the weak point in each division; the Object teaching is very fair; in other respects the children are satisfactorily trained and instructed.

HM Inspector reports that the Class-room of the Mixed School is ill-lighted and needs cleaning. The Attention of the Managers is requested to rule 9 of Section VII of the Code.

The Staff should be at once strengthened so as to meet the requirements of Art. 73 which are not at present satisfied (Art. 108). The Managers are reminded that Alfred Hawks is no longer recognised as forming part of the School Staff.

The Inspector reports that the girls are not taught cutting out. . . . The girls in the IV Standard and upwards must be taught cutting out in accordance with Schedule IIIB.

M. F. Hawks and S. Hawks are continued under Article 68.

Alfred Hawks (Certificated Master 1st Class).

23 Jan 1900   *First visit of Inspector Art. 84b.* [Written and signed by H.M. Inspector for Schools, Mr. W. Mulhall.]

20 Jun 1900   *School inspected.* [Written and signed by H.M. Inspector for Schools, Mr. Frederick Dugard.]

[The report was copied in the log book in 1901 by Alfred Hawks and signed by Rev. Armine G. Metcalfe.]

Copy of Report for 1900

Mixed School

The order is good and the instruction generally satisfactory. The Reading of the first Standard still needs attention and the Arithmetic of the upper class should be more intelligently taught. The Handwriting is good and the paper exercises neatly done. There is improvement in the oral answering, and needlework is now satisfactorily taught.

Infants' Class

There is room for improvement in the order, which is not of the best kind and the Reading of the first class is still a weak point. The writing is good, and the Object teaching, Singing and Varied occupations satisfactory. Some new large print Reading sheets are required.

The Mixed School accommodation is at present insufficient for the average Attendance. This should be at once remedied or the Grant next year will be endangered. HM Inspector reports that the Offices are not well kept, and are not protected from the public. These defects should be remedied by the Managers without delay.

The Inspector reports that the Second Standard is taught by an unqualified Monitress.

M. F. Hawks and S. Hawks are recognised under Art. 68.

A.G. Hawks is recognised under that Art., subject to her furnishing a satisfactory Medical Certificate on the Enclosed Form.

Alfred Hawks Certificated teacher (1st Class).

Spare the Rod and Spoil the Child

THERE IS NOTHING NEW about children behaving badly! Discipline in Victorian schools was very strict, as it was believed that if one spared the rod, or cane, then the child would be spoiled and bad behaviour encouraged. The cane was an important part of harsh Victorian school discipline, with boys being caned across their bottoms and girls across their hands or bare legs. Most parents accepted that their children should be treated firmly at school if they caused trouble. There are few mentions of behaviour and punishment in the log book, especially when Alfred Hawks was master. Martha Lovibond, when making her endowment for a school in 1820, had stipulated: *"That no Corporal punishment be allowed in the School."* Consequently, canings appear to be rare at the National School at Hadleigh, with very little mention of the use of a cane in the log book. This may be due to the fact that corporal punishment had to be recorded in a separate punishment book. In fact, in January 1874, Henry Yeaxlee decided to break up his cane, although he later regretted this decision, commenting in 1875: *" . . . my final conclusion is that children can never be properly managed without corporal punishment for a great length of time."* Twenty years later Alfred Hawks tried a similar experiment.

Log Book Entries

Miss Cecilia Miller had been appointed mistress in 1861

12 Jan 1863 — *Sent a boy home for bad behaviour.*

23 Jan 1863 — *James Dolby and James Griggs punished for taking two pens out of the box with intent to keep them.* [Both boys lived in Daws Heath Road. William James Dalby was the 6-year-old son of James and Jane Dalby. James was an agricultural labourer and his wife was a dressmaker. James Grigg was a year younger, and was the son of James and Hannah Grigg. His father was a hawker.]

12 Feb 1863 — *Thomas Choppen punished for coming to School at 5 minutes before 3.* [Thomas, aged about 8 years, lived with his grandparents, John and Mary Choppen. in the village street. John was the village wheelwright.]

13 Feb 1863 — *Kept nine children in to learn a lesson for talking.*

24 Feb 1863 — *Three boys kept in for playing during lessons.*

11 Mar 1863 — *James Dolby threw a stone and broke a square of glass.*

24 Mar 1863 — *Walter Hills got a task as a punishment for telling a lie.* [Walter, aged seven, was the stepson of Thomas Smith, a Hadleigh shoemaker, and his wife Mary, who lived in the village street.]

14 Apr 1863 — *Mary A. Smith pushed a pencil up her nose, which with some little difficulty was removed.* [Mary Ann Smith was just seven years old and the daughter of the village shoemaker, William, and his wife Mary Ann.]

22 Apr 1863 — *John Gilman threw a stone and cut Amy Chignell's forehead. Cautioned children never to throw stones.* [John was the 6-year-old son of John and Susan Gillman, who lived on the green in Hadleigh. His father was an agricultural labourer. Amy may have been the daughter of David and Elizabeth Chignell.]

7 May 1863 — *Phebe Adams very impudent – gave her a good caning.* [Phoebe Adams was the 10-year-old daughter of the village thatcher, James Adams, and his wife Sarah. They lived on Hadleigh Common.]

12 May 1863 — *Missed a half penny from the table – on searching found it in John Green's pocket –punished him for the theft.* [Aged six, John was the son of William and Ann Green, who lived in the village street. His father worked as an agricultural labourer and sometimes as a carter.]

21 May 1863 — *Sent Charles Coker home for bad behaviour.* [12-year-old Charles

lived on the Causeway at Hadleigh with his father William, a basket maker, and his mother Hannah, a laundress.]

11 Jun 1863   *Mr. Godson* [the curate] *cautioned children against using bad words and also about destroying shrubs in School yard.*

William Batchelor Kingswood appointed master 7 September 1863

7 Sep 1863   *Cautioned children against destroying the fences and laurels in and around the playground.*

9 Sep 1863   *Cautioned children as to behaviour in Church as suggested by Mr. Godson.* [The curate]

10 Sep 1863   *Gave general hints as to their general behaviour.*

1 Oct 1863   *Phoebe Adams was kept in for insubordination and idleness.* [Phoebe had been caned in May for insubordination.]

8 Oct 1863   *Severely reprimanded two Boys for swearing.*

26 Oct 1863   *Kept Geo. Thorington in for spending part of his schoolpence and telling a falsehood.* [7-year-old George lived in Daws Heath Road, the son of an agricultural labourer, George, and his wife Eliza.]

11 Nov 1863   *Punished Eliza Griggs for lying and misconduct.* [Now aged eight, Eliza had been in trouble before for truanting.]

1 Feb 1864   *I had to visit 2 parents at noon to-day in order to <u>quiet</u> them respecting their children who had to stay in at noon a few minutes for bad behaviour. This is the way <u>The Teachers</u> generally are thanked for their exertions.*

16 Feb 1864   *Severely reprimanded 2 Boys for getting over the school fence.*

17 Mar 1864   *M. A. Warren was caught actually destroying the Flowers and trees around the School grounds.*

10 May 1864   *Stephen Scudder was absent to-day on account of his being thrown at and hit in the head by the Boy Jas. Dalby who was kept in and had a task for doing it.* [Both boys were the sons of agricultural labourers living in Daws Heath Road. Stephen was the 8-year-old son of Richard and Amelia Scudder. While James was four years younger and the son of James and Jane Dalby.]

27 Jul 1864   *Cautioned children against throwing, running behind vehicles and interfering with the family of Warrens.* [This was probably the family of Samuel Warren, an agricultural labourer who lived in a cottage on Thundersley Common.]

Henry Yeaxlee appointed master 23 January 1865

4 Jan 1866	*I find the children very lax in their behaviour which obliges me to be more strict than usual.*
12 Apr 1866	*I find the children rather unruly after their holiday, which is uncommon.*

⁓✶⁓

14 Nov 1867	*Some trouble arose this afternoon in consequence of the obstinacy of a girl named Annie Green.* [Aged about nine years, Annie was the daughter of William and Ann Green. Her father was a carter and agricultural labourer.]

⁓✶⁓

20 Feb 1868	*One window broken by a stone. Cautioned the children about stone-throwing.*
8 Dec 1868	*Sent J. Steward home for stone-throwing.*

⁓✶⁓

30 Mar 1872	*I have found the school discipline very lax lately and I have been obliged to give it special attention.*
19 Jul 1872	*I have been very much troubled with lax behaviour in the lower classes.*

⁓✶⁓

11 Jul 1873	*I observe a great laxity of discipline in the children lately which I principally attribute to irregular attendance.*
19 Sep 1873	*The discipline is extremely lax.*
26 Sep 1873	*The discipline is improving.*
21 Nov 1873	*The discipline is more lax than usual; this is engaging my attention.*
5 Dec 1873	*The School-discipline has improved.*

⁓✶⁓

9 Jan 1874	*The discipline is very good – I have broken up the rod.*
16 Jan 1874	*I dismissed for a day one of the boys from the school, having heard him use foul language in the play-ground, and I reproved him. I admitted him again the next day, as he came to my house, begged pardon, and promised amendment.*
27 Feb 1874	*The discipline of the school is not so perfect as I could wish; the attempt to manage school entirely without a rod is a failure.*
29 May 1874	*I have found the school discipline rather lax this week. I am without a rod.*
11 Sep 1874	*The discipline of the children is very lax, principally owing to their long absence from school.*
25 Sep 1874	*The discipline is better.*

⁓✶⁓

19 Mar 1875   *I have been managing for a fortnight without a stick, and I think the children are not improved in discipline thereby. Having tried the same experiment very frequently during the past ten years, my final conclusion is that children can never be properly managed without corporal punishment for a great length of time, but if the discipline is well kept up, there may be occasional "interludes".* [This was Henry Yeaxlee's last entry in the log book.]

Alfred Hawks appointed master 17 May 1875

28 May 1875   *The children still continue very attentive both in their studies and discipline, corporal punishment being quite unnecessary.*

26 Nov 1875   *Alfred Bullock was severely punished for swearing yesterday.* [Alfred was the 9-year-old son of John and Eliza Bullock who lived in End Way. His father was an agricultural labourer.]

15 Dec 1876   *I had for some time been endeavouring to find how so many bricks get removed from the top of the closet; but on Wednesday Evening I caught one of the boys on the wall attending to a trap which he had skillfully* [sic] *made, with the aid of four bricks for each trap, which had been pulled off the Closet. I have strong hopes that such proceedings will not continue after the heavy punishment I felt compelled to . . .* [the last word is illegible.]

6 Feb 1880   *I have had to punish several children for using indecent language.*

4 Oct 1895   *Found the children had suffered considerably for the lengthened Vacation – I have adopted a new mode of punishment for the Children & found the experiment most Satisfactory. My object in so doing is to do away with corporal punishment altogether if possible. The boy Harold Nicklen has given very great trouble.* [Harold was the 9-year-old son of Jesse and Eliza Nicklen. The family had moved to Hadleigh from Dorset, where Jesse Nicklen had been a foreman in a brickworks. Presumably Jesse had moved to Hadleigh to work on the Salvation Army Farm Colony.]

11 Oct 1895   *The new method of punishment answers well.* [Unfortunately Alfred Hawks does not explain what this new method is.]

25 Oct 1895   *I am glad to record no case of corporal punishment since the re-opening of the School since the holidays.*

Here, Sir!

ALMOST EVERY ENTRY IN the school log book starts with a comment on the number of children who attended school. The main causes of absence from the National School were the weather, sickness and the work that was done by the children on the farms. The number of children attending school also fluctuated at different times of the year, depending on the weather and what seasonal jobs were available on the farms. Summer haymaking usually took away the largest number, and the managers of the National School tried to arrange the summer break, called the Harvest Vacation, to suit this work on the farms.

As Hadleigh was a farming community, families would move in and out of the village looking for agricultural work. If the head of the family could not find work in the winter months then, as the last resort, they would have to enter Rochford Workhouse. (When Rochford Union Workhouse was built in 1837 Hadleigh's workhouse was closed. Until the late 1860s the road in which it had been was known as Workhouse Lane. It was renamed Chapel Lane when the Methodist Chapel was built.) In the summer months new children would be admitted to the school as their families moved into the village for the harvesting. When children are named in the log book, I have attempted to find more details about them from the census, birth indexes and baptismal records. Unfortunately, with a fluctuating population in the village, this has not always been possible.

For the first twenty-three years or more, the National School, like most Victorian schools, encountered serious attendance problems. It took many years before parents and children accepted that schools were there to stay, and that going to school had to be seen as more important than going to the fairs, picking peas, or helping with the harvest. When the National School first opened in 1855 attendance at school was not compulsory. Sandon's Education Act in 1876 set up School Attendance Committees and placed the responsibility for ensuring school attendance firmly on the parents. Legal sanctions were introduced, enabling local authorities to employ attendance officers who would follow up absentees, visit homes and pursue prosecutions of parents. From the start, the range of penalties included fines, attendance orders and in extreme cases the removal of children from the parental home. The first mention of the school attendance officer in the log book is in February 1878. Summonses were issued by him and the parents fined by the magistrates at Rochford. Various loopholes were removed by the 1880 Education Act, which made attendance compulsory between the ages of five and ten. The minimum leaving age was raised to eleven in 1893 and to twelve in 1899. To meet the needs of the increased numbers of children attending school, Standard VII was added in 1882.

In the 1880s it became a requirement that the registers should be checked by the managers of the school at least once a quarter at irregular intervals. On 3 August 1883, Alfred Hawks recorded for the first time that Rev. A. J. Skrimshire had visited that week to check the registers.

Author's Note

Where sufficient data is provided on the weekly attendance averages, I have presented the data as a chart. To enable comparison of the values on the charts, the vertical axes have the same maximum value. For the years up to 1895 the maximum value is 100, which was the capacity of the school. From 1895 onwards the maximum value is 160, as the capacity had by then increased to 155. If no weekly average was given I have included the master's comment on attendance, which was recorded in the log book.

It is advisable to read this chapter in conjunction with the following chapters on sickness, the weather, children working and holidays.

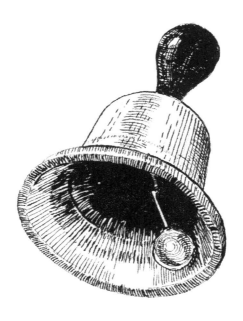

Log Book Entries

Miss Cecilia Miller had been appointed mistress in 1861

1 Jan 1863   *Attendance not very good.*

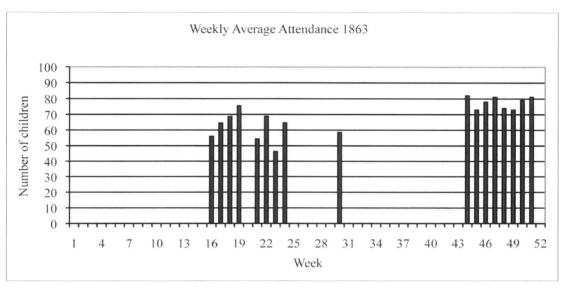

9 Jan 1863   *Average attendance good.*

16 Jan 1863   *Reproved a boy for playing truant.*

22 Jan 1863   *Alfred Hockley left the School.* [Alfred, who was aged about 9, had been living with his aunt and uncle, William and Eliza Grigg, on the Causeway. The Causeway was the stretch of the village street from what is now Chapel Lane to Victoria House Corner, so called because of its raised nature.]

3 Feb 1863   *Walter Hills punished for playing truant yesterday afternoon.* [Walter, aged 9, was the stepson of Thomas Smith, the shoemaker.]

4 Feb 1863   *On enquiring the cause of the absence of about a dozen boys this afternoon was told they had gone pigeon shooting.*

4 Mar 1863   *Eliza Dalby and Eliza Griggs played truant.* [The two girls both lived in Daws Heath Road, Thundersley and were aged seven. Eliza Dolby was the daughter of James and Jane Dolby, who worked as an agricultural labourer and a dressmaker.]

18 Mar 1863   *Eliza Griggs left at 3.30 to nurse her mother's baby.* [Eliza Grigg was the daughter of James and Hannah Grigg. James Grigg was a hawker.]

20 Mar 1863   *Charles Coker came to ask if he might come to School again.* [12-year-old Charles lived on the Causeway with his father William, a

basket maker, and his mother Hannah, a laundress.]

30 Mar 1863	*Four names added to the Register.*
21 Apr 1863	*Two names added to the Register.*
5 May 1863	*Attendance good. Two names added to the register.*
2 Jun 1863	*Half the children gone to Rayleigh Fair.*
4 Jun 1863	*School very thin all week owing to Fair and Circus at Rayleigh.*
16 Jun 1863	*About twenty children absent on account of a party at the Castle.*
18 Jun 1863	*Made out a list of absentees – found 23 children absent who ought to be at School.*
23 Jun 1863	*3 Gillmans absent because Cornelius Pepper yesterday threw the eldest boy's cap in the ditch.* [William, John and Henry Gillman were the three eldest sons of John and Susan Gillman. John was an agricultural labourer. Cornelius Pepper was the 9-year-old son of the village hurdle maker, James Pepper, and his wife Eliza. The family lived on the Causeway.]
25 Jun 1863	*School very thin on account of the Fair.*

Between 6 July and 27 July 1863, there was no official master or mistress
It is unclear who taught the children

20 Jul 1863	*Very few children present in the 1st class.*

William Batchelor Kingswood appointed master 7 September 1863

7 Sep 1863	*Attendance for first day after vacation 70.*
16 Sep 1863	*Gave James Bell and John Green a serious talking to for Truant playing which was chiefly through the instigation of a bigger boy (not a scholar).* [Both boys were aged about seven and were the sons of agricultural labourers living at Hadleigh. James' parents were Joseph and Ann Bell and John's were William and Ann Green. James' sister Emma would later teach at the school.]
28 Sep 1863	*A boy named John Harvey was admitted who had been to several schools for upwards of 8 years and was 12.9 years old, but could not do a compound subtraction sum or read or write at all nicely.*
5 Oct 1863	*Admitted Stephen Scudder aged 8 years who could neither read, write or cypher.* [Stephen was the son of agricultural labourer Richard Scudder, and his wife Amelia, who lived in Daws Heath Road.]

13 Oct 1863	*Kept Eliza Griggs in for Truant playing.* [Eliza had been punished in March by Miss Miller for the same offence.]
14 Dec 1863	*A beautifully fine day yet a great many Children absent, several from sickness and others I find running in the roads, with the consent of the Parents.*

⌒⅊⌒

| 4 Jan 1864 | *The School was begun to-day after the Xmas holidays. About 60 attended but on account of the severe weather and sickness many were absent.* |

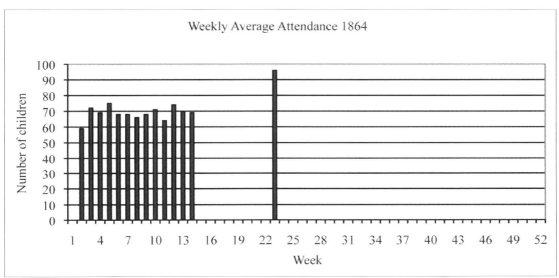

11 Jan 1864	*Admitted a boy – Geo. Finch – 11 years of age who does not know his Alphabet – the effects of having been taken to work so young.*
21 Jan 1864	*Most of the Daws Heath Scholars absent to-day, having gone to a treat given by the Minister of that place, at Rayleigh.* [This was probably the Minister of the Peculiar People Chapel which had been built in Daws Heath in 1852.]
5 Feb 1864	*Henry Snow poor attendance.* [Henry, aged about eight, was the son of an agricultural labourer, Henry Snow, and his wife Sarah who lived in End Way.]
10 Mar 1864	*A girl was also absent because she could not find her shoes which she pulled off the night before. <u>One</u> of the hundreds of excuses a Teacher's ears are pained with for irregular attendance at School.*
1 Apr 1864	*Several absent to-day for paltry reasons. This week being Easter the average was consequently reduced.*
9 May 1864	*The School has greatly increased in numbers, particularly among the Infants which last week attained the number of 40 in attendance.*

10 May 1864	*Leigh fair held to-day, several of the children absent on that account.*
11 May 1864	*A boy named John Felton who has not attended since Xmas came to-day of his own accord, saying he was tired of staying at home which he has done solely on account of the base indifference to the cause of education manifested by his parents.* [He was the 15-year-old son of John Felton, a Hadleigh agricultural labourer, and his wife Sarah.]
23 May 1864	*Thin School on account of Raleigh* [sic] *Fair.*
24 May 1864	*The School is thinner still to-day from the same cause.*
27 May 1864	*Fine weather during the week yet irregular attendance on account of the fair at Raleigh* [sic] *and its being the first week after the Holidays.*
30 May 1864	*Martha Lee re-entered after being absent for 5 or 6 months.* [Martha Lee was the 15-year-old daughter of Joshua Lee, an agricultural labourer who lived in Castle Lane. As her mother was dead, and she was the eldest daughter, she had probably been absent running the house.]
1 Jun 1864	*Had 100 in attendance in the afternoon.* [This was the maximum number the school had been built for.]
24 Jun 1864	*Several away to-day it being Hadleigh Fair.*
8 Sep 1864	*Several away for divers excuses "Blackberrying", "Gone out", "Truant playing", "Sick" &c. &c. &c.*
11 Oct 1864	*Several of Standards 3 and 4 away to-day.*
13 Oct 1864	*J. Green played truant for the third time this week.* [John Green was the 7-year-old son of Hadleigh agricultural labourer William, and his wife Ann. They lived in the village street.]
17 Oct 1864	*Several of higher standards away from various lessons picking up wood etc. etc. etc.*
2 Dec 1864	*Many little ones absent this week.*
6 Dec 1864	*General washing day in Hadleigh and many away in the morning especially in Standard I.*

Henry Yeaxlee appointed master 23 January 1865

23 Jan 1865	*My first day in School. Cold day and attendance about 60.*
3 Apr 1865	*School rather thin: on enquiring the cause I find that there is a report in the village that an infectious disease is going round in the school, and suspicion principally rests on two children.*
4 Apr 1865	*Many parents keep their children at home.*

6 Apr 1865	*Consult with Revd. J. Baines about the rumour.*
7 Apr 1865	*Visit some of the parents and speak to them about the prevailing opinion.*
10 Apr 1865	*I have refused admittance to the two children, and the attendance will I hope improve.*
11 Apr 1865	*School attendance still poor. Many children employed at home.*
5 Jun 1865	*Whit-Monday. School thin.*
12 Jun 1865	*Attendance poor.*
13 Jun 1865	*Raleigh [sic] Fair.*
14 Jun 1865	*Improved attendance.*
25 Jun 1865	*Hadleigh Fair-day. Attendance very low.*
4 Sep 1865	*Reopened school with an attendance a little exceeding 30. [After Harvest Vacation]*
8 Sep 1865	*Attendance poor all through the week.*
11 Sep 1865	*The attendance today improved.*
25 Sep 1865	*Some children returned to school who left some months ago and went to Raleigh [sic].*
21 Dec 1865	*Attendance unsatisfactory.*

1 Jan 1866	*Began this year with a moderately full school.*
3 Jan 1866	*Very much inconvenienced by having no registers, the managers having forgotten to get them for me in time.*
26 Jan 1866	*Several absent from infant room.*
7 Mar 1866	*Many children absent from 5th Class.*
9 Mar 1866	*Class 5 very thin indeed.*
13 Mar 1866	*Good first class attendance.*
19 Mar 1866	*Admitted Matilda Choppen into Class V.* [Matilda was probably a relative of the Choppen family who lived at Hadleigh, and worked as wheelwrights or blacksmiths.]
21 Mar 1866	*Infant attendance rather poor.*
23 Mar 1866	*A poor 1st Class all this week. The children seem always to stay away just before Easter.*
26 Mar 1866	*Admitted Mary Ann Colyer into the 5th Class.*
9 Apr 1866	*Admitted several small children.*
16 Apr 1866	*Admitted three more children into the 5th Class.*
23 Apr 1866	*Admitted William Carter. A rather thin first class.*
27 Apr 1866	*Only two first class children present this afternoon.*
30 Apr 1866	*Fifteen away from the Infant room.*
7 May 1866	*I have admitted three fresh children into the fifth class this morning.*

14 May 1866	*Admitted Elizabeth Gentry again after a long absence. Very good attendance.* [Elizabeth lived with her parents Daniel and Elizabeth in Chapel Lane. Aged six, her father was an agricultural labourer.]
15 May 1866	*Very full school.*
28 May 1866	*Falling off of 5th class attendance.*
2 Jul 1866	*Two fresh children in fifth class.*
9 Jul 1866	*Admitted a little girl Sarah Snow – but there were only 18 present out of 45 in Class 5.* [Sarah, the daughter of Henry and Sarah Snow, was only three years old. Her father was an agricultural labourer and lived in End Way.]
6 Aug 1866	*The attendance very low. Visited by Revd. T. E. Espin who spoke about the attendance.* [There was smallpox in the village.]
8 Aug 1886	*The attendance today was about 36 and the parents say that they think the children might as well be at home as the holidays are so near.*
10 Sep 1866	*Reopened school. Readmitted Ernest Gage and two little ones into Class 5.*
28 Sep 1866	*Good attendance. More children promised next week.*
1 Oct 1866	*Admitted several small children 5th class. Register quite filled up.*
2 Oct 1866	*Nearly 90 present this morning.*
5 Oct 1866	*The attendance this week has been better than I ever saw it.*
8 Oct 1866	*Admitted seven more children this morning.*
9 Oct 1866	*95 present in the morning.*

1 Jan 1867	*Reopened school with a very small attendance.*
4 Jan 1867	*There have been scarcely any children at school this week.*
5 Feb 1867	*Admitted Walter Hockley, re-admitted J. Dolby.* [Walter Hockley had moved into New Road from Rochford. Aged eight, his father David was a journeyman bricklayer, married to Mary. A resident of Daws Heath Road, 6-year-old James was the son of James and Jane Dalby. His father was an agricultural labourer.]
26 Mar 1867	*Much better attendance.*
29 Apr 1867	*Reopened the School – rather poor attendance in the upper classes.* [After Easter Vacation] *M. A. Stowers re-admitted – away three weeks at a dame's School because "she learnt nothing", and having learnt less there, she has returned.* [Mary Ann Stowers, aged seven, lived in Chapel Lane with her parents George and Elizabeth. Her father was an agricultural labourer. Dame Schools were small private schools,

usually taught by women and were often located in the home of the teacher.]

3 May 1867	*Scanty attendance in the upper classes.*
6 May 1867	*Admitted three Children.*
13 May 1867	*Attendance poor in the first Class.*
17 May 1867	*Attendance this week has been unsatisfactory, from weather & other causes – the Average only 57.*
21 May 1867	*Admitted three infants.*
27 May 1867	*Very many children absent this morning in consequence of an idle report of there being no school.*
29 May 1867	*Attendance still poor.*
10 Jun 1867	*Poor attendance – many children absent on account of home-work.* [This refers to the children working at home, doing chores for their parents.]
17 Jun 1867	*Raleigh* [sic] *fair-day – some absent for that reason.*
24 Jun 1867	*Hadleigh fair-day. Very poor attendance.*
26 Jun 1867	*Many children absent in consequence of an idle rumour of a half-holiday.*
27 Jun 1867	*The school has been very thin this week, in consequence of the two days' fair.*
1 Jul 1867	*Admitted Betsy Wilson.*
2 Jul 1867	*Attendance considerably improved.*
8 Jul 1867	*Admitted three children.*
9 Jul 1867	*Admitted another boy.*
12 Jul 1867	*Attendance this week 82.*
17 Jul 1867	*Attendance still poor.* [This was after a day's holiday.]
19 Jul 1867	*Average this week very low.*
25 Jul 1867	*Very many children absent this afternoon on the occasion of Rayleigh Anniversary.*
29 Jul 1867	*Attendance considerably improved.*
13 Sep 1867	*There have been very few children at school this week.* [First week after the Harvest Vacation.]
16 Sep 1867	*Better attendance this morning. Admitted Sarah Anderson, readmitted Philip Law.*
23 Sep 1867	*Obliged to refuse admission to a little girl she being too young.*
30 Sep 1867	*Admitted two children.*
8 Oct 1867	*Admitted two children.*
14 Oct 1867	*Admitted two children. Very good attendance.*
15 Oct 1867	*Attendance this morning 86.*

28 Oct 1867	*Attendance rather diminished.*
11 Nov 1867	*Obliged to refuse admission to some children.*
15 Nov 1867	*Average for the week 82.*
18 Nov 1867	*Attendance today rather diminished.*
25 Nov 1867	*Began School with good attendance.*
29 Nov 1867	*Week's average 81.*
3 Dec 1867	*Only six present out of 34 in V Register.*
12 Dec 1867	*Very few children present.*
13 Dec 1867	*Lowest weekly average of the quarter – 49.*
30 Dec 1867	*Re-opened School. Attendance rather poor.*

21 Jan 1868	*Hardly any children.*

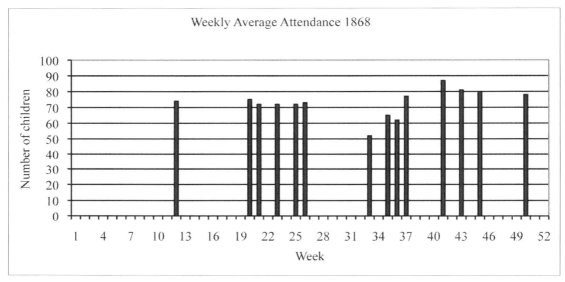

4 Feb 1868	*Attendance improved with the weather.*
18 Feb 1868	*73 present this morning.*
2 Mar 1868	*Very fair attendance this morning. Admitted Maria Spooner.*
12 Mar 1868	*Two boys (Davy) absent from school for some weeks, upon enquiring to-day I hear they have been playing in the roads.*
16 Mar 1868	*Admitted six children into Class V.*
27 Mar 1868	*Average for the past Quarter 63.*
30 Mar 1868	*Readmitted Martha Chignell.* [Martha was the 7-year-old daughter of Elizabeth Chignell, the widow of David Chignell, who had died in August 1866.]
20 Apr 1868	*Reassembled school. Attendance poor.* [After Easter Vacation]
4 May 1868	*Admitted B. Davy.*
11 May 1868	*Admitted Hester Cheshire.*

25 May 1868	*Admitted 2 Children.*
28 May 1868	*I was hindered for a long time this morning by a boy named Saward who refused to come to school till led: he having been allowed to run in the roads by his mother for some time previously.* [This was probably one of the three sons of Elijah and Susan Saward, who lived on Hadleigh Common. The agricultural labourer and his wife had three sons: George, Owen and Ernest.]
4 Jun 1868	*Admitted three children.*
25 Jun 1868	*Attendance rather poor in the lower classes.*
13 Jul 1868	*I find the attendance falling off very much; as some of the girls are sent out to be nurse girls, while parents work in the fields.* [At harvest time the women would work in the fields, leaving their daughters to look after the other children in the family.]
17 Aug 1868	*Reopened school with very few children.* [After Harvest Vacation]
24 Aug 1868	*Attendance much improved.*
2 Sep 1868	*Attendance diminished; but I cannot discover any cause.*
14 Sep 1868	*Admitted four children.*
21 Sep 1868	*Admitted J. Wallis.*
5 Oct 1868	*Admitted 3 Children.*
6 Oct 1868	*Admitted 2 Children.*
7 Oct 1868	*Admitted William Baldwin.* [William, aged about four years, was the son of William and Lavinia Baldwin, who lived in the village street. His grandfather, Thomas Baldwin, had been the village butcher for many years until his death in 1867. William's father had also worked as a butcher, but by 1871 he was working as a groom.]
12 Oct 1868	*Admitted Philadelphia Brown.* [Aged about thirteen, Philadelphia was the daughter of William Brown, a labourer.]
12 Nov 1868	*The average attendance of Infants has gone down very much this week.*
30 Nov 1868	*The 5th Class attendance has been very poor in the last week & continues so partly from weather & sickness.*
14 Dec 1868	*The attendance to-day is thin. Admitted W. Smith.* [William Henry Smith was the 11-year-old son of Alfred and Ellen Smith. His father was a bricklayer and the family had recently moved to New Road.]
4 Jan 1869	*Reopened school. Very few present.*

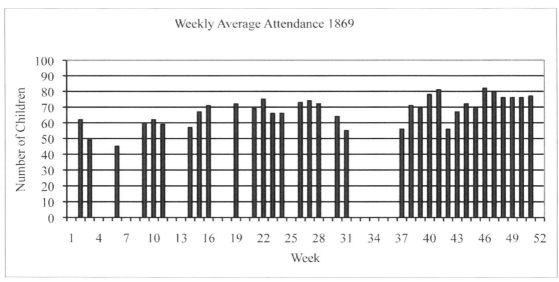

18 Jan 1869	*Began this morning with a small school.*
25 Jan 1869	*Attendance very bad indeed.* [Many of the children were sick.]
15 Feb 1869	*Attendance considerably improved.*
1 Mar 1869	*Attendance much improved.*
5 Apr 1869	*Recommenced the school with only a moderate attendance.* [After Easter Vacation]
14 Apr 1869	*One boy away all day "having his hair cut".*
19 Apr 1869	*Attendance good. Admitted 7 children.*
29 Apr 1869	*Attendance good, but many children are absent unnecessarily.*
3 May 1869	*Readmitted S. Wakeling.* [This was probably Sarah, the 4-year-old daughter of Henry and Mary Ann Wakeling who lived in the cottages next to the *Crown Inn*. Henry was an agricultural labourer.]
10 May 1869	*Admitted three children. Attendance rather thin.*
12 May 1869	*Rather poorer attendance. Leigh Fair-Day.*
18 May 1869	*Attendance very poor, partly through an idle report of there being a week's holiday in the Afternoon.* [Whitsun week]
25 May 1869	*Many away – it being Fair Day.*
1 Jun 1869	*Several children absent from small excuses.*
6 Jun 1869	*Rather poor attendance. Admitted E. Grubb.* [This was probably Eliza Ann, the 11-year-old daughter of William and Emma Grubb, who lived in Hart Road Cottages in Thundersley. Her father was an agricultural labourer.]
14 Jun 1869	*Readmitted O. Saward.* [Owen was the 9-year-old son of an agricultural labourer, Elijah Saward, and his wife Susan, who lived on Hadleigh Common.]

25 Jun 1869   *Very poor attendance. [Second day of Hadleigh Fair.]*

28 Jun 1869   *Admitted two small children.*

5 Jul 1869   *Attendance good. Admitted three children.*

6 Jul 1869   *One boy allowed to stay away to-day to lie about near the roads. This is only too common a thing.*

7 Jul 1869   *A number of Children absent to have a day's holiday, because there is a club-feast at Leigh, to which some of the parents go.*

21 Jul 1869   *A great many children absent from trifling excuses.*

22 Jul 1869   *Three or four children are away running about in the Castle Lane, because there are visitors (with the parents' consent).*

4 Aug 1869   *Very poor attendance indeed; only 19 out [of] 43 in Class V.*

13 Sep 1869   *Began school with 48 Children. [After Harvest Vacation]*

20 Sep 1869   *Attendance much improved. Admitted 3 Children.*

5 Oct 1869   *80 Present this morning.*

25 Oct 1869   *Attendance rather poor – many children playing in the roads & the parents quite indifferent.*

26 Oct 1869   *Some of the elder children absent at a tea-party.*

3 Nov 1869   *Attendance improved. 76 this morning.*

15 Nov 1869   *Attendance improving – 81. Readmitted some Daw's [sic] Heath children.*

24 Nov 1869   *Some children absent this afternoon at a tea-feast.*

13 Dec 1869   *Admitted Mary Hazleden, a girl of 15, who can barely write or read.*

3 Jan 1870   *Reassembled the School.*

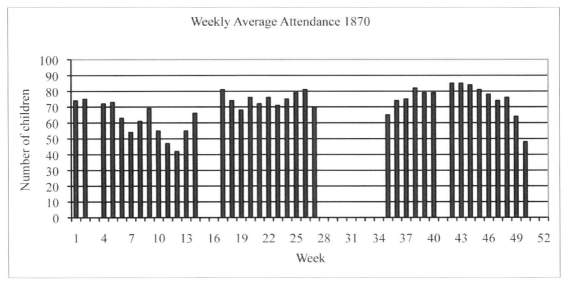

24 Jan 1870   *Admitted Ann and Emily Lincoln.* [Ann and Emily were the daughters of John and Emily Lincoln who had moved from

Rayleigh. John Lincoln was the occupier of 7 acres of land in Thundersley. His daughters were aged about nine and ten.]

25 Jan 1870   *Attendance not so good as it should be. Many children away from trifling excuses.*

9 Feb 1870   *Attendance very small in the lower classes.*

17 Feb 1870   *Very few present.*

29 Feb 1870   *Admitted G. Rankes & W. Tipthorp.* [George Rank, aged about eight, was the son of George and Elizabeth. His father worked as a blacksmith and they lived at Hart Road Cottages in Thundersley. Walter Tipthorp, aged about three, lived in the village street with his parents Charles and Rachel. His father worked as a hay-binder.]

15 Mar 1870   *Attendance very low: 12 present out of 48 in the Vth Register.*

28 Mar 1870   *Attendance slightly improved. Admitted Walter Lancaster.* [Walter, aged seven, was the son of James and Elizabeth Lancaster who lived at Thundersley. His father worked as an agricultural labourer.]

4 Apr 1870   *Attendance much improved. Readmitted two infants.*

25 Apr 1870   *Recommenced with good Attendance.* [After Easter Vacation]

2 May 1870   *Attendance poorer – several small children absent.*

5 May 1870   *A few children absent: some I saw to-day in the roads, playing, and with the parents' consent. This only too common a thing.*

6 May 1870   *Average for this week 74: the reduction owing partly to illness, and partly to the parents' indifference to learning.*

9 May 1870   *Admitted Julia Shelley.* [10-year-old Julia's father was a carpenter employing three men. Samuel and his wife Eliza lived with their family in the Hadleigh Road Cottages at Thundersley.]

10 May 1870   *Readmitted H. Russell & Wm. Snow. Attendance thinner this afternoon, because of Leigh Fair.* [Harriet Russell was the girl who survived small pox in 1866. She was now aged eight. 9-year-old William, like Harriet, lived in the village street. His father Henry Snow was an agricultural labourer and was married to Sarah.]

16 May 1870   *Admitted Keziah Dolbey.* [Kezia Dalby, aged three, was the daughter of James and Jane of Thundersley. Her father worked as an agricultural labourer and her mother as a dressmaker.]

23 May 1870   *Readmitted O & E Seaward.* [Owen and Ernest Saward were the sons of Elijah and Susan. Elijah, an agricultural labourer, rented a cottage in the village street. Owen was aged eight, and Ernest was two years younger.]

30 May 1870   *Many children absent – playing in the roads, and other things.*

1 Jun 1870	*One boy absent, having "gone for a ride". The children are frequently absent for such trivial causes.*
7 Jun 1870	*Attendance poor in the lower classes.* [There was fever in the village, with deaths later in the month.]
8 Jun 1870	*Readmitted Eliza Griggs and William Griggs. Several children away at "Southend Fair"* [Eliza and William, aged seven and four, were the children of a Thundersley agricultural labourer, William Grigg, and his wife Sarah.]
10 Jun 1870	*There are children playing in the roads; but when I write to the parents, I get no answer, and when I speak to them they promise and never perform.*
13 Jun 1870	*Admitted G. Robinson. Some of the elder boys absent at Rayleigh Fair – a <u>horse-fair</u>, with the parents' consent, I regret to say.*
17 Jun 1870	*There are still children absent unnecessarily.*
20 Jun 1870	*Admitted Emma Rivers.* [5-year-old Emma lived in one of the Hadleigh Road Cottages in Thundersley with her parents, Henry and Eleanor. Her father was a market gardener.]
21 Jun 1870	*Admitted Ellen French. A great many absent from the lower classes.* [Aged about four, Ellen was the daughter of Samuel and Hannah French. The family lived in Church Road, Thundersley and Samuel worked as an agricultural labourer.]
28 Jun 1870	*90 present this afternoon.*
22 Jul 1870	*The Attendance is rather poor this week – some children being unwell, and many employed at home.*
29 Aug 1870	*Recommenced school with an attendance of 61.* [After Harvest Vacation]
20 Sep 1870	*92 present this morning.*
28 Sep 1870	*Some children away playing in the roads – with the parents' knowledge and consent.*
26 Oct 1870	*Very good attendance 91 children present.*
9 Nov 1870	*I have been much troubled to-day by a boy named Whitehead who has been truant-playing, a rather unusual thing here.* [Alfred was the 8-year-old son of Robert and Louisa Whitehead. Robert was a farm bailiff and the family lived in Chapel Lane.]
28 Nov 1870	*The weather is cold, and there is more illness in the village; which together have considerably diminished the attendance, especially in Class V.*
8 Dec 1870	*Very bad weather and illness keep the Average low.*
13 Dec 1870	*Very poor attendance indeed.*

⌇

| 2 Jan 1871 | *Reopened the school with a small attendance. Admitted H, F & A Eaton.* [Henry Eaton, a bricklayer, had recently moved to Hadleigh from Leigh with his wife Maria and family. Harry was nine, Florence six and Arthur three.] |

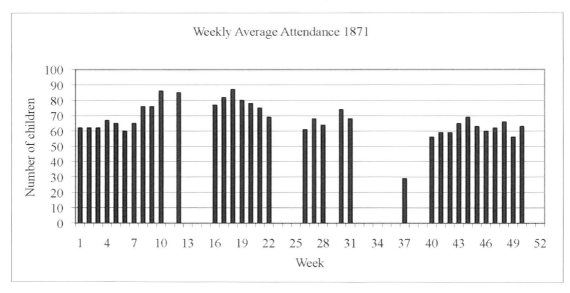

12 Jan 1871	*Some children away in the roads playing even in this severe weather.*
27 Jan 1871	*The Attendance is v. slowly improving. Some children are still unwell, & the weather is unfavourable.*
15 Feb 1871	*Some children absent from illness, some playing in the roads.*
20 Feb 1871	*Admitted three children.*
6 Mar 1871	*Admitted two children.*
24 Mar 1871	*I have admitted four children.*
31 Mar 1871	*I have re-admitted two young children, absent through the winter.*
15 Apr 1871	*I have admitted two children. The elder children are leaving school very fast.*
26 May 1871	*Several children are absent because of the indifference of their parents whether the children are educated or ignorant.*
30 Jun 1871	*The Average is still low 61. This is principally owing to the field-work, which takes parents from their homes and the Children are kept from School to mind each other, and for trifling errands.*
14 Jul 1871	*A great many children absent pea-picking and running in the roads, while the parents take no heed.*
16 Sep 1871	*I have reopened School this week, with a very low average (29) partly because the gleaning is not yet over.* [After Harvest Vacation]

⌇

8 Jan 1872   *The Average is rather low. I have admitted two children.*

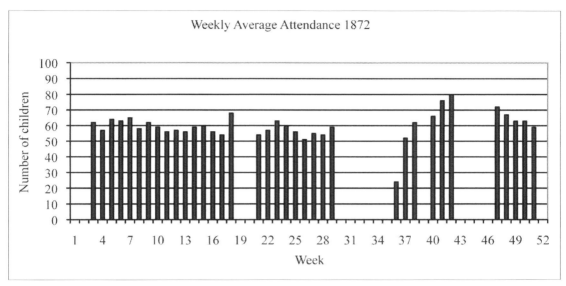

2 Feb 1872   *One child admitted.*

16 Feb 1872   *I have been obliged to reject some applications from other parishes.*

10 Apr 1872   *I have to refuse admission to several children from other parishes.*

19 Apr 1872   *Some of the children are allowed to play in the roads still, and the parents look quietly on.*

3 May 1872   *I have this week admitted eight children.*

7 Jun 1872   *I have admitted one scholar.*

26 Jul 1872   *The attendance was low on Monday because of a tea-feast held by the Banyards, which many of the children attended.* [The 'Banyards' were the Peculiar People, founded by James Banyard, who had a chapel at Daws Heath.]

13 Sep 1872   *The attendance has much improved.* [The previous week the school had closed after two days as so few children returned from the Harvest Vacation.]

27 Sep 1872   *On Wednesday Afternoon the attendance was very low owing to a Sunday-school tea-feast at Hadleigh Chapel.* [This was the Methodist Chapel in Chapel Lane.]

17 Oct 1872   *I have admitted some children this week.*

22 Nov 1872   *There has been a dame-school started in Hadleigh, and three of the children have gone there, that as their mother said, "they might set more comfortable in a cottage, and not be taught by girls."*

6 Dec 1872   *The upper classes have been very irregular, especially the girls who are employed at home.*

2 Jan 1873	*I have reassembled the school this week after the vacation, and the attendance was rather poor.*

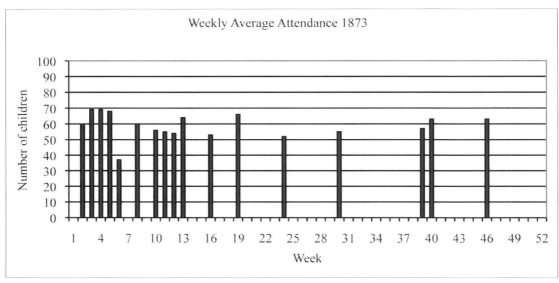

14 Feb 1873	*The attendance has been low, partly because of inclement weather, & partly through illness.*
3 Apr 1873	*The Average is again very low.*
10 Apr 1873	*The Average has improved.*
25 Apr 1873	*The Average has considerably improved.*
23 May 1873	*The Average has fallen considerably owing to severe weather and illness among the children.*
29 May 1873	*The average has improved with the improving weather, and decrease of illness.*
20 Jun 1873	*The Average this week is exceptionally high.*
27 Jun 1873	*The Average has fallen slightly.* [Hadleigh Fair]
4 Jul 1873	*The Attendance is still good. The school was visited by Mr. Tyrrell on Thursday Morning, and the attendance &c. commented on.*
18 Jul 1873	*The Average is very little raised.*
25 Jul 1873	*The attendance is falling off in the upper classes principally because the parents are absent from their homes at field work.*
8 Aug 1873	*The attendance has diminished very much. I intend to carry on the school for another week if possible.*
8 Sep 1873	*Reassembled the school. The Attendance very thin indeed.* [After Harvest Vacation]
19 Sep 1873	*The Average is still very low. Many children are absent from very trivial causes.*
17 Oct 1873	*The Average is rather lower.*

31 Oct 1873	*The Attendance continues good.*
21 Nov 1873	*There are still many children absent from trifling excuses.*
28 Nov 1873	*The Average for this week is very high.*
5 Dec 1873	*There are still many children absent from trifling causes – as running on errands, and the like.*
19 Dec 1873	*The Attendance has rapidly fallen off this week.*

⌒ℳ⌒

9 Jan 1874	*I have reassembled the School after the Vacation, and the attendance is not so good.*
16 Jan 1874	*The average is improving.*
23 Jan 1874	*The Average for the week is much improved.*
6 Feb 1874	*The Attendance has decreased this week owing to cold weather and illness in the village.*
13 Feb 1874	*The Average attendance is very low, partly caused by illness and partly by the coldness of the weather.*
20 Feb 1874	*The Attendance is considerably higher this week.*
6 Mar 1874	*The Attendance has considerably improved – though Children (a few) are allowed to play in the street.*
27 Mar 1874	*The average attendance this week is lower, and owing principally to the fact that so many parents will allow children to be absent from any trifling excuse.*
3 Apr 1874	*The average is rather higher.*
10 Apr 1874	*The Attendance is still very good. I have admitted three children this week.*
17 Apr 1874	*The Average is very high (71). I have admitted two children this week, and have refused admission to one.*
8 May 1874	*The Average is 73.*
15 May 1874	*The Attendance has been very good.*
22 May 1874	*The Average for the week is 69. I have been obliged to refuse admittance to several children (from Thundersley and Eastwood) as I am unable to take more children.*
29 May 1874	*The Average is rather lower than last week.*
5 Jun 1874	*This week occurred the annual fair at a neighbouring town, Rayleigh. The average has been considerably diminished by it.*
12 Jun 1874	*The Average has risen considerably. I have admitted one child this week and refused admission to a child from Thundersley.* [Thundersley had its own school.]
26 Jun 1874	*The Attendance this week has been very poor indeed, partly from weather and partly that there is much work in the fields done by women and the attendance suffers accordingly.*

3 Jul 1874	*The average continues very low.*
23 Jul 1874	*I have to-day dismissed the School for the Harvest Vacation, and given out the tickets of Admission to Lady Nicholson's tea to the best attendants at the school for the past year.*
28 Aug 1874	*The Attendance is still poor. I have never before had so few children in the school.* [After Harvest Vacation]
4 Sep 1874	*The attendance for this week has improved considerably though the average is not high.*
11 Sep 1874	*The attendance is slowly increasing. Many children are making a practise* [sic] *of coming late.*
18 Sep 1874	*The average has been considerably reduced this week by the absence of nearly the whole school at a school-feast in connection with the Chapel.*
25 Sep 1874	*The attendance is getting more regular than it has been.*
2 Oct 1874	*The attendance this week has been very good. I have admitted some young children this week.*
9 Oct 1874	*The Attendance has increased considerably: the average being the highest of the year.*
16 Oct 1874	*The average is higher than last week's.*
23 Oct 1874	*The attendance is not so good. I have admitted one girl.*
30 Oct 1874	*The Attendance is very good still (72).*
6 Nov 1874	*The attendance this week has been very good.*
13 Nov 1874	*The attendance still continues very good.*
20 Nov 1874	*This week's average is the highest of the year 83.*
27 Nov 1874	*The average is still very good. (80).*

| 8 Jan 1875 | *The attendance is very low this week.* |

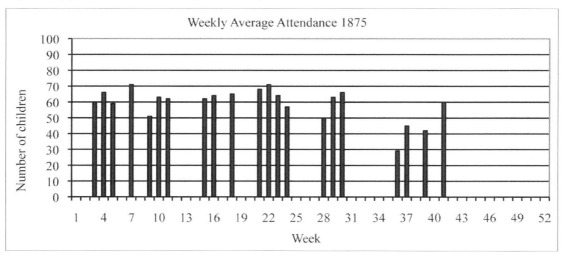

15 Jan 1875	*The average still continues low though better than last week.*
29 Jan 1875	*I have had several applications for admittance for children of other parishes – even from Eastwood, which I am obliged to refuse.*

Between 19 March and 17 May 1875, in the absence of a master, the rector ran the school

16 Apr 1875	*Admitted three children from Daws Heath.*
23 Apr 1875	*No falling off in the attendance which has been good.*

Alfred Hawks appointed master 17 May 1875

21 May 1875	*The average has been rather low, probably owing to the Vacation.* [After Whitsun Vacation]
28 May 1875	*I have refused to take several children as the average is still high.*
16 Jul 1875	*Two children have been admitted from the village. Christopher Thorington has again been playing truant, being an old offender of the late master. I intend locking him up on Saturday (if I can get him here).* [Aged about 9 years, Christopher was the son of George and Eliza Thorington of Daws Heath. The family was also known as Carey. George was an agricultural labourer.]
23 Jul 1875	*Several of the old children returning to the village have again been admitted to the School.*
30 Jul 1875	*William Tilstone was admitted on Tuesday.* [This was probably the young son of William Tilston, who until recently had been a gunner in the Royal Artillery at Shoeburyness.]
10 Sep 1875	*Attendance very bad – late harvest. Average 29. We opened School on Monday morning, after a month's Vacation, with 21 children.*
8 Oct 1875	*The attendance continues fair. Several children have been refused entrance to the School. Yesterday (Thursday) many of the children were at Rochford, being the Annual Sale.*
5 Nov 1875	*Attendance good – admitted several children.*
19 Nov 1875	*Admitted Charles Ebon.*
17 Dec 1875	*Attendance greatly improved – still a few children absent for very poor causes.*
14 Jan 1876	*The School was re-opened on Monday with a good attendance. On Wednesday I was called home and obliged to close the School for the rest of the week.* [This was due to the death of Gertrude Ann

Hawks, Alfred's 13-year-old sister, at Snodland in Kent.] *The Rector promised to manage School for me till I returned on the following Wednesday, but on reaching the Station, I heard of his death, consequently the School was closed for a week.* [Rev. William Metcalfe died on 17 January 1876, aged 45 years of pleuritic effusion, after an illness of three days.]

31 Mar 1876   *The average has decreased considerably this week; the children have attended very irregularly.*

28 Apr 1876   *As is very common the average after the Easter Vacation is somewhat lower than usual 58. The children seem none the worse for their holliday* [sic].

5 May 1876   *The average for past week has increased to 66 the children having attended very regularly.*

9 Jun 1876   *The attendance has been somewhat low and irregular, which is, no doubt owing to the Whitsun-tide hollidays* [sic]. *I have received a note from Mrs. Howlett stating that Emma her daughter had obtained a situation and obliged to leave School. She was one of my fifth Standard girls for Examination.*

23 Jun 1876   *The attendance up to this afternoon has been very good, but I have on several occasions sent for the absentees, and have luckily been successful in getting them to School.*

30 Jun 1876   *Admitted 5 children in the Infants room.*

7 Jul 1876   *The School has been quite full this week especially with the smaller children.*

21 Jul 1876   *The attendance has been rather irregular this week, several children been out holliday-making* [sic].

28 Jul 1876   *Admitted Ernest Shelley.* [Ernest Shelley was the illegitimate 9-year-old son of Eliza and lived at Thundersley with his grandparents, Samuel and Eliza. Samuel Shelley was a carpenter.]

4 Aug 1876   *I have dismissed the children for the usual Month Vacation.*

8 Sep 1876   *The School was re-opened on Monday with very low numbers (35), consequently the general routine has been somewhat lax and unmethodical.* [After Harvest Vacation]

15 Sep 1876   *The numbers have greatly increased this week, and the general routine is carried on.*

6 Oct 1876   *The attendance has been very irregular this week partly owing, I believe, to a very large annual sale at Rochford.*

27 Oct 1876   *I have admitted three Children this week from the parish but have been obliged to reject one boy out of the parish.*

3 Nov 1876	*The attendance has been very good having at one meeting of the School 76 Children.*
12 Jan 1877	*The School was re-opened on Monday, after the usual fortnight Vacation, with 60 children. I have great hopes from the appearance of the weather we shall have an increase in numbers next week.*
26 Jan 1877	*The School has not been quite so well attended this week, as the two preceding weeks.*
2 Feb 1877	*The attendance is on the decrease: Sickness is spreading through the village: the highest number present at any meeting of the School has only been 56.*
16 Feb 1877	*The Attendance has slightly improved this week. The Attendance in the Infant-room has been very low during the past few weeks.*
2 Mar 1877	*The attendance has been very good this week.*
16 Mar 1877	*The attendance has been very good this week up till this afternoon, when I have only 10 present in the two upper classes.*
23 Mar 1877	*The attendance has not been quite so good this week, the weather being unsettled and several Children Sick.*
13 Apr 1877	*The School has been well filled during the past week. I have admitted several fresh children, chiefly in the Infant department & re-admitted Eliza Morley.* [Eliza, aged about seven, was the daughter of Joshua and Emily Morley, who lived in Chapel Lane. Joshua died at the age of 45 years, and was buried on 19 April 1877.]
25 May 1877	*The attendance has been rather below the average. The School was closed on Monday this being Whitsun week, which accounts no doubt for the attendance not being so good.*
20 Jul 1877	*In the early part of the week the attendance was very good owing to the promise of a treat on Wednesday but on Thursday and Friday the numbers went down rapidly. Many of the children are engaged in the fields pea-picking.*
27 Jul 1877	*Attendance very good.*
21 Sep 1877	*The numbers are still very low which caused the instruction to be somewhat lax.*
28 Sep 1877	*The attendance has improved this week considerably.*
11 Jan 1878	*The School was re-opened on Monday with a fair attendance.*
8 Feb 1878	*I have several applications for admittance to the School from Daws Heath, but have been obliged to refuse – the School being full.*

22 Feb 1878	*The numbers are on the increase. The officer to hunt up the absentees is working with great good energy in the village.*
26 Apr 1878	*The attendance is still very good, but now the hot weather is coming I begin to feel the effects of the insufficient staff of teachers, especially now the numbers are increasing, from the energy of the Officer of* [the] *School Attendance Committee.*
3 May 1878	*I have had a little trouble this week with a truant boy.*
10 May 1878	*Admitted eight children on Monday.*
24 May 1878	*Several children are leaving the village. Sarah and Emily Plaile, both qualified for Examination, have left.* [Sarah and Emily, aged about nine and five, were the daughters of a gamekeeper, John Playle, and his wife Emma.]
31 May 1878	*The attendance has been rather irregular this week, especially in the upper classes.*
4 Jun 1878	[Her Majesty's Inspector wrote the following comment in the log book.] *Visited the School. I have no confidence in the Registers.*
21 Jun 1878	*The School has been fairly attended this week. Admitted Ada Brown.* [Ada was the 3-year-old daughter of William and Elizabeth Brown, who lived in New Road. Her father was an agricultural labourer.]
28 Jun 1878	*The attendance has not been nearly so good this week. On Monday afternoon there were only seventeen children present, owing probably to the village fair. The School was not opened on Monday Morning, the Managers having given me <u>full</u> permission to close the School. Average for the week 62.*
12 Jul 1878	*Notwithstanding the determination of many of the parents to keep their children at home, while they are themselves working in the hayfields, I have succeeded in keeping the average up to a good point – 71.*
19 Jul 1878	*Admitted Thirza French and Edith Eaton.* [Thirza was the 3-year-old daughter of George and Harriet French, and lived in Pleasant Row, the cottages between the school and the school house. Edith Eaton was not yet three years old, the daughter of Henry, a bricklayer, and his wife Maria. They lived in the village street.]
26 Jul 1878	*I have, this afternoon, punished Eliza Nelson for "playing truant" this morning.*
2 Aug 1878	[The HMI report on the inspections on 4 and 17 June severely criticised the registration of the children.] *The manner in which the Registers have been kept I consider most discredible.* [Word illegible] *feel compelled to order a deduction of one tenth to be made from the grant for faults of Registration (Article 32b). An*

	Assistant Teacher (Article 79) should be appointed at once or a Pupil Teacher transferred from some other School if the average Attendance during the current year is to exceed 60.
13 Sep 1878	*The School was re-opened on Monday with very low numbers indeed. In addition to the usual Month's holliday* [sic] *we were obliged to close the School another week on account of the late Harvest.*
20 Sep 1878	*The numbers continue to be very low indeed. Average 45.*
27 Sep 1878	*The numbers have increased considerably this week. All the Eatons are leaving the School; their parents having hired a house at Southend. Average 60.*
4 Oct 1878	*The average for the week has increased considerably viz. 73 against 60. There are still 24 children who have either not been at all during the week or are very irregular.*
25 Oct 1878	*Admitted several fresh children.*
29 Nov 1878	*The attendance does not increase much at present, the highest number present during the week was 68, which is poor against 100 on books. Numbers of children have not yet sufficiently recovered to leave their houses, especially as the weather has been so very wet for this last week. Admitted Emma Sandon on Monday.* [Measles had been in the village for eight weeks and had led to the school being closed for nearly three weeks.]
6 Dec 1878	*The Attendance has improved this week, the highest number present was 78.*

⌇

3 Jan 1879	*The School was re-opened on Monday with a fair attendance, which increased on Tues. and Weds.; but the numbers were brought down to 54 this morning and 60 this afternoon showing a weekly average of 69.*

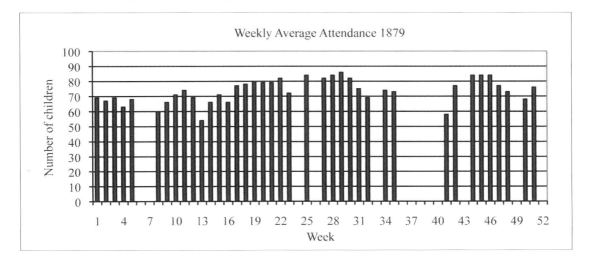

17 Jan 1879	*The Attendance has improved a little this week.*
31 Jan 1879	*Alfred Allen and Frank Bowyer left the School the latter having left the district.*
7 Feb 1879	*Admitted Henry Bond.*
28 Feb 1879	*The Attendance has improved a little this week but it is still low compared with no. on Registers. Average 66. Number on Registers 98.*
15 Mar 1879	*Admitted Fred Balls and William Stibbards.* [Fred Balls, aged about three years old, was the son of John and Maria, who lived in the village street. His father was an agricultural labourer. There were two William Stibbards living in the village at this time, either William John who was the 3-year-old son of Samuel and Ann Stibbards, who lived on the Common; or William Charles, nearly three years old, the son of James and Emily, who lived in Pleasant Row. Both their fathers were carpenters and wheelwrights. In 1867 Samuel Stibbards had started his undertaking business, which is still owned by the family today. Samuel Stibbards was the uncle of James Stibbards.]
28 Mar 1879	*Admitted Harriett Mathews and Ellen Turner.*
25 Apr 1879	*The Attendance has been very good this week, on Thursday morning I had 83 present and there has not been less than 75 at one meeting throughout the week.*
2 May 1879	*James and William Law began playing truant this week – I have succeeded in getting William but James is still "running the streets".* [The brothers were the sons of Henry Law, the village baker, and his wife Fanny. They lived next to the *Crown Inn*. James was aged twelve, and would soon start to work as a baker with his father. William was two years younger.]
9 May 1879	*There are several children who have nearly made their times still absent, and I am very much afraid I shall lose them; the Attendance officer has issued a final notice to them but the Parents absolutely disregard them.*
16 May 1879	*Admitted Edith Miller.*
23 May 1879	*The highest number in attendance was 89 on Tuesday morning.*
30 May 1879	*The Average for present week is the highest since I have had charge of the School (82). Admitted Jessie Reid on Monday.*
13 Jun 1879	*Two summons have been issued for neglecting to send children to School.*
20 Jun 1879	*The Attendance has been remarkably good this week, but for some unaccountable reason it always falls on Friday afternoons.*

4 Jul 1879	*Admitted Sarah Gillman this morning.* [Sarah Ann was the 6-year-old daughter of Joseph and Sarah Gillman, who lived in Rectory Road. Joseph was an agricultural labourer.]
18 Jul 1879	*We have succeeded in getting Joseph Gillman to School who has for some time been playing truant.* [Joseph was the 9-year-old brother of Sarah.]
10 Oct 1879	*After 5 weeks Vacation the School was re-opened on Monday with 52 Children – the highest number present during the week was 63.*
24 Oct 1879	*The School Attendance Officer called this week and took several absent Childrens' names and sent in final notice to the parents.*
31 Oct 1879	*On Wednesday Afternoon there were 91 present. Re-admitted Matilda Stowers and Edith Miller.* [Matilda Ann Stowers was aged about 11 years and was the daughter of an agricultural labourer, who lived on the Common by Solby's Farm. Her parents were George and Hannah.]
12 Dec 1879	*Admitted Florence Miller.* [Florence and Edith were the step-daughters of Lewis Ridgwell.]
19 Dec 1879	*Admitted three Gibson's* [sic].

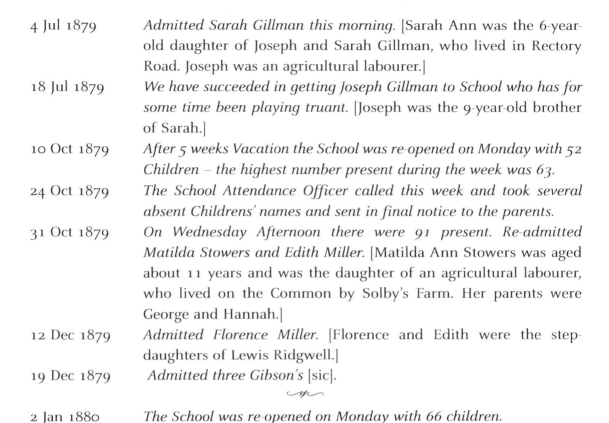

2 Jan 1880	*The School was re-opened on Monday with 66 children.*

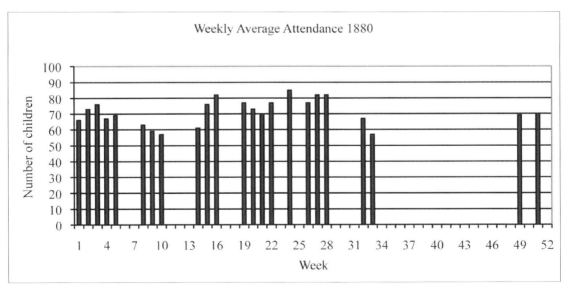

9 Jan 1880	*Re-admitted Edw. Smith an old III Standard boy.*
16 Jan 1880	*Admitted two Sawford's* [sic]. [Isaac Sawford, a gamekeeper, his wife Selina and four of their children, lived at Scrub House in Scrub Lane. Aged from ten to four years, the children were Isaac, Florence, Agnes and Ernest.]

13 Feb 1880	*The Attendance is still far from satisfactory, many of the Children are still sick, and others are absent from very trivial causes.*
5 Mar 1880	*The three Gibsons have left the School having removed to Benfleet.*
12 Mar 1880	*The Attendance is still low.*
2 Apr 1880	*Admitted William Cates. The Attendance of Standard II has been very irregular this week.* [William was the 4-year-old son of the bailiff at Pratts Farm in Daws Heath. His parents were John and Susanna Cates who had moved from Great Wakering.]
16 Apr 1880	*Admitted Florence and May Hall on Monday. The highest number present 88 on Wednesday morning.*
21 May 1880	*The Average is still lower this week owing to Bank Holliday* [sic].
11 Jun 1880	*On Wednesday afternoon 92 were present. Admitted 9 children this week.*
18 Jun 1880	*The Attendance continues to be good. Admitted John and Henry Widdicombe on Tuesday.* [John and Henry, aged seven and eleven, were the sons of Robert Churchward Widdicombe and his wife Mary Ann, who lived in the house next to the *Waggon and Horses*. Their father was a newspaper editor and proprietor.]
2 Jul 1880	*Admitted three children this week.*
23 Jul 1880	*The Attendance has improved this week, consequently the general routine of the School has been more regular.*
6 Aug 1880	*Admitted Emily Widdicombe on Monday.* [Emily was the eldest daughter of Robert Churchward Widdicombe. She was aged ten years.]
24 Sep 1880	*Re-opened School on Monday with only 57 children and throughout the week the numbers were very low.* [After Harvest Vacation]
1 Oct 1880	*The numbers have increased this week, but they are far below the mark. Admitted Frederick Edmonds on Monday.*
8 Oct 1880	*The Average has increased considerably, on Tues. morning I had 93 present. Admitted 3 Kings, 2 Murrays and 2 Nunns.* [Elizabeth, Henry and John were the three eldest children of John King, an agricultural labourer, and his wife Elizabeth, who lived in Castle Lane. Isaiah and Joshua were the two sons of Ephraim Murray and his wife Sarah. The family lived in the village street and Ephraim worked as an agricultural labourer.]
22 Oct 1880	*Admitted Rosa Murray.* [Rosetta was the sister of Isaiah and Joshua.]
19 Nov 1880	*Mary Ann Bullock has left the School, having moved to Canvey Island. Fred Edmonds is also leaving for Southend.* [Mary Ann Bullock, of End Way, moved with her parents, John and Eliza. Fred

Edmonds went to live at 5 Belmont Villas with his aunt and uncle, Jonathan and Mary Ann Wood.]

7 Jan 1881   *Re-opened School on Monday with 69 Children. The Fever is still in the Village hence the low numbers. Admitted George Wayland on Monday.* [There had been fever in the village for three months and the outbreak would continue until February. George Henry Wayland was the nine-year-old son of George, an agricultural labourer, and his wife Sarah, who lived at Daws Heath.]

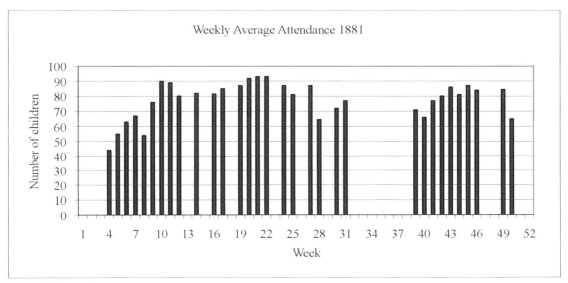

Weekly Average Attendance 1881

4 Feb 1881   *The numbers are still very low compared with the no. on books.*
11 Feb 1881 *The Average for past week is 63 which is the highest for some weeks past.*
4 Mar 1881   *The Attendance Officer is hunting up the Children again.*
11 Mar 1881 *Admitted several fresh children this week.*
18 Mar 1881 *Admitted Hortense Clark.* [Hortence was the 13-year-old daughter of widower Robert Clark, the bailiff at Sayers Farm. By the time of the census, on 3 April, she was listed as a domestic servant.]
8 Apr 1881   *Admitted Lewis Upson and Elizabeth Baker on Monday also Alfred King and Fred Elsdon.* [Lewis was the 12-year-old son of George and Mary Ann Upson who ran the *Waggon and Horses* beer house. Elizabeth's father, Edward Baker, was a gardener. The family lived in Benfleet Road, near to Hadleigh House, where he probably worked. Elizabeth was aged seven. Alfred, aged four, was the son of John and Elizabeth King, who lived in Castle Lane. His father was an agricultural labourer. 3-year-old Fred Elsdon lived on Hadleigh

	Common with his parents George and Mahala. George was a bricklayer's labourer.]
22 Apr 1881	*On Wednesday Afternoon we had 90 present being the highest for some weeks.*
20 May 1881	*On Wednesday we had 100 present at each meeting of the School being the highest on record.*
27 May 1881	*Highest number present 101.*
3 Jun 1881	*Admitted Lottie Dean.*
17 Jun 1881	*The Attendance has not been so good this week owing, no doubt, to the Agricultural Show at Southend. Admitted three children.*
24 Jun 1881	*The Attendance is very poor this afternoon, owing to the village Fair.*
22 Jul 1881	*Considering the time of year the numbers keep up very well.*
16 Sep 1881	*The School was re-opened on Monday.* [After Harvest Vacation]
30 Sep 1881	*Many of the children are absent from the most trivial reasons.*
7 Oct 1881	*Admitted four children.*
14 Oct 1881	*Admitted 8 children this week.*
11 Nov 1881	*The Attendance has been very good indeed this week the lowest no. present at one meeting of the School being 81 & the highest 92.*
18 Nov 1881	*For this time of year the attendance is remarkably good. Re-admitted Caroline Parish.* [Aged about 12 years, Caroline was the only daughter of George and Sarah Parish of Daws Heath. Her father was a wood merchant.]
25 Nov 1881	*Attendance continues good.*
22 Dec 1881	*Attendance not good.*
6 Jan 1882	*Re-opened School on Monday with very fair numbers.*

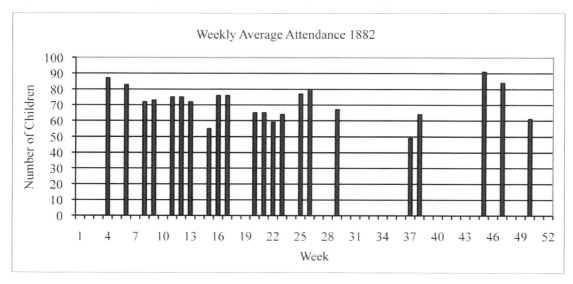

13 Jan 1882	*Attendance continues good.*
20 Jan 1882	*Attendance continues about the same.*
27 Jan 1882	*The attendance has been very regular the lowest number at one meeting being 83 and the highest 93.*
3 Feb 1882	*The Attendance has not been quite so good this week. Several children have been absent from the most trivial causes.*
24 Feb 1882	*Several boys are away from the upper Standards.*
3 Mar 1882	*I have sent off a list of irregular children to the School Attendance Officer. Admitted John Whitlock.*
10 Mar 1882	*The Average is about the same as last week.*
17 Mar 1882	*Several children have been playing truant.*
6 Apr 1882	*Attendance continues about the same.*
14 Apr 1882	*Re-opened School on Tuesday with 61 children.* [After Easter Vacation]
21 Apr 1882	*Admitted Annie & Harry Tesier.* [Annie, born at Dalston in London, was aged about twelve, while her 5-year-old brother Harry had been born at Prittlewell. Their father, Henry Tessier, was an oil and colourman which meant he was in the hardware trade, and was married to Annie.]
28 Apr 1882	*Attendance continues about the same.*
12 May 1882	*Attendance still very poor.*
9 Jun 1882	*Monday and Tuesday being Rayleigh fair many children were absent on that account.*
16 Jun 1882	*Attendance getting a little better.* [Measles in the village for the last month.]
7 Jul 1882	*The Attendance continues to be very fair. Admitted Ethel Wyborn and Florence Mansfield.* [4-year-old Ethel was the daughter of George and Emily Wyborn, who lived in Chapel Lane. Her father was a grocer's assistant, probably in James Swain Potter's grocery. Florence was a year older and was the daughter of George Mansfield, a baker, and his wife Ellen. They lived in the village street.]
14 Jul 1882	*Attendance fair, several children away for the most trivial causes.*
21 Jul 1882	*This afternoon I have only 35 children present, owing to a Chapel School treat in the village. Admitted Alice Raison.* [Alice was the 3-year-old daughter of Stephen and Eliza Raison, who lived in the village street. Her father was a sawyer.]
28 Jul 1882	*Attendance about the same.*
4 Aug 1882	*Attendance poor. Admitted Alice & James Hawk.*

15 Sep 1882	*Re-opened school on Monday with only 56 children, and during the week the Attendance has been very poor.* [After Harvest Vacation]
22 Sep 1882	*I have sent a list of irregular children to the School Attendance Officer.*
29 Sep 1882	*The Attendance is improving.*
6 Oct 1882	*Attendance still very fair. The Attendance Officer has been looking up a good many Children, with a satisfactory result.*
13 Oct 1882	*Average on the increase, and the Attendance is good.*
20 Oct 1882	*Attendance about the same. I have had some trouble with the boy Morley for playing truant.* [Herbert was the 8-year-old son of Emily Morley, a widow who lived in Chapel Lane. Since her husband's death, she had been working in the fields to support her family.]
27 Oct 1882	*Attendance still very fair. Morley still absenting himself from School.*
3 Nov 1882	*Mr. Millar was Summoned for neglecting to send his daughter Edith to School and fined 5/-. This has had a good effect on the others.* [The weekly wage for an able-bodied farm worker would be about 9/- at this time. This was worth £21.74 in today's money.]
10 Nov 1882	*Admitted four children by the name of Winnall on Monday.*
17 Nov 1882	*Re-admitted Edith Millar.* [Edith Miller was the 11-year-old daughter of Elizabeth Miller who was the common law wife of Lewis Ridgwell, a basket maker.]
1 Dec 1882	*Attendance continues very fair.*

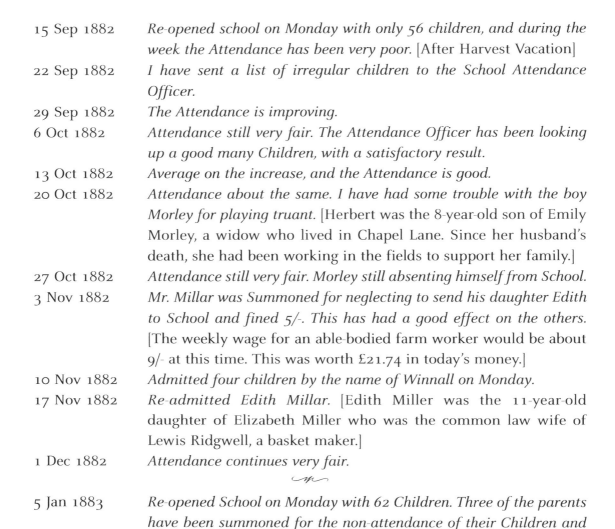

| 5 Jan 1883 | *Re-opened School on Monday with 62 Children. Three of the parents have been summoned for the non-attendance of their Children and each fined 5/-.* |

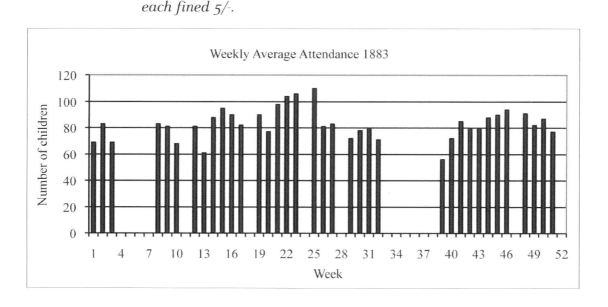

12 Jan 1883	*Admitted Joseph Tookey.* [Joseph was the son of William and Ann Tookey. When he was born, in about 1873, his family was living at Hadleigh, but in 1881 Ann and three of her children were inmates at the workhouse at Uppingham in Leicestershire. Ann's family, the Griggs, lived at Thundersley and in 1883 Joseph was lodging with them. It is unclear where Joseph's father was living.]
9 Feb 1883	*Attendance still poor.*
16 Feb 1883	*The Attendance has improved a little but still low.*
2 Mar 1883	*Admitted Edith Potter and Albert Brett.* [Albert was the 5-year-old son of Henry Brett, a shepherd, who lived with his wife Emma in the village street.]
9 Mar 1883	*Admitted Dorothy Appleton.* [Dorothy was nearly three years old and the daughter of William and Mary Ann Appleton. Her father, a market gardener in the village, was over sixty when his daughter was born.]
16 Mar 1883	*The average is still poor. I had only 57 this afternoon. Admitted Harry Fox and Herbert & Kate Anstee.* [Herbert and Kate, aged seven and five, had moved into the area with their mother, Esther Anstee, from Shopland. Their father William, an agricultural labourer, had recently died.]
23 Mar 1883	*Admitted Emily, William & Matilda French.* [Samuel French, an agricultural labourer, had recently moved from Vange into the area with his family. His wife Martha had been born at Hadleigh. The children were aged about eight, six and five.]
30 Mar 1883	*I have again sent a list of Absentees to the Attendance Officer.*
13 Apr 1883	*I had @ one meeting of the School during the week 107 children which is certainly the highest number ever present. Admitted three Infants.*
11 May 1883	*Admitted Martha Snow, Mary Gilman & Edith Petchey on Monday.* [Martha was the 4-year-old daughter of Henry and Sarah Snow, who lived on the green in the village street. Her father was an agricultural labourer, as was Joseph Gillman, the father of 5-year-old Mary. Mary's mother was Sarah and the family lived in Rectory Road. Edith Petchey probably only moved into the village for the summer as her father was a shepherd. John and Emma Petchey's daughter was aged five.]
18 May 1883	*Opened School on Tuesday with 68 children. Admitted Ch. Goss.* [Charles was the 5-year-old son of Henry and Emily Goss. His father was an agricultural labourer who moved to find work.]

25 May 1883	*Admitted five children this week.*
8 Jun 1883	*Admitted William Price.*
15 Jun 1883	*The Attendance continues to be very good. Admitted Emily Petchy.* [Emily was the 12-year-old sister of Edith Petchey admitted in May.]
29 Jun 1883	*Admitted Alice Smith and Fred. Smith in the Infant room.* [Alice and Frederick were the children of William Smith, a baker, and his wife Philadelphia. They lived in the village street.]
6 Jul 1883	*Admitted Alfred Augustus Hawks and Arthur Lambert.* [Alfred was the 3-year-old son of the school master and his wife Sarah. Arthur was nearly three years old, and the son of an agricultural labourer, Henry Lambert, and his wife Emma. They lived in the village street.]
20 Jul 1883	*Admitted two children on Monday Caroline Smith and Mary Lewsey.* [Mary Ann was the 3-year-old daughter of Henry and Eliza Lewsey. Her father was a farm bailiff at Hadleigh.]
27 Jul 1883	*Although the Attendance has been better this week it is far below the mark with 122 on the books.* [This was above the capacity of 100 for the school so it must have been very crowded.]
3 Aug 1883	*Admitted Amy Ridgwell and Charlie Francis.* [Amy, aged nine, was a member of the Ridgwell family, the village basket makers. Charlie was the 3-year-old son of James and Ellen Francis, the licensed victuallers at the *Crown Inn*.]
10 Aug 1883	*Re-admitted Fred Walliss.* [Fred Wallis, aged six, was the son of the village tailor, Stephen Wallis, and his wife Julia. They lived in the village street.]
28 Sep 1883	*Re-opened School Monday with only 45 children. Admitted Florence Gentry.* [Florence's father, Daniel Gentry, was an agricultural labourer. He lived with his wife Elizabeth and 7-year-old daughter in a cottage at End Way.]
5 Oct 1883	*Admitted five children this week.*
12 Oct 1883	*Admitted five children.*
26 Oct 1883	*Compared with the numbers on Registers the Attendance is not good. Admitted Gertrude Durrant.* [Gertrude entered the Infants class at the age of three. She was the daughter of John, an agricultural labourer, and his wife Ann who lived in the village street.]
2 Nov 1883	*Admitted two Humphreys.*
9 Nov 1883	*Admitted Emily and Alice Rodwell and Charles Knightsbridge.* [Emily and Alice, aged six and four, were the daughters of William

Rodwell, an agricultural labourer, and his wife Eliza, who lived at Daws Heath.]

23 Nov 1883 — *Attendance very good. Had 101 children present on Tuesday.*

30 Nov 1883 — *Admitted Eleanor Hodge.* [In 1881, at the age of seven, Eleanor had been an inmate in the Rochford Union Workhouse. She was born at Thundersley.]

14 Dec 1883 — *Herbert and Sarah Cockman leave the School this week having removed near to Rayleigh.*

4 Jan 1884 — *Re-opened School on Monday. Attendance poor.*

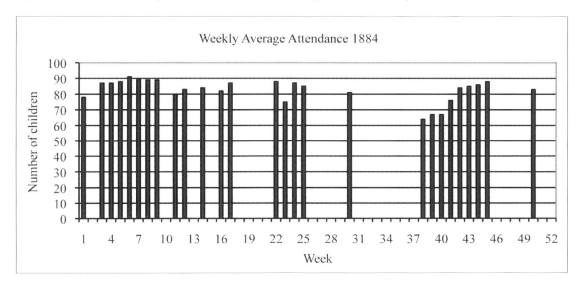

25 Jan 1884 — *Admitted Kate and Alice Ansty.* [Esther Anstee had moved into the area after the recent death of her husband William at Shopland. Kate was aged about six and her sister three. Kate had been admitted during the previous March and had presumably left for a while.]

7 Mar 1884 — *Attendance very fair.*

14 Mar 1884 — *Admitted Kate Prudry.*

18 Apr 1884 — *Re-opened School on Tuesday with 82 children.* [After Easter weekend]

25 Apr 1884 — *Highest number present 96.*

2 May 1884 — *Attendance very fair.*

9 May 1884 — *Children have been very irregular this week. The Attendance Officer has called and taken some of the names which may have a good effect.*

16 May 1884 — *Attendance very fair.*

143

28 May 1884	*The Attendance Officer called on Wednesday.*
6 Jun 1884	*The School re-opened on Tuesday with 68 Children. The Attendance has been poor, owing no doubt to the hollidies* [sic]. [Whitsun Vacation]
4 Jul 1884	*The Attendance has been rather poor this week.*
11 Jul 1884	*The Average is still on the decrease. Admitted 14 Children this week.*
18 Jul 1884	*Attendance only fair. The School Attendance Officer called on Wednesday, but there is little chance of getting the Average up before the hollidies* [sic].
1 Aug 1884	*The numbers have decreased considerably towards the end of the week. 91 Present on Tuesday and only 58 this afternoon.*
19 Sep 1884	*Re-opened School on Monday with 65 and the numbers throughout the week have been very low. Admitted Edward and John Monk on Monday.* [After Harvest Vacation]
26 Sep 1884	*The Attendance continues very poor. Admitted Alice Beale on Monday.* [Edmund and Jane Beale had moved from Rettendon to Castle Lane. Edmund worked as an engine driver on a farm. Alice was aged about four.]
3 Oct 1884	*The Attendance Officer called on Wednesday and took a long list of Absent Children. Admitted Frederick Watson in the Infant Room.* [As Frederick was about eight years old, he should have been in either Standard I or II. Living in Castle Lane, he was the son of William, an agricultural labourer, and his wife Eliza.]
10 Oct 1884	*Admitted Harry Richardson and Thomas Guy.* [5-year-old Harry was the son of Henry and Fanny Richardson. His father was an agricultural labourer.]
17 Oct 1884	*Admitted John, Annie & Ernest Edwick. Kate Welton has been Summoned for irregular Attendance.* [The children of William Edwick, a farm bailiff, and his wife Annie, were aged about ten, eight and six. They had moved from Bishops Stortford to Hadleigh.]
24 Oct 1884	*Several children are still absent from the most trivial causes.*
31 Oct 1884	*Admitted Arthur Richardson & Alice Smith. The School Attendance Officer called on Wednesday and took a list of Absentees.* [Arthur was the 3-year-old brother of Harry, who had been admitted earlier that month. Alice was the 6-year-old granddaughter of William Smith, the village bootmaker, and his wife Mary Ann. Her father was their son John, who was a shoemaker.]
7 Nov 1884	*I have heard to-day that Kate Welton who has given so much trouble*

is leaving the village.

14 Nov 1884   *Admitted Thomas Adams. Kate Welton has returned to the School.*

21 Nov 1884   *Attendance continues about the same.*

28 Nov 1884   *Many of the Children are still irregular.*

5 Dec 1884   *The Average is about the same.*

12 Dec 1884   *The School Attendance Officer called on Wednesday and took a list of Absentees.*

2 Jan 1885   *The Attendance has been rather poor this week.*

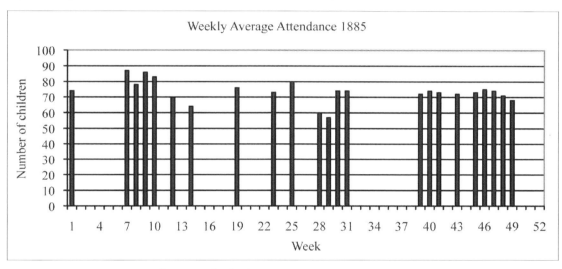

9 Jan 1885   *Attendance a little better.*

30 Jan 1885   *The Attendance is still very fair. The Attendance Officer called this week and looked up some of the Absentees.*

20 Feb 1885   *The Attendance has been very irregular this week, having had as low as 62 and on Thursday 97.*

12 Mar 1885   *Attendance is falling off considerably.* [Whooping cough in the village.]

27 Mar 1885   *The Attendance is still poor especially in the Infants and lower Standards.*

9 Apr 1885   *The Attendance continues poor.*

16 Apr 1885   *Admitted two Lindsells. Infants very low.*

23 Apr 1885   *The Attendance is slowly improving.*

15 May 1885   *Attendance about the same.*

12 Jun 1885   *The Attendance has slightly improved.*

3 Jul 1885   *The Attendance is rather Small now.*

10 Jul 1885   *Admitted Alice Lindsell, and Charles Millar.* [Charles Miller was probably the 4-year-old son of Lewis Ridgwell, a basket maker, and his common law wife Elizabeth Miller, who lived in the village street.]

24 Jul 1885	*Admitted Fred Snow & Fred Watson.* [Fred Snow was the 4-year-old son of Henry, a baker in the village, and his wife Elizabeth. Fred Watson, aged about nine, lived in Castle Lane with his father William, who was an agricultural labourer, and his mother, Eliza.]
18 Sep 1885	*The School was re-opened on Monday, but the Attendance has been very poor. Nearly all the Children examined in Standard III have left the School.* [After Harvest Vacation]
2 Oct 1885	*Admitted Fred Smith on Monday. John and Thurza French left this week and I am expecting another family or two to leave shortly.* [Fred was the 5-year-old son of William, a village baker, and his wife Philadelphia. John and Thirza were the children of George and Harriet French, who lived in Pleasant Row. George was an agricultural labourer and the family moved to Eastwood.]
9 Oct 1885	*The Attendance Officer called on Wednesday and took a list of Absentees.*
23 Oct 1885	*The Attendance Officer called on Monday and took a list of Absentees.*
6 Nov 1885	*Three of the children are Summoned for Wednesday next at Rochford.*
11 Dec 1885	*Attendance very irregular I have sent a list of Absentees to the Officer.*
18 Dec 1885	*Attendance a little improved but still not up to the mark.*
23 Dec 1885	*The Attendance continues about the same.*

⁓⁂⁓

8 Jan 1886	*Admitted Alfred & Henry Vaughan & Mary Parish.* [Mary, who was aged about ten, lived on Thundersley Common with her parents, Charles and Sarah Parish. Her father was a hurdle maker.]

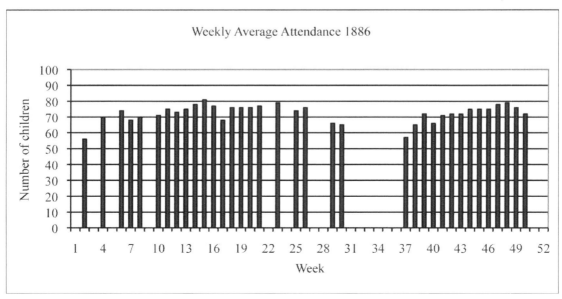

22 Jan 1886	*The Attendance is Considerably better this week.*
12 Mar 1886	*Admitted William Morris.*
26 Mar 1886	*Admitted Alice Law, Alice Beale & Jenny Cracknell.* [All three girls lived at Hadleigh. Alice Law was the 6-year-old daughter of Henry, a baker, and his wife Fanny. They lived in the village street. Edmund Beale had moved his family from Rettendon to Castle Lane for a new job as an engine driver on a farm. Alice was aged five. Jenny had also recently moved to Hadleigh with her parents John and Charlotte from Prittlewell. A former groom, John Cracknell was the new publican at the *Castle Inn.* Jenny was aged nearly five.]
2 Apr 1886	*Several parents have received notice of their children's irregularity from the Attendance Officer.*
9 Apr 1886	*Admitted Olive Potter.* [Olive was the 5-year-old daughter of George Wayland Potter and his wife Agnes. George was a grocer in the village street like his father James Swain Potter, who was now living at Hadleigh Hall.]
16 Apr 1886	*The Attendance of Infants has been very good indeed.*
30 Apr 1886	*Re-opened School on Tuesday morning with 70 children. The Attendance has been very fair for Easter Week.*
7 May 1886	*Admitted Clarissa Wood.* [Clarissa was the 9-year-old daughter of Ernest Augustus Wood and his wife Clarissa. Ernest was a member of the Wood family, who had owned many of Hadleigh's farms. He had been brought up on Park Farm, but had left Hadleigh in the early 1870s, married Clarissa Power, and worked as a baker at Reading. Their daughter was born at Thundersley in 1876.]
28 May 1886	*Several parents have received notices from the Attendance Officer.*
16 Jul 1886	*The Attendance has been very poor this week. Many of the Children who passed IV Standard have already left.*
17 Sep 1886	*Re-opened the School on Monday with 57 Children. Admitted 7 children.* [After Harvest Vacation]
24 Sep 1886	*Admitted Alice Lewsey & Leonard Smith.* [Alice, aged about five, was the daughter of Henry, a farm bailiff, and his wife Eliza. Leonard was the son of William and Philadelphia Smith. Aged about four, his father was a baker in the village street.]
1 Oct 1886	*Admitted 2 children in the Infant room and 1 in the Vth Standard. I have sent a list of Absentees to the Attendance Officer.*
8 Oct 1886	*Admitted Emily & Alice Rodwell and Fred. Lambert.* [Living at Daws Heath, Emily and Alice were the daughters of William Rodwell, an

agricultural labourer, and his wife Eliza. They were aged nine and seven.]

5 Nov 1886   *Admitted Susannah and Mary White.* [The daughters of an agricultural labourer, Philip White, and his wife Maria, the family had moved to Church Road, Thundersley from North Benfleet. They were aged about seven and five.]

26 Nov 1886   *Ernest Law has left the School.* [Ernest, now aged nearly eleven, went to work as an assistant in his father's bakery in the village street.]

17 Dec 1886   *Jessie & Arthur Vaughan have left the School. Parents removed from the parish.*

7 Jan 1887   *The Attendance has been very poor.*

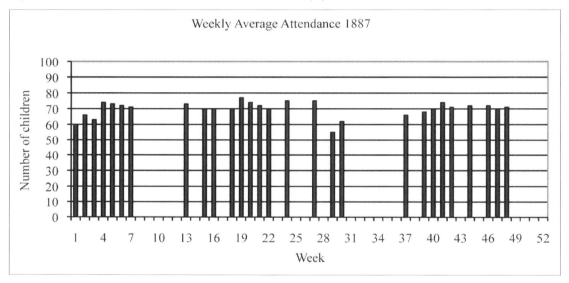

Weekly Average Attendance 1887

4 Feb 1887   *The Attendance in the V Standard has been very irregular this week.*

4 Mar 1887   *The Attendance has been irregular this week. I have sent a List of Absentees to the Attendance Officer.*

11 Mar 1887   *The Attendance is still poor.*

18 Mar 1887   *Attendance improving but still low. 2 Admitted (Barbers).*

25 Mar 1887   *Clarissa Wood & Alex Wood left the School.* [The children of Ernest Augustus Wood, born at Park Farm. The family moved to Mile End Old Town.]

22 Apr 1887   *Admitted Clement Buckingham.* [5-year-old Clement lived with his parents Henry and Matilda Buckingham at Blossoms Farm. James Tyrrell had farmed the land prior to his death in 1886, but the farm was owned by his brother Eleazar. He rented out the farm to Henry

	Charles Buckingham, a local cattle dealer.]
13 May 1887	*Admitted Thomas & George Cook.*
10 Jun 1887	*The Attendance has been irregular this week.*
17 Jun 1887	*The Jubilee Yacht-Race affected the School on Tuesday.* [The Prince of Wales was due to start this race at Southend to celebrate Queen Victoria's Golden Jubilee. Unfortunately, he was unable to sail to Southend because of the fog, and the race started without him.]
24 Jun 1887	*The Queen's Jubilee has greatly affected the School this week, but we were obliged to give two days holiday.*
1 Jul 1887	*The Attendance has improved this week.*
15 Jul 1887	*The Attendance has been very good this week.*
16 Sep 1887	*Re-opened School on Monday with 71 Children, but the Attendance has been poor throughout the week. Admitted 6 children.* [After Harvest Vacation]
7 Oct 1887	*The Attendance has improved a little this week – the Attendance Officer has been busy in the Village.*
14 Oct 1887	*Two Cooks left the School.* [Thomas and George admitted five months earlier.]
21 Oct 1887	*Sent a list to Attendance Officer.*
28 Oct 1887	*Admitted two Newman's* [sic]. *Admitted Alice Jefferies.* [Alice was the 9-year-old daughter of Eliza Jeffries, a widow. Eliza worked as a sick nurse and lived with her children in Rectory Road.]
4 Nov 1887	*Admitted Harry Choppin.* [Harry Alfred Choppen was the son of Thomas and Emma Choppen, who lived at Grays Thurrock. Aged six, Harry was probably staying with one of his Choppen relatives at Hadleigh.]
11 Nov 1887	*Admitted E. Groves.*
2 Dec 1887	*Florence Gentry left the School.* [Aged nearly twelve, Florence went into domestic service, working for the Rev. William Talfourd at Thundersley Rectory.]
9 Dec 1887	*The Attendance has been irregular.*

⁓⁓

6 Jan 1888	*I have made a list of Absentees for the Attendance Officer and hope to have a much better Attendance next week. Admitted Ch. Offord.* [Charles Offord, born at Clapton in about 1880, was the nephew of the village blacksmith, William Mansfield, and his wife Mary Ann.]

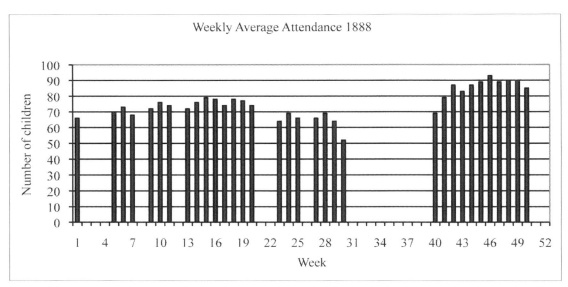

Weekly Average Attendance 1888

13 Jan 1888	*The Attendance has improved slightly but is far from good.*
3 Feb 1888	*I have sent a list of Absentees to the Attendance Officer and hope to have a better Attendance next week.*
10 Feb 1888	*The Attendance has been considerably better this week.*
17 Feb 1888	*Admitted five of the Faux family.* [John Faux, a master carpenter, moved with his wife Eliza and six children from Hornsey in Middlesex to the village street. The five eldest children – John, Jane, William, Fred and Stanley – became pupils at the school.]
6 Apr 1888	*Admitted 3 Infants.*
13 Apr 1888	*Admitted 2 Infants.*
20 Apr 1888	*The Attendance is now good. Admitted 1 Infant.*
27 Apr 1888	*I have sent a list of Absentees to the Att. Officer as the Attendance has been irregular during the past week.*
4 May 1888	*Mr. Judd called on Tuesday and warned a number of irregular children.* [Mr. Judd was the Attendance Officer.]
25 May 1888	*The Attendance has been very poor during the week owing in a great measure to the Whitsuntide holiday.*
28 Sep 1888	*Re-opened School on Monday when the numbers were low.* [After Harvest Vacation]
5 Oct 1888	*Admitted Joseph Durrant on Monday morning.* [Although registered as Walter, the 3-year-old son of John and Ann Durrant was known by his middle name. The family lived in the village street, with John working as a general labourer.]
12 Oct 1888	*Admitted 4 Emsons.* [John and Emma Emson had at least thirteen children. John was a dealer at Daws Heath with a shop. The four children who attended the school were probably Ida, Emily, Willie

and Nellie.]

19 Oct 1888   *Admitted three Theobalds.* [Eunice Theobald, the widow of the former farm bailiff of Jarvis Hall Farm at South Benfleet, lived in the village street, and possibly these were three of her grandchildren who were staying with her.]

2 Nov 1888   *Admitted Edith Hawks.* [Aged seven, Edith was the daughter of Alfred Hawks, the school master, and his wife Sarah. She joined her elder sisters, Alice and Minnie, and her elder brother Alfred, as a pupil at her father's school.]

9 Nov 1888   *Average still increasing.*

16 Nov 1888   *Admitted Alice Bennett. Mr. C. Judd the new Atten. Officer called on Tuesday.*

~~

4 Jan 1889   *Re-opened School on Monday morning.*

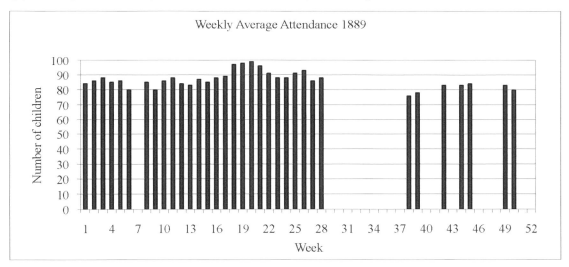

22 Feb 1889   *School opened again on Monday with a good Attendance.* [It had been closed for a week due to inclement weather and sickness.]

15 Mar 1889   *Attendance now good. Admitted Mary Gillman & Bithia and Bertha Monk.* [Mary was the 10-year-old daughter of Joseph Gillman, a farm servant, and his wife Sarah, who lived in the village street. Bithia and Bertha, aged about six and four, were the daughters of William Monk, a baker, and his wife Emily. The family had moved into the village street from Shoebury.]

5 Apr 1889   *Admitted Bertie Hills.* [The bootmaker Walter Hills and his wife Clara were the parents of 4-year-old Bertie. This was the same Walter Hills who had been punished in March 1863 by Miss Miller for telling a lie.]

12 Apr 1889	*The School Attendance Officer called on Tuesday and is doing good work for the School.*
18 Apr 1889	*Admitted Montague Potter & Herbert Lewsey.* [Montague was the 5-year-old son of George Potter, a village grocer, and his wife Agnes. Herbert Lewsey's father was a farm bailiff at Hadleigh. Henry and Eliza Lewsey's son was also aged five.]
26 Apr 1889	*Admitted Louisa and Jane Tuck.*
3 May 1889	*Admitted Evelyn & Violet Mitchell, Kate Hawks, & Alice Buckingham & Eveline Barber.* [Evelyn and Violet were brother and sister, the children of James and Ellen Mitchell of Castle Lane. Aged seven and five, their father was a farm bailiff. Kate Hawks was the 5-year-old daughter of the master. 5-year-old Alice Buckingham lived at Blossoms Farmhouse in the village street. Her father Henry was a cattle dealer.]
10 May 1889	*The School is now quite full.*
17 May 1889	*Average 99. This is the highest average during the year. Fred Snow and his sister left the School to-day.* [Fred and his sister were the children of Henry and Elizabeth Snow, who moved to nearby Leigh. Their father was a baker.]
14 Jun 1889	*The School Attendance Officer called on Wednesday and intends looking up some Absentees.*
28 Jun 1889	*The School year ends to-day. Average for year 83 being the highest ever reached.*
20 Sep 1889	*School re-opened on Monday with very fair numbers. Admitted Thomas Marshall.* [Albert Marshall, a journeyman carpenter, had moved his family into the village street from Rayleigh. Thomas was aged about five.]
27 Sep 1889	*Admitted Jessie Raisin & Henrietta Brown. Several large families are leaving the village this week.* [Jessie was the 6-year-old daughter of Stephen and Eliza Raison. The Raison family had been bricklayers in the village for many years.]
4 Oct 1889	*The Attendance is still on the increase.*
11 Oct 1889	*The Attendance Officer is doing good work for the school by occasionally calling and sending in notices. Admitted Alice Anstey.* [Alice Anstee, who was being readmitted, was the 9-year-old daughter of Esther Thorington. Her widowed mother had married William Thorington, a Thundersley labourer, in 1884.]
1 Nov 1889	*Mr. Judd (Att. Off.) called on Tuesday and* [took] *the names of a few irregular children.*

22 Nov 1889   *The Average still keeps above 80 which is satisfactory during this*
                season of the year.

                ⟿

3 Jan 1890   *Re-opened School on Monday. Attendance not very good.*

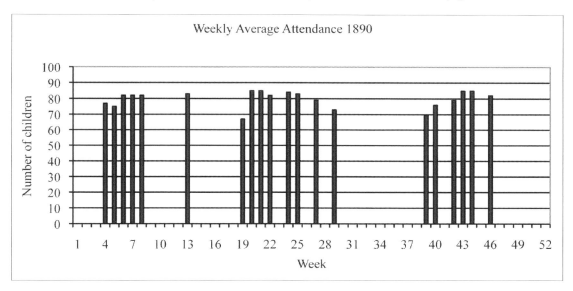

14 Feb 1890   *Re-admitted Martha Snow.*
28 Mar 1890   *The Attendance falls off considerably in the upper Standards.*
6 Jun 1890   *Attendance very fair.* [The school had been closed for three weeks
               in April and May due to a measles epidemic.]
28 Jun 1890   *The School was opened this morning (Saturday) in order to meet the*
               requirements of the Department with regard to opening 400 times –
               without which extra meeting the number of times opened would be
               399. The work of the <u>Time Table</u> for Monday morning being carried
               out.
11 Jul 1890   *The Attendance has been irregular owing to sickness and the wet*
               weather.
25 Jul 1890   *The School was inspected on Monday . . . The Attendance has been*
               very poor the remainder of the week.
1 Aug 1890   *The Attendance has been very poor since the Examination.*
26 Sep 1890   *The School re-opened on Monday after being closed 7 weeks with 64*
               children. [After Harvest Vacation]
3 Oct 1890   *Many of the children are away from most trivial causes.*
17 Oct 1890   *The Attendance continues to improve – but several children are very*
               troublesome.

                ⟿

| 2 Jan 1891 | *The School re-opened on Monday and the Attendance has been very poor.* |

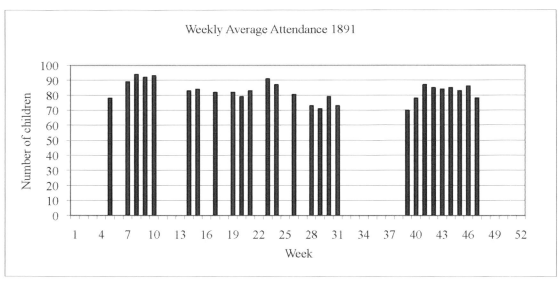

16 Jan 1891	*The Attendance continues to be very low especially in the Infant room.*
6 Feb 1891	*Admitted Jessie Faux and Alfred Ball.* [Jessie was the 5-year-old daughter of John Faux, a master carpenter, and his wife Eliza, who lived in the village street. Alfred was still only aged four, the son of John and Maria Balls. His labourer father rented a cottage next to the *Castle Inn.*]
13 Feb 1891	*Admitted Binah Monk & Annie Playle.* [Binah was the 4-year-old daughter of William and Emily Monk, who lived in the village street. Her father was a baker, while Annie's father was a blacksmith. The 4-year-old lived in Chapel Lane with her parents, William and Polly.]
20 Feb 1891	*The Attendance has very greatly improved this week. On Thursday only one child was absent.*
13 Mar 1891	*Ethel and Willie Knight left the School.*
10 Apr 1891	*Admitted Arthur Lodge on Monday.* [4-year-old Arthur lived with his parents, George and Sarah, in Castle Lane. George was a labourer.]
1 May 1891	*Several families are leaving the Village "General" Booth having purchased farms, several families which were employed on them have had to seek work elsewhere.* [By March 1891 the Salvation Army had purchased Castle, Park and Sayers Farms in order to open a farm colony.]
15 May 1891	*Ada, Albert & William Chambers left the School. Admitted Fred. Hawks & Frank Smith.* [The Chambers family had been living in the village street next to the blacksmith's. As their father William Chambers was an agricultural labourer, he may have been one of

22 May 1891	*School was re-opened on Tuesday with 73 children.* [After Spring Bank Holiday]
12 Jun 1891	*Admitted three Brockwells.*
17 Jul 1891	*Admitted Hugh Buckingham.* [Hugh was the 4-year-old son of the cattle dealer, Henry Buckingham, who lived at Blossoms Farm.]
24 Jul 1891	*Eve Barber left the School to go to Miss Bell's.* [Miss Bell was the former infant teacher and had probably set up her own dame school at South Benfleet, where she lived.]
31 Jul 1891	*I have lately had several interviews with the Attendance Officer and our united efforts have had a good effect upon the Attendance. There are three children who utterly ignore the notices and we hope to get a summons for them.*
2 Oct 1891	*The school was re-opened on Monday with 67 children. The School is now free.* [The Education Act of 1891 provided for the state payment of school fees.]
9 Oct 1891	*Admitted Miriam Rivers, Agnes Scudder & Ernest Allen. The Att. Officer called this morning and took a list of Absentees.* [Miriam lived at Daws Heath with her parents Walter and Ellen Rivers. Aged only three, her father was an agricultural labourer. Agnes was nearly four, and also the daughter of a labourer who lived in Castle Lane. Her parents were Joseph and Emily Scudder. Ernest also entered Miss Bragg's infant class as he was three. He lived in the village street with his parents, James and Sarah Allen. His father was a bricklayer.]
16 Oct 1891	*Admitted three Broughtons, John Lambert & Emma Chambers.* [4-year-old John lived with his parents, William and Emma Lambert, in Chapel Lane. His father was a bricklayer's labourer.]
23 Oct 1891	*Admitted Jane Taylor & Maud Mary Dale. Re-admitted Miriam Stibbards.* [Miriam Stibbards was the 8-year-old daughter of Samuel Stibbards, a carpenter and wheelwright by trade, who had also set up a business in Commonhall Lane as a funeral director.]
30 Oct 1891	*Three children were summoned for irregular Attendance – two fined the other case adjourned.* [On 30 October the *Chelmsford Chronicle* reported on the case at the Petty Sessions at Rochford on 28 October: "John Balls and William Playle, labourers, were fined 1s. and 4s. costs for neglecting to send their children to school".]
6 Nov 1891	*Arthur Playle has not yet attended in spite of the fine imposed upon*

The text at top (continuation): the workers forced to seek work elsewhere. Frederick Hawks was the 4-year-old son of the master. Frank Smith was the son of Alfred, a bricklayer, who was a widower with four young sons.]

his father last week for absenting himself from School. [Arthur was ten years old and lived in Chapel Lane with his parents, William and Polly Playle. William was a blacksmith]

⟋⟍

15 Jan 1892   *The school was re-opened on Monday and the average for week is only 51.* [The school had been closed since 30 November because of an outbreak of diphtheria.]

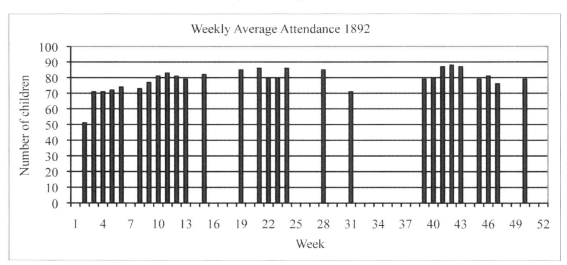

22 Jan 1892   *The Attendance has improved but it is still very bad.*
5 Feb 1892   *Emily Jefferies has left the School.* [Sadly Emily's mother, Eliza, who was a widow, had died.]
12 Feb 1892   *Arthur Watson has left the school.* [William Watson, Arthur's father, had also died. As he was a widower, it is unclear who would have looked after Arthur, who was only about ten. He had two older brothers who worked as farm labourers, or he may have had to enter the Rochford workhouse. By 1901 Arthur was working as a greengrocer's assistant in Prittlewell.]
19 Feb 1892   *The Attendance in the Infant room is still very poor.*
11 Mar 1892   *Admitted three Woods.* [This may have been Emily, Jenny and Percy who briefly lived in the village, having moved from Kent with their parents, Thomas and Louisa Wood.]
25 Mar 1892   *We are trying to get a summons for the Scudders the only family in the village who are giving any trouble.* [Joseph and Emily Scudder of Castle Lane had three children who should have been attending school – Agnes, Herbert and Frances.]
29 Apr 1892   *Admitted two Johns.* [Possibly Frederick and James Johns.]
6 May 1892   *Admitted Harriet Matthews, Nellie Sims, Sidney and Alice Wiggins.*

Attendance very fair. [Harriet was the 5-year-old daughter of William and Ellen Matthews. As an agricultural labourer, William had moved his family from Thundersley and South Benfleet in search of work. Nellie, or Ellen, was the 4-year-old daughter of Jeffrey and Martha Sims. The family lived in the village street near to Blossoms Farmhouse and, as Jeffrey was a farm servant, he may have worked there.]

20 May 1892   *The Attendance is fairly good. Admitted Herbert and William Shove.*

10 Jun 1892   *Admitted Richard and Wilfred Schooling.* [James Schooling, a carpenter and joiner, moved his wife Marion and family from Tottenham in London. Richard was aged eight and Wilfred was six.]

24 Jun 1892   *The attendance is now fairly good although @ times irregular.*

5 Aug 1892   *Attendance poor.*

30 Sep 1892   *Re-opened school on Monday with 72 children. Admitted twelve fresh children.* [After Harvest Vacation]

7 Oct 1892   *The Attendance is very fair. Admitted four fresh children.*

21 Oct 1892   *Admitted Sarah Wood & Annie Beale.* [Annie was the 5-year-old daughter of Edmund and Jane Beale, who lived in Castle Lane. Edmund worked as an engine driver on a farm.]

18 Nov 1892   Admitted Gertrude Hinton, Nellie Simms, Alfred Bainbridge & Alfred Allen. [Nellie Sims had first been admitted to the school in May. Alfred Bainbridge was the 4-year-old son of Alfred and Emily Bainbridge, who lived in the village street. His father was a sweep. Alfred Allen also lived in the village street. Aged three, he was the son of James, a bricklayer, and his wife Sarah.]

6 Dec 1892   *School Attendance Officer called on Wednesday.*

6 Jan 1893   [The school re-opened after a week's holiday for Christmas.]

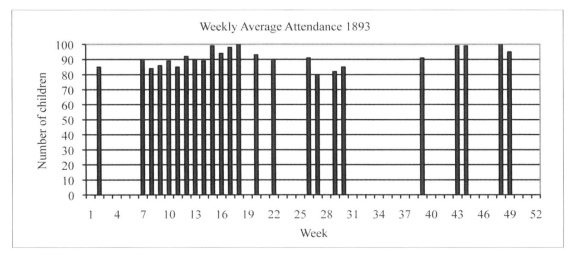

13 Jan 1893	*Admitted 2 Johns.* [Possibly Frederick and James.]
20 Jan 1893	*The Attendance continues about the same. The Attendance Officer called on Tuesday.*
27 Jan 1893	*Attendance good.*
10 Feb 1893	*Admitted Lily Littlewood. The average is now good.*
17 Feb 1893	*Admitted four children on Tuesday.*
24 Feb 1893	*Admitted Jenny Cracknell.* [Registered as Virginia, Jenny was nearly twelve and lived with her parents John and Charlotte at the *Castle Inn*, where her father was the publican.]
10 Mar 1893	*Admitted Ernest Balls.* [5-year-old Ernest lived in the cottage next to the *Castle Inn* with his parents John and Maria. His father was a labourer.]
8 Apr 1893	*Admitted Grace Becker & A. Buckingham.* [9-year-old Alice lived with her parents Henry and Matilda Buckingham at Blossoms Farmhouse, where her father was a cattle dealer.]
15 Apr 1893	*This week has the highest average of the year (99). Admitted Wm. & Emma Stitt.* [Their father was the Farm Colony Governor.]
13 May 1893	*The Attendance continues to be good.*
2 Jun 1893	*Admitted 3 Burnetts from Salvation Army.*
23 Jun 1893	*I have sent a list of irregular children to the Att. Officer as we have several troublesome ones.*
14 Jul 1893	*Attendance only fair.*
28 Jul 1893	*Admitted May Thomas on Monday. I have sent a list of Absentees to the Attendance Officer.*
29 Sep 1893	*Re-opened School on Monday with 89 children. Admitted 8 fresh children.* [After Harvest Vacation]
6 Oct 1893	*Attendance good. Admitted 3 fresh children.*
13 Oct 1893	*Admitted 3 fresh children. Average good.*
20 Oct 1893	*Admitted Wm. Thorington. Attendance fairly good.* [5-year-old William had been born at Thundersley, where the Thorington family had lived for many years. His father William, a labourer, moved his family from South Benfleet to Hadleigh. He was the stepfather of the Anstee children who were also pupils at the school.]
27 Oct 1893	*Admitted Nos. 291 to 294 on Ad. Register.*
17 Nov 1893	*Admitted Dorothy Whittaker & Agnes Johns. Average very fair.* [Agnes was probably the 5-year-old daughter of George and Ellen Johns, and had been born at Wood Green in Middlesex.]
24 Nov 1893	*Annie Gillman left the district.* [Annie was the 7-year-old daughter

of Joseph and Sarah Ann Gillman. Joseph was a farm servant.]

21 Dec 1893   *Attendance is irregular.*

5 Jan 1894   *Re-opened School on Monday. Admitted Frank Highman.*

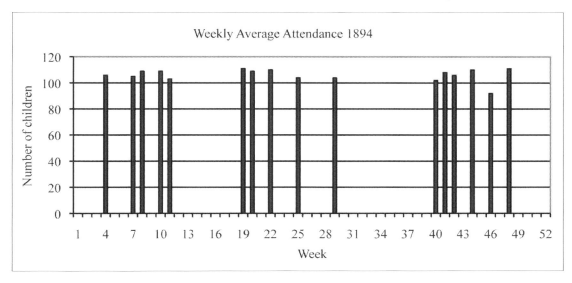

12 Jan 1894   *The Attendance is fairly good.*

19 Jan 1894   *Admitted Dorothy Ansell & Albert Baker. Attendance good.*

2 Feb 1894   *Admitted 3 Fosters from the Farm Colony.*

9 Feb 1894   *The Attendance is now very good.* [The average attendance was now regularly above 100, the capacity for the school.]

23 Feb 1894   *Admitted Francis Knightsbridge & Ernest Harvey.*

2 Mar 1894   *Attendance still very good.*

6 Apr 1894   *Re-opened School on Monday with 107 children. Admitted two Wards & Walter Miller. Several children have left the Village viz. The Brockwells, Balls & Hughes.* [Walter Miller was the son of Lewis Ridgwell and his common law wife Elizabeth Miller. His father was a basket maker.]

13 Apr 1894   *Attendance still good. Admitted 3 Calverleys, Mahala Elsden & Ethel Beale.* [Henry Calverley moved his family from the East End to Hadleigh. He was a zinc worker and married to Emma. The three children were Violet, Constance and Stewart. 3-year-old Mahala was the daughter of George and Elizabeth Elsdon who lived in Castle Lane. George was a bricklayer. Ethel Beale was the 4-year-old daughter of Edmund and Jane Beale of Castle Lane. Her father was an engine driver on a farm.]

20 Apr 1894   *Attendance good.*

27 Apr 1894	*Although the general Attendance is good several children are very irregular.*
4 May 1894	*The Attendance continues to be good.*
18 May 1894	*Admitted Raymond & Ernest Bradley.*
25 May 1894	*Attendance very good. Admitted Florence Hinton in the Infant room.*
8 Jun 1894	*Admitted Edith Fearley. Attendance good with the exception of a few children.*
15 Jun 1894	*The Attendance is not quite so good – several children are very irregular and I have again seen the Attendance Officer who has promised to write to the parents and send notices. This all the help we can get and some of the parents persist in keeping their children from school.*
22 Jun 1894	*Admitted Geo. Saunders on Tuesday.*
6 Jul 1894	*The Attendance Officer called to-day but we have the greatest difficulty to keep up the Attendance.* [There was sickness in the village, including measles.]
28 Sep 1894	*The School was re-opened on Monday with 100 children. The Attendance has been very fair for the first week. Admitted 11 children.* [After Harvest Vacation]
12 Oct 1894	*The Attendance Officer called yesterday and took the names of a few absentees.*
19 Oct 1894	*Admitted Beatrice Turtle.*
26 Oct 1894	*The Attendance continues to be good with a few exceptions. Admitted 2 Astburys & 3 Tuckers.*
9 Nov. 1894	*The Attendance is good, but a few are still very irregular. The Attendance Officer called.*
23 Nov 1894	*The Average is still good. Admitted 2 Cowells. Admitted Dora Baker.* [John and Mary Cowell had moved to Hadleigh from Little Bardfield in Essex. John was a stockman on a farm, and the family lived in a cottage next to the *Castle Inn*. The children were probably their daughters Mary and Emily.]
30 Nov 1894	*Admitted two Butchers.*
7 Dec 1894	*The Attendance is fairly good. Attendance Officer called to-day and took the names of some absentees.*

⁓

4 Jan 1895	*Re-opened School on Monday. Admitted James Webster.* [James was the 5-year-old son of Jonathan and Ellen Webster. His father had opened up a butcher's shop on the corner of the village street and Castle Lane, converting Hadleigh Lodge.]

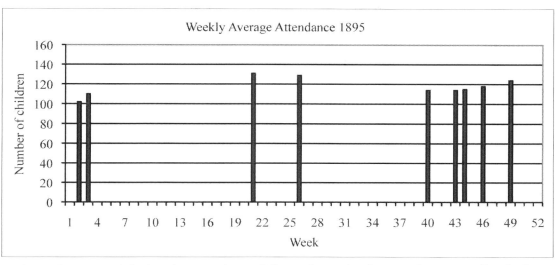

11 Jan 1895	*Admitted two Feltons.* [The Feltons had moved into Hadleigh from Thundersley. John Felton, himself a former pupil, was a stockman on a farm, and was married to Sarah. The two children were Alice and Edward, aged about eight and six.]
15 Feb 1895	*The Attendance has been better this week. Admitted Rose Cowell.* [Rose was the 12-year-old sister of Mary and Emily Cowell who had joined the school the previous November.]
22 Feb 1895	*The Attendance has improved.*
22 Mar 1895	*Attendance improving.*
29 Mar 1895	*Average going up. I have sent a list of very irregular children to the Att. Officer.*
5 Apr 1895	*Attendance good. Every available seat is occupied in the School.*
11 Apr 1895	*Attendance good.*
19 Apr 1895	*The Attendance is good.*
26 Apr 1895	*Highest average on record – had over 130 children at School. Several Sal. Army children are giving trouble – very irregular.* [There was now serious overcrowding in the school with an extension due to be built during the Harvest Vacation.]
10 May 1895	*The Attendance is good but several children are still irregular. The Att. Officer has summoned Whittaker for the non-attendance of his daughter Dorothy.*
17 May 1895	*The Attendance is very good. The Att. Officer succeeded in getting a Conviction in the case of Dorothy Whittaker.*
7 Jun 1895	*Re-opened School on Tuesday with 105 children.* [After Spring Bank Holiday]
21 Jun 1895	*Attendance good.*
5 Jul 1895	*Attendance fairly good. Admitted James Bowman.*

26 Jul 1895	*The Attendance is not good.*
27 Sep 1895	*Re-opened School on Tuesday morning not a very good Attendance.* [After the Harvest Vacation the new extension meant the school could admit up to 155 children.]
18 Oct 1895	*Attendance improving. I have sent in a good list of Irregular Children and intend pushing forward the cases if the notices are not responded to.*
25 Oct 1895	*The notices sent by the Att. Officer have had the desired effect several of the irregular children having shown up this week.*
1 Nov 1895	*I have been obliged to complain to the Att. Officer about a few irregular children. Admitted two Cotterells & Lily Havis.* [George and Fanny Cotterill moved to Hadleigh from Whitchurch in Hampshire. George worked as a foreman on a farm. The two children were probably Edith and Ethel. Lily was the 6-year-old daughter of Herbert and Alice Havis. They lived in Castle Road, with Herbert working as a general labourer.]
8 Nov 1895	*Attendance fairly good.*
15 Nov 1895	*The Attendance Officer called on Wednesday & took the names of Absentees.*
22 Nov 1895	*The Attendance is fairly good. A few are very irregular.*
29 Nov 1895	*Attendance very fair.*
6 Dec 1895	*Attendance Officer has been busy among the Absentees.*
13 Dec 1895	*The Attendance is fairly good. Attendance Officer called and took list of Irregular Children.*
19 Dec 1895	*Attendance irregular.*

3 Jan 1896	*Re-opened School on Monday with a poor Att. Average fairly good.*

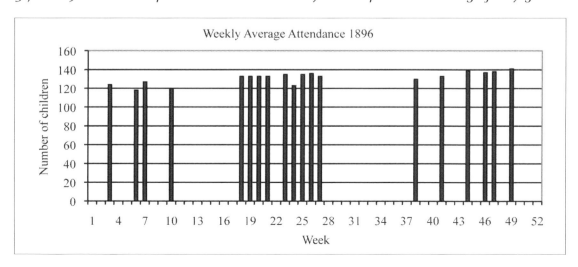

162

10 Jan 1896	*Average for week very fair. Attendance Officer called and took list of Absentees*
17 Jan 1896	*The average is still good.*
21 Feb 1896	*The Attendance Officer called Wednesday and took list of Irregular Children.*
28 Feb 1896	*The Attendance has much improved. The Attendance Officer has been putting pressure on several families & with good effect.*
13 Mar 1896	*Attendance good. All the Fosters have left the school & also the two Noyes.*
20 Mar 1896	*Attendance Officer called on Wednesday.*
27 Mar 1896	*Attendance has been fairly good.*
10 Apr 1896	*The Attendance has been somewhat irregular and I have again sent in a list of irregular children.*
17 Apr 1896	*Attendance very fair.*
24 Apr 1896	*The Attendance has been very good this week up till to-day & this afternoon we have over 40 children absent. I have consequently sent a list to Att. Officer asking for special attention to this fact as it greatly interferes with the general progress of the School. This Friday-afternoon irregularity has been growing worse for some weeks.*
1 May 1896	*I am glad to say the Att. on Friday was better.*
29 May 1896	*The Attendance has not been so good this week owing to the Holiday. Several families are very indifferent with regard to their children's Attendance and we hope shortly to get a conviction against one or two.* [After Spring Bank Holiday]
17 Jul 1896	*The Attendance is going down.*
24 Jul 1896	*The Attendance has been poor.*
18 Sep 1896	*School re-opened on Monday. Admitted a good number of Children.* [After Harvest Vacation]
2 Oct 1896	*Attendance on the increase. Attendance Officer has been busy with some success.*
9 Oct 1896	*Admitted a number of fresh children.*
23 Oct 1896	*The Attendance has been very good all the week till this afternoon when over 40 children were absent.*
30 Oct 1896	*The numbers are rising rapidly.*
13 Nov 1896	*Numbers still increasing.*
4 Dec 1896	*The Attendance is very fair indeed the Authorities at Rochford are looking up the irregular Children.*

8 Jan 1897   *The school re-opened on Monday with a good attendance.*

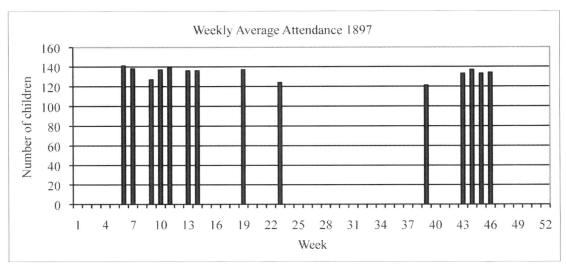

22 Jan 1897   *Attendance very fair indeed. Attendance Officer called to look up irregular children with some good results.*

19 Feb 1897   *I am losing the two Astburys.*

26 Feb 1897   *The Average has not been quite so good.*

5 Mar 1897   *The Attendance has been bad during the past week & I have been obliged to draw the attention of the Att. Officer to the fact.*

19 Mar 1897   *The school is getting very full. Mr. Judd called on Friday & I am hoping the Attendance will now be more regular.* [Mr. Judd was the Attendance Officer.]

2 Apr 1897   *I have again had to call in the Attendance Officer for several cases of irregularity.*

23 Apr 1897   *There is much irregularity in the Attendance.*

30 Apr 1897   *The Attendances are not yet come up to a good point. I have again asked the Att. Officer to look up irregular Children.*

7 May 1897   *Several children are leaving parish. The Attendance in Infant-room is very good.*

21 May 1897   *The Attendance is not so good as it should be & I have written to the Attendance Officer on the subject.*

28 May 1897   *The Attendance has not been good and I have again approached the Officer to take out Summonses.*

4 Jun 1897   *The Attendance is not good.*

2 Jul 1897   *Re-opened School 28th of June with a very fair number.* [After Diamond Jubilee week]

10 Sep 1897   *Commenced School with a fair number which increased throughout the week.*

17 Sep 1897	*The School is again increasing in numbers. Admitted eleven children this week & few are leaving the village at present.*
5 Nov 1897	*The Atten. Officer called yesterday & took a list of Absentees.*
3 Dec 1897	*The Attendance Officer called yesterday and took a list of Absentees.*
17 Dec 1897	*The Attendance is falling off considerably.* [There had been whooping cough in the village for several months.]

| 7 Jan 1898 | *Re-opened School on Tuesday with 118 children. The Sch. Atten. Officer called yesterday.* |

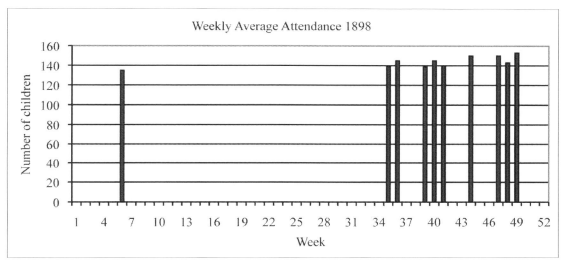

18 Feb 1898	*The Attendance is not so good as it might be.*
25 Feb 1898	*The Average has improved.*
4 Mar 1898	*The Attendance has been poor owing partly to the weather & partly to bad colds.*
11 Mar 1898	*Attendance fairly good. The Attendance Officer called on Wednesday & took a list of Absentees.*
25 Mar 1898	*Average fairly good.*
7 Apr 1898	*The Average is by no means good.*
22 Apr 1898	*Re-opened School on Monday with 134 children. Admitted several fresh Children.* [After Easter Vacation]
29 Apr 1898	*The Attendance is not so good as it should be I have again sent in a list to Att. Officer.*
13 May 1898	*The Attendance is improving.*
20 May 1898	*The Attention of the Att. Officer has had some effect on the Attendance.*
19 Aug 1898	*The School re-opened on Monday.* [The school was closed for eleven weeks due to an outbreak of measles and then the Summer Vacation.]

26 Aug 1898	*We have admitted a good number of children.*
9 Sep 1898	*The Average is still good.*
14 Oct 1898	*Attendance improving. The Attendance Officer has been working in the village.*
21 Oct 1898	*Average still increasing. Several children are causing a good deal of trouble in absenting themselves and we hope to have a case for the Magistrates next week.*
4 Nov 1898	*The Attendance continues to be good.*
18 Nov 1898	*The Att. Officer called to-day and took a list of Absentees. A half-holiday was given to-day as a reward for good attendance.*
9 Dec 1898	*Attendance very good.*
16 Dec 1898	*The Average has gone up considerably and the Att. Officer is doing some good work.*

13 Jan 1899	*The School re-opened on Monday with 150 children. Several children have left the School owing to the long journeys.* [Thundersley had a National School and so the Daws Heath children may have enrolled there.]

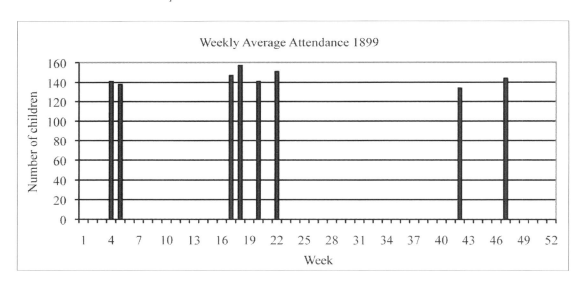

20 Jan 1899	*Attendance slightly improved but still poor.*
10 Feb 1899	*The Attendance is gradually improving. The Att. Officer is doing some good work.*
17 Feb 1899	*Attendance still good although there are* [a] *few irregular ones.*
24 Feb 1899	*This afternoon I have nearly 40 children absent this is generally the case on Friday afternoons in the fine weather.*
14 Apr 1899	*The Attendance has not been good.*

21 Apr 1899	*We are admitting a great many fresh children.*
28 Apr 1899	*I have admitted three more children this week.*
5 May 1899	*The Attendance is increasing and children are still being admitted.*
12 May 1899	*Attendance still good although several children are irregular.*
26 May 1899	*Owing to the holiday on Monday the Attendance has been poor.* [Spring Bank Holiday]
9 Jun 1899	*The average has again increased and the attendance is now good.*
23 Jun 1899	*The Attendance is only fairly good.*
20 Jul 1899	*The Attendance has been poor all week.*
8 Sep 1899	*The School re-opened on Monday with a very fair Attendance. The numbers are increasing but the Attendance is somewhat irregular. I have sent in a list of Absentees to the Att. Officer.*
15 Sep 1899	*Attendance still increasing.*
22 Sep 1899	*The Att. Officer is improving the Attendance and on the whole it is satisfactory.*
29 Sep 1899	*Since the holiday a good number of Children have been admitted.*
20 Oct 1899	*The Attendance Officer is hunting up absentees.*
27 Oct 1899	*The Attendance has improved this week several children have been admitted.*
3 Nov 1899	*I am still admitting fresh children.*
17 Nov 1899	*The Attendance Officer has been busy in the parish with some good results.*
22 Dec 1899	*The Attendance has been very bad and the progress of work suffered in consequence.*

҈

12 Jan 1900	*The School re-opened on Monday with 135 Children and the average for the week is 137.*
26 Jan 1900	*The Attendance has been better during the past week.*
9 Feb 1900	*Attendance is improving – Attendance Officer is looking up Absentees.*
2 Mar 1900	*The Attendance has improved.*
9 Mar 1900	*Attendance fairly good.*
27 Apr 1900	*The Average is increasing.*
4 May 1900	*The School is now quite full and no more children outside the village will be admitted. Although the Average Attendance does not exceed the number allowed the children are much crowded for work.*
11 May 1900	*The Attendance is on the increase, although many of the children are irregular.*
25 May 1900	*Attendance about the same. Average 151.*

8 Jun 1900	*School was closed on Monday (Whit) and the Attendance has been very irregular during the week. Average 139.*
13 Jul 1900	*Attendance still improving. The Attendance Officer is working hard to improve the Att.*
7 Sep 1900	*The School re-opened on Monday with a fair Attendance.*
21 Sep 1900	*The Attendance Officer called yesterday and we hope with his aid to bring the average up to a good standard. The school will be closed this afternoon as a reward for regular Attendance.*
28 Sep 1900	*The Attendance is improving and the Att. Officer is doing some good work.*
5 Oct 1900	*The Attendance is now good.*
12 Oct 1900	*Attendance satisfactory.*
26 Oct 1900	*The School is now full for Older Scholars and outside children are refused. The Attendance however is not quite so good.*
2 Nov 1900	*Average for week 133.*
9 Nov 1900	*The Attendance is now fairly good the Attendance Officer is doing some good work.*
23 Nov 1900	*Average 139.*

In the Midst of Life We Are in Death

ONE OF THE MOST common causes of poor attendance at the National School was sickness. In particular, attendance was always low in the winter months due to coughs and colds, plus the inclement weather. In Victorian times infants and children were the most vulnerable to disease because of their weak immune systems. Despite improvements in housing conditions and medicine, death rates remained relatively the same in 1901 as they had been in 1837, with about twenty-five per cent of infants still dying before the age of one. The chart below shows that proportionally more children under the age of five were buried at St. James the Less than children of school age, aged five to twelve.

One would expect absences due to colds, influenza and gastric complaints, but the Hadleigh National School log book records epidemics of measles, mumps, whooping cough, scarlet fever, diphtheria and smallpox, which occasionally caused the death of the pupils. With the exception of smallpox, no vaccines were developed in Victorian times to prevent these childhood diseases.

Measles was a major killer at this time, as cramped living conditions allowed the virus to spread quickly. Many children died of complications such as meningitis and pneumonia. Outbreaks of measles occurred at Hadleigh in 1865, 1870, 1878, 1882, 1890, 1894 and 1898. The outbreaks were so severe in 1878, 1890 and 1898 that the

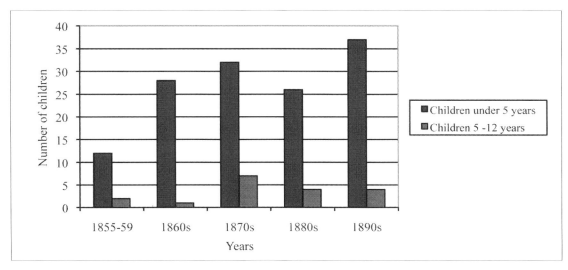

20. Child burials at St. James the Less, 1855-1899

school had to be closed. There were fewer cases of mumps, with only the outbreak of 1884 being recorded by Alfred Hawks.

Whooping cough accounted for about forty per cent of all deaths in Victorian England of children under the age of five. A highly contagious disease, it was spread through coughing and sneezing. Hadleigh suffered outbreaks of whooping cough in 1864, 1870, 1880, 1885, 1890 and 1897, with one 4-year-old girl dying in 1864.

Cases of fever are recorded in the log book, and the term fever could have included a number of different diseases. Five of the pupils died from fever in 1870. Ten years later fever reduced the attendance by about fifty per cent and led to the death of one boy from scarlatina. This outbreak lasted for four months until the end of February 1881. The log book records that in 1888 the children were too afraid to attend school in case they caught the fever which had broken out in the village. A common disease among children at this time was scarlet fever, with outbreaks in the village in 1864 and 1879. As well as a rash, the symptoms included chills, aching bodies, nausea and vomiting, and often led to death.

Although outbreaks of diphtheria at the school only occurred in 1891 and 1900,

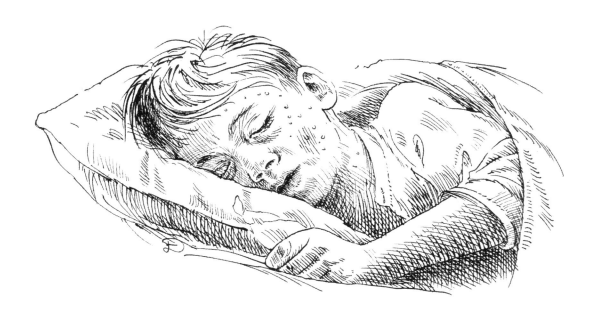

they caused the school to be closed for many weeks and led to the deaths of at least three of the children. The infection blocked the nose and throat, making breathing and swallowing difficult, but was more likely to affect children under the age of five.

Smallpox was another disease which was feared in Victorian times, and was especially fatal to young children. It was a highly contagious disease and killed over thirty per cent of those who caught the disease, and left many of the survivors blinded or scarred. In 1796 Edward Jenner had successfully vaccinated a boy against smallpox. The Vaccination Act of 1853 introduced compulsory vaccination against smallpox of infants within three months of birth. In 1867 a further parliamentary act extended the age limit for compulsory vaccination to 14 years. There was considerable opposition to these laws and many people, especially the poor, simply ignored them. In June 1863 Dr. Byass of Rayleigh visited the school to carry out a vaccination programme and several children stayed away from school. It was not until the 1870s that the vaccination programme was effectively implemented. There was an outbreak of smallpox at Hadleigh in 1866, which led to the school being virtually empty, but 1871 was the last time any of the masters recorded an outbreak of the disease.

In Victorian times there was no National Health Service and so medical treatment had to be paid for. In the 1860s Dr. Robert Bakewell lived at Hadleigh Lodge. There was no chemist in the village until after 1901 and, if they could afford it, villagers generally had to send to Rayleigh for medical help.

Log Book Entries

Miss Cecilia Miller had been appointed mistress in 1861

22 Jan 1863	*During play time John Adams, in jumping over the ditch, fell, and put his wrist out of joint.* [John was the 8-year-old son of John and Sarah Ann Adams, who lived in the village street, next to the blacksmith's. His father was an agricultural labourer.]
25 Feb 1863	*Elizabeth Polly taken ill in School this morning.*
26 Feb 1863	*John Adams began to write today for the first time since breaking his arm more than a month ago.*
25 Mar 1863	*Thomas Felton pinched a piece of his finger in putting up the desk.* [Aged eight, Thomas was the son of John and Sarah Felton who lived on the green at Hadleigh. Like most fathers, John was an agricultural labourer.]
1 Jun 1863	*Several children absented themselves afraid of Mr. Bias vaccinating them.* [Dr. James Byass of Rayleigh Weir was the nearest doctor.]

William Batchelor Kingswood appointed master 7 September 1863

4 Jan 1864   *Emily Harris was forced to go home from school because of the cold; it making her ill.*

11 Jan 1864   *Several are away through sickness, especially a Kind of Epidemic called "breathing-out" which the children all are or have been more or less afflicted with.*

28 Jan 1864   *A great deal of sickness among the children this week. 11 are at home ill.*

12 Feb 1864   *Several at home with the Ague.*

21 Jun 1864   *Several children sick today.*

27 Jun 1864   *Little Henry Rivers of the Infants died on Saturday of a fever.* [Henry was the 6-year-old son of Henry and Ellen Rivers of Daws Heath Road. On the death certificate the cause of death was consumption of many months. His father's occupation was given as farmer and carter. He was buried on 1 July at St. Peter's Church, Thundersley.]

11 Jul 1864   *Another death of an infant named Emma Griggs from Low Fever and Hooping [sic] Cough.* [Emma, the daughter of James and Hannah Grigg of Daws Heath Road, was only four years old. Her father's occupation was given as a huckster. She died on 8 July of whooping cough and was buried four days later at St. Peter's, Thundersley.]

15 Jul 1864   *Smaller attendance this week on account of the Hooping [sic] Cough, particularly among the Infants.*

22 Sep 1864   *Great deal of sickness among the children.*

21 Nov 1864   *Scarlet fever very prevalent in the place. The Hicks all ill.* [The Hicks family lived at Workhouse Lane in Hadleigh. Joseph Hicks was an agricultural labourer and his 13-year-old daughter Caroline was buried at St. James the Less on 23 November.]

23 Nov 1864   *Wet and cold and many children ill.*

5 Dec 1864   *More present. Several who had been ill for intervals of 2, 3 or 4 weeks.*

10 Jan 1865   *Measles among the children at the Hamlet of Daws Heath.*

Henry Yeaxlee appointed master 23 January 1865

23 Jan 1865   *Obliged to refuse admittance to J. Hicks on account of fever.*

26 Feb 1866   *One of the children hurt by falling in the ditch.*

3 May 1866   *I hear there is talk of small pox going about and that parents dislike*

	to send their children to school.
4 May 1866	*I have begun a system of cleanliness in the school, dirty hands etc. are sent out to be washed, hair combed etc. but we are obliged to get water from the school-yard ditch.*
29 May 1866	*More talking about smallpox – it has reached the villages round but not come to Hadleigh yet.*
18 Jun 1866	*Smallpox in the village and I fear the attendance will fall off.*
22 Jun 1866	*Harriet Russell away because her father has the smallpox.* [Harriet Russell was the 4-year-old daughter of James Russell, a labourer. Sadly, James Russell died aged twenty-seven, leaving his widow Emma to work as a charwoman.]
25 Jun 1866	*A wretched attendance of infants 12 in the morning, 9 in the afternoon. No. on register 42 – partly bad weather.*
26 Jun 1866	*There seem hardly any children at all.*
28 Jun 1866	*School going on to get empty.*
3 Jul 1866	*Another family attacked with the disease: this will keep three more children away from school.*
10 Jul 1866	*There seems nothing to write about now but that the school is nearly empty and the small pox continues. A little girl Harriet Russell is so ill that she is not expected to live another hour.*
12 Jul 1866	*Visited by Mr. Tyrrell, who specially requested me to keep away from school all children from infected houses.*
23 Jul 1866	*The Attendance nearly the same as last week.*
27 Jul 1866	*Only 16 present in 5th class.*
17 Sep 1866	*Harriet Russell has come back to school again.*

23 Jan 1867	*Emma Sewell taken ill in school.* [Possibly Emily, the 5-year-old daughter of William Sewell, and his wife Sarah.]
20 May 1867	*Elizabeth Savard taken in a fit of nearly an hour's duration.* [Aged about eleven years, Elizabeth Saward lived with her parents David and Martha in Chapel Lane. Her father was a shepherd.]

1 Jan 1868	*Two children taken ill in School today.*
29 Oct 1868	*One of the infants accidentally fell into the school-yard ditch & was hurt.*
17 Nov 1868	*Some of the smaller children are ill.*
23 Nov 1868	*A great many children absent from sickness & inclement weather.*

8 Jan 1869	*The Average this week is very low. Many children are ill.*
13 Jan 1869	*Some children ill in school.*

15 Jan 1869	*Many children still ill, 4 taken ill this week.*
19 Jan 1869	*Poor Attendance – very many children ill.*

✳

25 Jan 1870	*Many children ill at home at this time, mostly from colds.*
7 Mar 1870	*Attendance very low. Many children ill.*
10 Mar 1870	*A great number of children ill.*
18 Mar 1870	*Average for week 47. This low Average is owing to the rapid spread of measles in the parish. A boy taken ill in school this afternoon, and sent home:- the second case this week.*
29 Mar 1870	*One of the children taken ill in school this morning.*
1 Apr 1870	*The illness in the village is slowly abating.*
11 Apr 1870	*Obliged to refuse Attendance to a boy because of a death from fever near his home.*
3 May 1870	*Sent three children home, because of the fever in an adjoining house.*
20 May 1870	*Another family seized with fever, 3 children thereby absent.*
30 Jun 1870	*Two children died last night of fever and cold.* [John Gentry and Elizabeth Bullock, both aged five and the children of farm labourers, died on 30 June and were buried on 3 July. John, the son of Daniel and Elizabeth Gentry of Chapel Lane, died of fever of the brain. Elizabeth died of convulsions in the cottage of her parents John and Eliza Bullock in End Way.]
8 Jul 1870	*Dismissed E. Smith this morning from school, because of fever at her home.* [Probably Eliza Smith, aged eight years.]
11 Jul 1870	*More illness in the parish.*
30 Aug 1870	*Some absent through illness.*
30 Sep 1870	*One of the children died this morning from fever.* [8-year-old Jane Grigg, who lived in Daws Heath Road with her parents James and Hannah, had been suffering from scarlet fever for ten days. She was buried on 1 October at St. Peter's churchyard by the curate, Rev. E. E. B. Salisbury. Her parents had lost another daughter Emma in July 1864. James worked as a huckster, selling small items door-to-door.]
3 Oct 1870	*Another of the children died from fever.* [On 1 October William Grigg died of scarlet fever after an illness of several days. He was the 5-year-old brother of Jane. There is no record of his burial, so he may have been buried in the coffin with his sister.]
7 Oct 1870	*Some children still ill, and one more has died.* [Sadly, James and Hannah lost a third child from scarlet fever on 5 October. This was 3-year-old Arthur who was buried the next day. James and Hannah must have worried about their six other children, especially baby

Alfred who was only a few months old.]

1 Nov 1870	*Some of the smaller children are ill.*
23 Nov 1870	*The attendance is much poorer in the lowest class. Hooping-cough* [sic] *is very common.*
13 Dec 1870	*A great number ill.*
14 Dec 1870	*I have just counted 38 children ill.*

<hr>

24 Mar 1871	*Some throat-illness has thinned the upper classes.*
5 May 1871	*I have by the direction of the Revd. W Metcalfe refused admission to Jemima Harrod, a Banyard's daughter, because of the small-pox at her home.* [Jemima was the 9-year-old daughter of Samuel and Eliza Harrod. Samuel worked as a gardener and the family lived in the Hart Road Cottages at Thundersley. Jemima was described as 'a Banyard's daughter' as the family attended the chapel of the Peculiar People at Daws Heath, which had been founded by James Banyard.]
4 Aug 1871	*The Small-pox has visited a house adjoining the School-yard, and some Children are kept away to prevent infection.*
8 Aug 1871	*I have closed the school this morning - at Mr. Tyrrell's suggestion, because of the spread of disease in the village.*

<hr>

7 Feb 1873	*There have been three children taken ill in school this week and sent home.*
14 Mar 1873	*The average is still very low (55). This is principally owing to ill health among the children, and cold weather.*
16 May 1873	*The attendance has slightly fallen off, owing to illness principally.*

Alfred Hawks appointed master 21 May 1875

19 Nov 1875	*We have lost one little one from the Infants Willie Wallis, who died on last Friday.* [William Wallis Cook, the 4-year-old son of Julia Cook, a housekeeper, died on 12 November from pneumonia after being ill for five days. His death was certified by Francis Dorrell Grayson, a general practioner from Rayleigh. Willie was buried on 18 November by the rector.]

<hr>

2 Feb 1877	*The attendance is on the decrease: Sickness is spreading through the village.*
9 Feb 1877	*The attendance still continues to decrease the sickness not having abated.*

⁂

11 Jan 1878	*A great many children are absent from sickness.*
18 Jan 1878	*Mary A. Bullock was sent home yesterday on account of having a ring worm on the face.* [Mary Ann Bullock was aged about six years old and lived with her parents John and Eliza in End Way.]
22 Mar 1878	*A few children have been absent this week from sickness.*
11 Oct 1878	*The attendance continues to be good, but the Measles has prevented a great many from attending.*
18 Oct 1878	*The Measles still keeps a great many children absent. Average for week 64.*
25 Oct 1878	*The Measles has brought the average down to 37, consequently the general routine has been somewhat interfered with.*
1 Nov 1878	*The School was closed on Tuesday on account of Measles. Average for the two days 28.*
22 Nov 1878	*The School was re-opened on Monday, and although the attendance was not up to its old standard, most of the children which* [sic] *have recovered from the Measles were present.* [The school had been closed for nearly three weeks.]
29 Nov 1878	*Numbers of children have not yet sufficiently recovered to leave their houses, especially as the weather has been so very wet for this last week.*

⁂

17 Jan 1879	*Several children are sick.*
14 Feb 1879	*There is one case of Scarlet Fever in the village and a great number of children sick. I have been instructed by the Inspector of Nuisances to forbid any child attending, which appears to be sickening for any disease.* [The Inspector of Nuisances was employed by a parish to inspect for breaches of law regarding insanitary conditions, which were known as 'nuisances'.]
21 Feb 1879	*The irregular attendance, which to a great extent arises from sickness, greatly hinders the progress of the School.*
4 Apr 1879	*A great many of the children are sick, both among those who have been in attendance this week and those who have not.*
31 Oct 1879	*William Morley, one of my brightest children in Standard III was buried on Wednesday.* [William, aged eight, was the son of Emily Morley, a widow living in Chapel Lane. She supported her family by working in the fields, following the death of her husband Joshua in 1877. William died of pneumonia on 24 October after an illness of seven days, and was buried by the rector five days later.]

❦

23 Jan 1880	*A great many Children are suffering from bad colds.*
30 Jan 1880	*Many of the Children are ill with colds and bad throats.*
20 Feb 1880	*A great many of the Children have got the whooping-cough.*
19 Mar 1880	*[There] is still a great deal of sickness among the younger Children.*
22 Oct 1880	*Several children are sick, and it is feared with Fever.*
29 Oct 1880	*The numbers are very low. Many of the children are sick with Fever. Only about half the Children on Register are present.*
5 Nov 1880	*The numbers are still very low and I find that the Fever is very much in the village.*
12 Nov 1880	*Fever no better. Lost one of the Infants on Wednesday with fever.* [Alfred George Clark had been ill with scarlatina for one month and, although attended by Dr. F. D. Grayson of Rayleigh, died on 10 November. He was the 6-year-old son of William and Louisa who lived in Pleasant Row at Hadleigh. Three days later, this agricultural labourer's son was buried in the village churchyard.]
19 Nov 1880	*I think the Fever is gradually abating.*
26 Nov 1880	*The Fever has broken out in several fresh houses.*
3 Dec 1880	*Fever is subsiding.*
10 Dec 1880	*There are two fresh cases of Fever, but the others are recovering.*
17 Dec 1880	*The Fever has greatly interfered with the progress of the School. It is now over two months since it broke out.*

❦

7 Jan 1881	*The Fever is still in the Village hence the low numbers.*
28 Jan 1881	*The Fever has not yet left the village.*
4 Feb 1881	*Several cases of Fever.*
11 Feb 1881	*There are no fresh cases of Fever this week.*
25 Feb 1881	*No fresh cases of Fever.*

❦

24 Mar 1882	*There are several cases of Measles in the village.*
19 May 1882	*Many of the Children have measles.*
26 May 1882	*There are a great many children ill with Measles; and others staying away from fear.*
2 Jun 1882	*Attendance still very bad, owing to Measles.*
9 Jun 1882	*Still many cases of Measles.*
16 Jun 1882	*Several fresh cases of Measles.*
15 Dec 1882	*Several children are suffering from colds.*

❦

26 Jan 1883	*Many children are suffering from bad colds.*

~

21 Mar 1884	*Many of the children are sick.*
4 Apr 1884	*The Attendance has suffered considerably from the mumps, which has been among the children for some time.*

~

16 Jan 1885	*Many of the children are absent with bad colds.*
27 Feb 1885	*Many of the children are at home with bad colds.*
6 Mar 1885	*Many of the children are suffering with colds and coughs.*
12 Mar 1885	*Attendance is falling off considerably. Many of the children are still suffering from severe colds, there are one or two cases of whooping cough.*
19 Mar 1885	*The whooping-cough is in the village, and the Attendance is most irregular in consequence.*
2 Apr 1885	*Infants and Standard I exceptionally low, the whooping cough is very much in the village.*
16 Apr 1885	*Whooping cough is better.*

~

12 Mar 1886	*Several of the children are at home suffering from chilblains.*

~

11 Mar 1887	*Many of the children are suffering from colds.*
16 Dec 1887	*Many children are absent with bad colds.*

~

1 Jun 1888	*A Low Fever which has broken out in the place is seriously affecting the School.*
8 Jun 1888	*Many children are either sick or afraid to attend the School on account of the Fever.*
15 Jun 1888	*Several Children have recovered from the Fever and are now attending School.*
22 Jun 1888	*Many children are down with Fever.*
29 Jun 1888	*The Attendance is still low. Alice Rodwell is now down with Fever and Olive and Bertha Potter.* [Alice was aged nine and the daughter of an agricultural labourer. She lived with her parents William and Eliza at Daws Heath. Bertha and Olive, aged eight and seven, were the daughters of George and Agnes Potter. George Wayland Potter owned a grocer's shop in the village street. All three girls recovered.]

~

11 Jan 1889	*Several children are suffering from bad colds.*
25 Jan 1889	*A great many children are suffering from bad colds which has brought down the average.*

31 May 1889	*Several children are sick.*

⁓⁋⁓

17 Jan 1890	*The Attendance is very poor owing to sickness.*
31 Jan 1890	*Several children are still away ill.*
28 Feb 1890	*Several children are sick.*
21 Mar 1890	*There is a good deal of sickness in the village.*
11 Apr 1890	*Attendance decreasing – many of the children are now down with Measles and there is every appearance of the School being greatly affected thereby.*
9 May 1890	*The School was closed on Monday April 14 owing to an Epidemic of Measles, and re-opened on Monday May 5th. Several of the children have not yet sufficiently recovered to attend School.* [The school was closed for three weeks.]
30 May 1890	*Several children are sick and unable to attend School.*
4 Jul 1890	*Several children are still sick.*
18 Jul 1890	*There is a good deal of sickness among the Children (whooping cough) and the Attendance is suffering in consequence.*
14 Nov 1890	*Numbers have fallen off this week. There are several cases of sickness in the parish.*
5 Dec 1890	*Several children are sick.*

⁓⁋⁓

23 Jan 1891	*There is a good deal of sickness in the village chiefly among the younger children.*
20 Mar 1891	*Several children are sick.*
3 Apr 1891	*Several Children suffering from bad colds.*
8 May 1891	*The Attendance is not good – several Children are still sick.*
22 May 1891	*Two cases of influenza are reported in the village.*
26 Jun 1891	*Several children are sick.*
20 Nov 1891	*Several children have bad colds which keeps them from School.*
27 Nov 1891	*The average is reduced owing to several children having colds.*
30 Nov 1891	*The School was closed to-day by the Rector's order owing to an outbreak of Diphtheria.* [The school did not re-open for six weeks.]

⁓⁋⁓

22 Jan 1892	*There is a great deal of sickness in the village.*
29 Jan 1892	*The Attendance has not improved. Many of the children are suffering from severe colds.*
29 Apr 1892	*The Attendance is irregular – several children are sick.*
3 Jun 1892	*There is a good deal of sickness in the village, and the attendance is poor in consequence.*

28 Oct 1892	*Several children are sick.*
11 Nov 1892	*Several children are sick.*
9 Dec 1892	*Several children sick.*

3 Feb 1893	*The Attendance is improving although several children are still sick.*
3 Mar 1893	*There is still a good deal of sickness in the village.*
26 May 1893	*Several children are absent from sickness.*
16 Jun 1893	*Attendance only fair. Several children are sick.*
3 Nov 1893	*A good number of children are absent through sickness.*
10 Nov 1893	*The Average is not so good – sickness among the children seems to be on the increase.*
24 Nov 1893	*The Average does not improve. A good deal of sickness still prevails among the children.*
8 Dec 1893	*Many of the children are suffering from colds.*
15 Dec 1893	*There is a good deal of sickness in the village.*

26 Jan 1894	*There is still a good deal of sickness in the village.*
29 Jun 1894	*Several cases of Measles in the village.*
6 Jul 1894	*There is a good deal of sickness among the children consequently the attendance is irregular.*
13 Jul 1894	*The Attendance is very fair considering the amount of sickness in the village.*
23 Nov 1894	*There are several cases of sickness in the village.*

15 Feb 1895	*There is a good deal of sickness in the village.*
1 Mar 1895	*Sickness together with the bad weather is still affecting the Attendance.*
8 Mar 1895	*Average improving slightly – but a great many children are still sick.*
15 Mar 1895	*Average is slightly improving but there is a good deal of sickness in the village.*
7 Jun 1895	*The Attendance is not quite so good – several children are sick.*
14 Jun 1895	*Attendance good with the exception [of] a few children who are sick.*
22 Nov 1895	*Several children are sick.*
22 Nov 1895	*Still have sickness among the children.*

3 Jan 1896	*Several children are sick.*
31 Jan 1896	*The Attendance has been poor – many of the children have very bad coughs.*

9 Jul 1897	*The Attendance is by no means good several children are sick.*
24 Sep 1897	*Many of the children are suffering from Whooping cough and the Attendance is considerably affected.*
1 Oct 1897	*A good deal of sickness prevails.*
8 Oct 1897	*The Attendance is fairly good considering the number of children sick with whooping cough.*
15 Oct 1897	*The sickness is abating gradually and although the Attendance is not good it is better.*
12 Nov 1897	*A good number of children are suffering from whooping cough and soars* [sic].
26 Nov 1897	*A good deal of sickness prevails in the village.*
22 Dec 1897	*Many of the children are sick especially in the Infant Class.*

ୟ

7 Jan 1898	*A great many children are suffering from bad colds consequently the Attendance is not so good as it should be.*
14 Jan 1898	*A great many Children are sick consequently the Attendance is affected.*
28 Jan 1898	*A good deal of sickness prevails in the village and the Attendance is irregular.*
1 Apr 1898	*The Attendance has been irregular. Many of the children are absent with colds.*
6 May 1898	*Many of the children are suffering from bad colds which affect the Attendance.*
19 Aug 1898	*Finding the School could not re-open after the Whitsuntide holiday* [because of an outbreak of measles] *an order was obtained "on the recommendation of the Medical Officer for the District" from the Authorities at Rochford to close the School – at the expiration of the order the summer holidays were given as it was considered to be better for the Children than to open School for about 3 wks and then have them, thus giving them a good opportunity for getting quite strong.* [The school was closed for eleven weeks.]
16 Sep 1898	*The Attendance is not quite so good but there is a little sickness in the village which accounts for the falling off of Att.*

ୟ

3 Mar 1899	*The Attendance has not been so good this week. A good number of children are sick.*
10 Mar 1899	*A great deal of sickness prevails in the village. Many of the children are down with influenza.*
17 Mar 1899	*The Attendance is still poor owing to sickness.*
30 Mar 1899	*The Attendance has suffered the last few weeks considerably from*

sickness. [The master had also been sick for nearly two weeks.]

21 Apr 1899   *There is a good deal of sickness in the village and the attendance suffers in consequence.*

19 May 1899   *The Attendance is not so good as it should be – but there is still sickness among the children.*

14 Jul 1899   *Several children are sick.*

6 Oct 1899   *There is a good deal of sickness in the village which affects the Attendance.*

13 Oct 1899   *There is a good deal of sickness in the village & the Attendance is irregular.*

10 Nov 1899   *There is a good deal of sickness in the place, which interferes with the work.*

1 Dec 1899   *There is a good deal of sickness in the village.*

8 Dec 1899   *The work of the school is suffering considerably from the sickness which prevails in the village.*

15 Dec 1899   *To-day I have less than 80 Children out of 173 on the books. There is quite an Epidemic of Influenza among the children.*

19 Jan 1900   *The Attendance is not good, but there is still a good deal of sickness in the village.*

16 Mar 1900   *The Attendance is somewhat irregular and I hear there is a good deal of sickness in the village.*

23 Mar 1900   *A great many children are still sick and the Attendance is still very irregular, especially among the smaller children.*

30 Mar 1900   *Very little improvement in the Attendance. Many of the Children are suffering from bad colds.*

6 Apr 1900   *The Attendance is not good – a good deal of sickness prevails in the village.*

30 Nov 1900   *The Attendance is poor owing to sickness. Several cases of Diphtheria have been notified and there have been two deaths.* [On 29 November Frederick and Alice Franklin, of Kent Terrace at Hadleigh, buried their 5-year-old daughter Ada and their 4-year-old son Jack. Frederick Franklin worked as a bricklayer in the village.]

5 Dec 1900   *The School was closed to-day by order of the Medical Officer of the District owing to an outbreak of Diphtheria.* [The school did not reopen until 14 January 1901. During this time at least two more children died in the village – Maggie Went and Lily Mays, who were both four.]

Come Rain or Shine

When writing their entries in the log book, the mistress and the masters were often preoccupied with the weather as it influenced the attendance, which consequently had an effect on the grant awarded by the government. Many of the children had a long walk to school, especially if they lived at Daws Heath. It was quite a struggle for a child as young as three or four to walk to and from school in snow or pouring rain, often in the dark, on unlit muddy roads or across fields. So it was very common for the children to stay away from school when the weather was bad. Another factor was the lack of warm and waterproof clothing, particularly boots, leading to the children getting chills. School closures were frequent in the winter with both staff and children unwell with bad colds.

Log Book Entries

Miss Cecilia Miller had been appointed mistress in 1861

13 Jan 1863   *Weather prevented some of the children attending.*

20 Jan 1863   *Morning wet and stormy, lower classes thin. Three squares of glass out, attempted to paste them up with brown paper.*

12 Mar 1863   *Cold and rainy – very poor attendance.*

16 Mar 1863   *Morning wet – attendance poor.*

30 Apr 1863   *Very cold day – unable to open coal house door, consequently could have no fire.*

19 May 1863   *Attendance very small owing to the bad weather. 29 in the morning. 31 in the afternoon.*

19 Jun 1863   *Wet morning – fifteen children present.*

Between 6 July and 27 July 1863, there was no official master or mistress. It is unclear who taught the children

22 Jul 1863   *A very wet morning – scarcely any children present at 9 o'clock.*

William Batchelor Kingswood appointed master 7 September 1863

2 Dec 1863   *Fearfully wet and very dark, especially in Afternoon.*

3 Dec 1863   *Scarcely any school on account of Wet Weather.*

5 Jan 1864   *Weather very severe.*

6 Jan 1864   *Several away on account of the weather.*

11 Jan 1864   *Very fine day and consequently better attendance.*

20 Jan 1864   *Very wet in morning and rather bad attendance in consequence.*

19 Feb 1864   *Very little done to-day. The weather being so bad and Snowy. Few here. The average was reduced greatly by the very inclement weather.*

25 Feb 1864   *The weather very wet and cold and consequently a poor school.*

9 Mar 1864   *Still very wet and snowy especially in the afternoon.*

11 Mar 1864   *Weather very stormy. Attendance this week very irregular and bad.*

13 May 1864   *Fine weather and good attendance during the past week.*

3 Nov 1864   *A beautifully fine day and many children absent in consequence.*

17 Nov 1864   *Wet day. Poor attendance.*

22 Nov 1864   *Very stormy day and few in afternoon.*

23 Nov 1864	*Wet and cold and many children ill.*
28 Nov 1864	*Very wet, many little children away.*
13 Dec 1864	*Fine day, more present.*

⁓

2 Jan 1865	*Weather very snowy and cold. Many sick and thin School.*
6 Jan 1865	*Poor school to-day. Very blusterous morning.*
13 Jan 1865	*Very stormy morning and consequently thin School.*

Henry Yeaxlee appointed master 23 January 1865

23 Jan 1865	*My first day in School. Cold day and attendance about 60.*
26 Jan 1865	*Very snowy consequently a thin school.*
27 Jan 1865	*Again a very stormy day. The number very small in the afternoon.*
30 Jan 1865	*Roads still very snowy – school thin.*
1 Feb 1865	*Weather finer and school fuller.*
6 Feb 1865	*Finer weather and better attendance.*
13 Feb 1865	*Very heavy snowstorm. Number very small.*
17 Feb 1865	*Weather very unfavourable. The school has this week been very thin indeed.*
24 Feb 1865	*Very wet and the attendance very thin.*
27 Feb 1865	*Finer weather – attendance improved.*
20 Mar 1865	*An extremely cold day – east wind. School very thin.*
23 Oct 1865	*Unfavourable weather, very thin school.*
1 Nov 1865	*Went to church alone this morning the weather being too unfavourable to take the Choir.*
6 Nov 1865	*Very stormy weather.*
30 Nov 1865	*Many children absent.* [The weather had been unfavourable the day before.]

⁓

8 Jan 1886	*The Attendance has been extremely low owing to the inclemency of the weather. School closed two days.*
10 Jan 1866	*Several children absent on account of unfavourable weather.*
11 Jan 1866	*Weather still stormy. Attendance very low.*
12 Jan 1866	*Very few children at school on the same account.*
15 Jan 1866	*Several absent from the infant school.*
19 Jan 1866	*Average this week less than usual, the weather being very unfavourable.*
22 Jan 1866	*Finer weather and the attendance improved.*
9 Feb 1866	*Exceedingly stormy: scarcely any infants present.*

13 Feb 1866	*The weather unsettled – several children absent.*
19 Feb 1866	*Began this week with a better school though the weather is far from favourable.*
11 May 1866	*A very wet morning. In the infant room <u>8</u>.*
30 May 1866	*Rather rough weather, and consequently a poor school.*
31 May 1866	*Finer weather and a better school.*
25 Jun 1866	*No. on register 42 – partly bad weather.* [Also smallpox in the village.]
2 Aug 1866	*A very wet day.*
6 Aug 1866	*Stormy weather again.*
11 Sep 1866	*The weather rough again, many infants away.*
14 Sep 1866	*A wet morning, but the attendance has improved.*
17 Sep 1866	*The smaller children are beginning to come back again to school.*
30 Oct 1866	*Rather a dull day – only moderate attendance.*
4 Dec 1866	*Very inclement weather.*
7 Dec 1866	*Average much thinned by the storm.*

ᴍ

7 Jan 1867	*Weather very cold and snowy – 8 children present in 5th Class of 44.*
14 Jan 1867	*Attendance improved, but almost all the infants are absent on account of the severity of the weather.*
18 Jan 1867	*A sharp snow storm, only 38 present this afternoon.*
30 Jan 1867	*Stormy weather in the morning.*
5 Feb 1867	*Very inclement weather.*
4 Mar 1867	*Very cold weather. Several absent from the upper classes.*
7 Mar 1867	*Very cold and snowy in the morning: only twenty-eight present.*
8 Mar 1867	*School much reduced on account of the weather.*
12 Mar 1867	*Hardly any present on account of the snow and rain.*
15 Mar 1867	*The average this week very low in consequence of the inclement weather.*
20 Mar 1867	*Very inclement weather.*
25 Mar 1867	*The weather is much milder, but the attendance has improved but little.*
8 Apr 1867	*The weather rather dull. Attendance not very good.*
17 Apr 1867	*Dull weather – attendance poor.*
14 May 1867	*The weather rather severe, & the attendance limited.*
16 May 1867	*Attendance poor from the severity of the weather.*
23 May 1867	*Very inclement weather, many absent.*
3 Jun 1867	*Very dull heavy weather, children very listless.*
15 Jul 1867	*Very wet weather. School much reduced.*

6 Aug 1867	*A very wet morning, many absent.*
29 Oct 1867	*Wet weather. More absent.*
2 Dec 1867	*Very inclement weather. Many children absent.*
6 Dec 1867	*Very bad weather this week and consequently a very poor attendance. Average 59.*
9 Dec 1867	*Severe weather. 3 present out of 45 in Class V.*

⸎

1 Jan 1868	*Small attendance from cold weather.*
3 Jan 1868	*Very cold and snowy. Many absent.*
17 Jan 1868	*Very wet weather.*
27 Jan 1868	*Very wet this afternoon – few present.*
13 Feb 1868	*The attendance has improved this week in consequence of fine weather.*
27 Feb 1868	*School rather poorly attended from cold weather.*
4 Mar 1868	*Very stormy morning.*
26 Mar 1868	*The school thinned today because of wet weather.*
15 Sep 1868	*A wet morning. 84 Children present.* [A good attendance considering the weather.]
30 Sep 1868	*Very wet this morning. Some absent. A great many in the afternoon.*
9 Nov 1868	*The attendance diminished by rainy weather.*
25 Nov 1868	*Wet weather, the attendance diminished, several children ill.*
4 Dec 1868	*The Average this week is low principally from inclement weather.*

⸎

1 Feb 1869	*Wet weather. Attendance still poor.*
3 Feb 1869	*A very wet day – very few children.*
22 Feb 1869	*Very rough weather.* [This continued for three days, affecting the attendance.]
15 Mar 1869	*Very cold weather. Attendance thin.*
4 May 1869	*Very bad weather, hardly any present.*
19 May 1869	*Rather a wet morning; poor attendance.*
16 Jun 1869	*Very wet morning.* [This was the third day of rain.]
13 Jul 1869	*Attendance thinned by wet weather.*
3 Aug 1869	*A wet day. No school in the morning, very few in the Afternoon.*
13 Sep 1869	*Very stormy weather.*
18 Oct 1869	*Very wet weather.* [Lasted two days and made weekly average low.]
8 Nov 1869	*A wet morning and the numbers diminished.*
22 Nov 1869	*Attendance diminished by wet weather.*
10 Dec 1869	*Attendance thinned this morning by wet weather.*
21 Dec 1869	*Some of the smaller children absent on account of wet weather.*

꘠

5 Jan 1870	*Several of the smaller children absent this morning on account of Wet Weather.*
11 Feb 1870	*Attendance very low to-day in consequence of a snow-storm.*
15 Feb 1870	*Very poor attendance in consequence of inclement weather. Only 52 present this morning and 60 in the afternoon.*
21 Feb 1870	*The attendance still very low, in consequence of the continuance of bad weather.*
4 Jul 1870	*Rather a wet day. Attendance lower.* [The wet weather continued for another two days.]
4 Nov 1870	*There was no school on Monday because of the heavy rain.*
5 Dec 1870	*A wet and cold day. The attendance much poorer.*
6 Dec 1870	*A very wet dismal day. The Attendance very low.*
8 Dec 1870	*Very cold day. Only 14 present of 42 in Class V.*
13 Dec 1870	*The weather very stormy.*
16 Dec 1870	*The School has been closed on Monday and this afternoon, the wet weather keeping so many absent.*

꘠

16 Jan 1871	*The school was closed before time because of the extremely wet weather.*
23 Jan 1871	*A very wet day.*
8 Feb 1871	*A wet day. Very few children still.*
21 Apr 1871	*The average has been diminished by extremely wet weather, and the school closed for 2 half-days on the same account.*
1 Jun 1871	*The school was closed on Monday on account of weather.* [The school should have been closed on the Monday anyway, as it was the first Spring Bank Holiday.]
23 Jun 1871	*The Average is very much lower, mostly in consequence of wet weather.*
28 Jul 1871	*The attendance is rather low to-day because of wet weather.*
29 Sep 1871	*The rain-storms have kept the attendance lower in this week.*
17 Nov 1871	*To-day being cold and snowy, the attendance is very much reduced.*
8 Dec 1871	*The severe weather has reduced the Average to 56.*
22 Dec 1871	*The Average has again decreased, principally owing to weather.*

꘠

26 Jan 1872	*The Average is low, owing to bad weather.*
22 Mar 1872	*Average 57, low – owing to severe weather.*
1 Nov 1872	*The Average is lower than last week – principally owing to unfavourable weather.*
15 Nov 1872	*The average is much lower, and the attendance very irregular this*

week on account of wet and cold weather.

29 Nov 1872   *The Average has fallen to 67 – principally owing to inclemency of weather.*

20 Dec 1872   *The average is very low for this week – 59 – principally owing to wet weather.*

7 Feb 1873   *The weather has been so severe that the Average has fallen to 37 this week. The school was closed on Monday.*

7 Mar 1873   *The School was closed last week in consequence of the inclement weather, the children being unable to attend.*

28 Mar 1873   *The Average for the week has gradually improved principally owing to the return of fine weather. 64.*

27 Feb 1874   *The Average has decreased again, because of inclement weather.*

13 Mar 1874   *The attendance this week is very low indeed – owing to inclement weather – I cannot get the work done so well in such weather, as the children suffer severely from cold.*

30 Oct 1874   *The very wet weather has slightly interfered with the attendance.*

13 Nov 1874   *The weather being very cold, we began fires yesterday.*

27 Nov 1874   *The weather being severe some of the smaller children are kept at home because of it.*

4 Dec 1874   *The attendance is slightly lower this week because of severe weather.*

11 Dec 1874   *The average attendance is considerably lower (73) principally owing to inclement weather.*

18 Dec 1874   *The average has fallen considerably owing to inclement weather. The school was closed yesterday morning on the same account.*

12 Feb 1875   *The Attendance has fallen off a little, owing partly perhaps to wet weather.*

26 Feb 1875   *The Average has been considerably reduced by a few days of rough weather. On fine days the Attendance was very good.*

6 Mar 1875   *The Average for this week was very considerably reduced by the coldness of the weather.*

Alfred Hawks appointed master 17 May 1875

4 Jun 1875   *The attendance continues good, but the work has not been so thoroughly executed as that of the preceding week, on account of the intense heat during the last few days.*

11 Jun 1875	*The rough winds and heavy showers to-day have brought the average for past week down to 64.*
2 Jul 1875	*The average is again brought down considerably by the heavy rains.*
30 Jul 1875	*On account of the intense heat the work has not been so readily entered into, especially among the younger children, several of which [sic] have been sent home through Sickness.*
24 Sep 1875	*The attendance is getting very fair, considering the wet days we have had during the week.*
26 Nov 1875	*Owing to the unsettled weather the attendance has been irregular.*
3 Dec 1875	*Attendance very irregular, owing to bad weather.*
10 Dec 1875	*Attendance still very poor. The School was closed on Monday and Tuesday on account of the bad weather.*

26 May 1876	*The average has increased to 61 notwithstanding the very heavy rains which have fell [sic] during the week.*
29 Sep 1876	*The attendance has not been quite so regular as the preceding week, on account of the very unsettled weather.*
3 Nov 1876	*The weather has been very cold but remarkably bright. Began fires in the School on Monday.*
10 Nov 1876	*The average is not quite so good this week, as the weather has been very severe, the ground has been covered with snow two days.*
17 Nov 1876	*Attendance again increased to a good average, the weather being fine.*
1 Dec 1876	*The School has been very well attended considering the great amount of rain which has fallen during the past week.*

12 Jan 1877	*On Thursday the attendance was very poor owing to the inclement weather.*
8 Jun 1877	*Weather very hot.*
9 Nov 1877	*The School was well attended in the early part of the week, but the heavy rains have brought the numbers down for the last two days.*
14 Dec 1877	*Considering the very unsettled weather the children have attended well.*
21 Dec 1877	*The attendance has not been quite so good this week, owing to the very foggy weather.*

3 Jan 1879	*The falling off of attendance in very bad weather seems to be the difficulty most difficult to guard against in these scattered country villages.*
10 Jan 1879	*The weather has been very severe the last few days.*
24 Jan 1879	*The Average has decreased this week being only 63, owing, no doubt, to the very sharp weather.*

28 Mar 1879	*The Attendance has been very poor this week, the highest number being 54. The weather has been very severe.*
4 Jul 1879	*Notwithstanding the heavy rains the Attendance has been very regular.*
21 Nov 1879	*Owing to the severe weather the average has considerably decreased this week (77).*
28 Nov 1879	*Weather very severe.*

✿

30 Jul 1880	*The Attendance has been very irregular. I have only 47 present this afternoon and this morning School was not opened on account of the very heavy rain.*

✿

14 Jan 1881	*Weather intensely cold.*
21 Jan 1881	*The School was closed on Tuesday afternoon on account of the inclemency of the weather and not opened again during the week.*
28 Jan 1881	*The weather is still very severe.*
25 Feb 1881	*The Attendance is very poor again (54) owing to the severe weather.*
9 Dec 1881	*The Attendance for the first four days of the week has been exceptionally good, but to-day the heavy rains have reduced it considerably.*

✿

28 Apr 1882	*This morning being very wet the numbers were brought down to 60.*
8 Dec 1882	*Attendance irregular owing to inclement weather.*
15 Dec 1882	*The weather has been very severe.*

✿

26 Jan 1883	*The Attendance is anything but good owing I believe in a great measure to the bad weather.*
9 Mar 1883	*The Average is low this week owing to the inclemency of the weather.*
19 Oct 1883	*Only 61 present this afternoon, very wet.*
7 Dec 1883	*Attendance not quite so good this week, owing to the severe weather.*

✿

27 Nov 1885	*The dull, foggy weather has affected the Attendance this week.*

✿

8 Jan 1886	*The Attendance has been extremely low owing to the inclemency of the weather. School closed two days.*
15 Oct 1886	*The weather has affected the Attendance considerably this week.*
10 Dec 1886	*Owing to the inclemency of the weather on Monday the School was not opened.*
23 Dec 1886	*The Attendance has been considerably affected by the inclemency of the weather.*

꧁

21 Jan 1887	*The weather is still keeping many from School.*
11 Feb 1887	*The bitterly cold weather has affected the Attendance this week.*
1 Apr 1887	*The weather has affected the Attendance this week.*
6 May 1887	*The weather has greatly affected the School this week. The attendance was very poor in the early part of the week.*

꧁

17 Feb 1888	*The School was not opened on Thursday owing to the inclemency of the weather.*
24 Feb 1888	*The Attendance still continues to be very poor owing to the inclemency of the weather.*
23 Mar 1888	*The Attendance has been poor owing to the inclement weather.*
14 Dec 1888	*The Attendance has not been so good owing to wet weather.*

꧁

15 Feb 1889	*School closed during the whole of the [week] on account of the inclemency of the weather and bad colds among the children.*
1 Mar 1889	*The bad weather has again affected the attendance.*
13 Dec 1889	*The weather has affected the attendance this week.*

꧁

7 Mar 1890	*The inclemency of the weather has greatly affected the Attendance. Not opened on Monday.*
28 Nov 1890	*Closed the school on Thursday & Friday, owing to severe snow storm.*
5 Dec 1890	*The attendance has not been good – weather very severe.*
18 Dec 1890	*Numbers low – weather very severe.*

꧁

9 Jan 1891	*The Attend. is still very poor, owing to the inclemency of the weather.*
17 Jul 1891	*Only 59 Children present this afternoon owing to thunderstorm.*
23 Oct 1891	*The Attendance is good though it was affected yesterday by the inclemency of the weather.*
13 Nov 1891	*The severe gale on Wednesday affected the Attendance 68 in the afternoon.*

꧁

28 Oct 1892	*The weather has greatly affected the Attendance.*

꧁

6 Jan 1893	*Considering the inclemency of the weather the Attendance has been very fair.*

꧁

5 Jan 1894	*The School was closed to-day owing to the inclemency of the weather.*
16 Nov 1894	*The bad weather has affected the Attendance considerably.*

꧁

25 Jan 1895	*The Attendance has not been quite so good this week owing to the inclemency of the weather.*
1 Feb 1895	*The Attendance is very poor. Owing to the severe weather the School was not opened to-day (Friday).*
8 Feb 1895	*Through the inclemency of the weather we have been obliged to close the School since Tuesday, & on Monday & Tuesday the Attendance was very small.*
11 Oct 1895	*The Attendance has not been quite so good this week owing to the wet.*

꧁

3 Jan 1896	*The weather has greatly affected the Att.*
6 Mar 1896	*On Tuesday morning the inclemency of the weather greatly affected the Attendance.*
20 Mar 1896	*The Attendance has been irregular owing to the weather.*
12 Jun 1896	*The Attendance has been affected by the heavy rain this week.*
18 Sep 1896	*The Attendance has not been quite so good owing to the excessive wind & rain.*
6 Nov 1896	*The inclemency of the weather has affected the Attendance this week.*
18 Dec 1896	*The weather has affected the attendance this week.*

꧁

8 Jan 1897	*The school re-opened on Monday with a good attendance which has since been much affected by the bad weather.*
3 Feb 1897	*Considering the very bad weather during the week the Attendance has been creditable.*
26 Mar 1897	*The weather has somewhat affected the regularity of Atten.*

꧁

25 Mar 1898	*The school was not opened to-day (Friday) owing to the inclemency of the weather.*
18 Nov 1898	*The wet weather has greatly affected the attendance.*

꧁

13 Jan 1899	*The inclemency of the weather has greatly affected the attendance throughout the week.*

꧁

2 Feb 1900	*The weather has affected the Attendance considerably.*
23 Feb 1900	*The inclement weather has caused the Attendance to be very irregular.*
1 Jun 1900	*The School was closed on Monday and Thursday. Owing to the weather the Attendance has been irregular.*

Down on the Farm

IN RURAL VILLAGES LIKE Hadleigh, the older children were needed at various times of the year to help with seasonal farming jobs. Agricultural labouring was the main occupation at Hadleigh in 1861, with about forty-four per cent of the working men of the village employed on the farms, which included Blossoms, Sayers, Park, Castle, Solby's and Hall Farms. The wages for an agricultural labourer were often insufficient to maintain a large family, so the women and children traditionally carried out weeding, stone picking, planting and harvesting on the farms. Many girls would be absent from school, not because they were working on the farms, but because they had to run the household while their mothers worked.

The harvest always took priority over school lessons. At first the National School would be closed for about four or five weeks each summer for the Harvest Vacation, but by the 1880s this had been extended to six or seven weeks. The date of the Harvest Vacation was variable, depending on the weather. However, when the school reassembled in September or October, the attendance was always very low because the older children were still gleaning in the fields after the harvest.

By the end of the 19th century fewer children were being employed on the land. This was due to the introduction of compulsory education for children in 1880 and the employment of School Attendance Officers from 1876. Other factors were the invention of labour-saving agricultural machinery and an improvement in men's wages. The opening of the Salvation Army Farm Colony in 1891 also had an effect on the employment of children and, by the 1890s, truancy was usually confined to fruit-picking.

Log Book Entries

William Batchelor Kingswood appointed master 7 September 1863

18 Sep 1863   *Several stayed away this week "Potato Picking".*

28 Sep 1863   *Several of bigger children Potato picking.*

29 Feb 1864   *Re-admitted the boy George Barker scarcely 7 years of age who has been away 3 months to work in the fields.*

4 Apr 1864   *Several children away potatoe* [sic] *dropping.*

29 Aug 1864   *Began school to-day with only 34 small children. Gleaning not being over generally.*

30 Aug 1864   *Few more attended to-day but some absent who were here yesterday.*

5 Sep 1864   *More children at school to-day, but many still away, gleaning and some sick.*

27 Sep 1864   *Several children absent in afternoon blackberrying.*

4 Oct 1864   *Several absent picking up potatoes.*

Henry Yeaxlee appointed master 23 January 1865

29 Jun 1865   *Attendance very low. Several at work.*

6 Sep 1865   *Gleaning not yet finished.* [Attendance poor all week.]

15 Sep 1865   *Attendance this week has improved but still there are many absent gleaning, gardening, etc.*

16 Oct 1865   *Improved attendance. Some boys returned from work.*

23 Jul 1867   *Upon enquiry, I find that Henry Petts was kept from school "to gather groundsel".* [Henry was the 6-year-old son of Ann Petts, a charwoman, who lived in End Way. His father James, an agricultural labourer, had died in 1862.]

5 Aug 1867   *Harvesting began, and the school therefore slightly diminished.*

9 Sep 1867   *Began school with only eighteen this morning the harvest being still unfinished.*

10 Sep 1867   *Almost all the children away.*

21 Aug 1868   *Attendance very low again – some children gleaning.*

19 Jul 1870   *Not a good attendance – partly owing to the coming harvest.*

30 Aug 1870   *Some children still gleaning.*

1 Nov 1870	*A few of the older boys are at plough.*

~

14 Jul 1871	*A great many children absent pea-picking.*
16 Sep 1871	*I have reopened School this week, with a very low average (29) partly because the gleaning is not yet over.*

~

21 Jun 1872	*The Average is 56; lower, because some children of the ages of Six & Seven are employed by a farmer named Manning to go in his fields to pick peas.* [Frederick Manning was a young man who farmed 320 acres at Hadleigh.]
28 Jun 1872	*Many children still at work in the fields.*

~

1 Aug 1873	*The attendance diminishes rapidly as the harvest-time approaches. The usual school-routine has been carried on, and the defective-attendance children are doing their best to make up the number of attendances.*

~

20 Mar 1874	*Even now, (a few minutes ago) One of the parents sent word to me that she wanted her boy and girl (Ages 5 & 6) to go out with her a "stone-picking".* [One of the jobs on the farm left to women and children was picking out the stones from the fields.]
17 Jul 1874	*The attendance is falling off as usual as the harvest comes on, the average this week being very low.*
21 Aug 1874	*The Attendance this week has been very low indeed, the children having not yet finished gleaning.*

Alfred Hawks appointed master 17 May 1875

18 Jun 1875	*Owing to pea-picking, the average is brought down to 57.*
9 Jul 1875	*The attendance is still getting lower, on account of the great amount of work done in the fields.*
5 Aug 1875	*On account of the approaching Harvest the attendance has been rather poor.*
10 Sep 1875	*Attendance very bad – late harvest. We opened School on Monday morning, after a month's Vacation, with 21 children.*

~

29 Jun 1877	*The attendance has been rather low, many of the children are pea-picking.*
6 Jul 1877	*Some of the elder children are engaged in the fields pea-picking.*

20 Jul 1877	*Many of the children are engaged in the fields pea-picking.*
14 Sep 1877	*The School was re-opened on Monday after the usual Month's Vacation, but the numbers are low, especially in the higher Standards, which can I think be attributed to the hop-picking having commenced at which many of the children are engaged.*
2 Aug 1878	*The attendance has been very poor this week when compared with preceding week, owing to the Harvest.*
13 Sep 1878	*In addition to the usual Month's holliday* [sic] *we were obliged to close the School another week on account of the late Harvest.*
25 Jul 1879	*Several of the children are engaged in the fields hay-making.*
8 Aug 1879	*The Attendance continues to decrease, and although there is a great amount of haying being done, there appears to be no signs of closing the School for the Harvest Vacation for several weeks.*
15 Aug 1879	*The Attendance is good considering the amount of haying that is being carried on.*
16 Jul 1880	*The Attendance has been exceptionally bad this week, owing to the pea-picking in which so many children are engaged. The highest number present was 65.*
6 Aug 1880	*The Attendance is getting poor as the Harvest is approaching. We shall endeavour to carry on the School another week if possible.*
8 Jul 1881	*The children are employed in the fields pea-picking.*
16 Sep 1881	*The numbers have been succeedingly low during the week, owing to the hop-picking, 32 present this afternoon.*
17 Feb 1882	*Many of the children are working in the fields for a week or two.*
31 Mar 1882	*I have again sent a list of boys who are working in the fields to the Attendance Officer.*
27 Apr 1883	*I have sent another list of Absentees to the School Attendance Officer as several children are engaged in the fields stone picking.*
4 May 1883	*Many of the children are still engaged in the fields.*
13 Jul 1883	*Attendance again low. Many of the children are engaged in the fields fruit and pea-picking.*
19 Oct 1883	*Many of the children go "Blackberrying".*

11 Jan 1884	*Attendance not good, many of the Children engaged in the fields "bird minding".*
11 Jul 1884	*Many of the children are engaged in the fields fruit and pea-picking.*
1 Aug 1884	*The Harvest is commencing.*
26 Sep 1884	*Many of the Children are absent picking blackberries.*

10 Jul 1885	*The bad attendance is owing, I believe, to the hay-making in which many of the children are engaged.*
17 Jul 1885	*Many of the children are engaged picking Currants for Market.*
25 Sep 1885	*Many of the Children are still Absent picking Blackberries, and I intend sending a list of Absentees to the Attendance Officer on Monday with a hope of improving the Attendance.*

| 9 Jul 1886 | *Many of the children are engaged in the fields pea-picking.* |
| 17 Sep 1886 | *The gleaning is not quite over but I hope to have more next week.* |

| 27 Jul 1888 | *Many of the children are engaged picking fruit.* |
| 28 Sep 1888 | *School was closed 7 weeks owing to late Harvest.* |

| 24 Jul 1891 | *The Attendance has been fairly good considering the time of year. [There may have been less work in the fields for the children with the opening of the Salvation Army Farm Colony.]* |

| 22 Jul 1892 | *The Attendance has fallen off this week owing to the Currant-picking and pea-picking.* |

| 13 Jul 1894 | *Fruit-picking is affecting the attendance especially among the children connected with the Salvation Army.* |

| 7 Oct 1898 | *A great many children are absent picking blackberries.* |

| 30 Jun 1899 | *The Attendance has been affected by the fruit-picking.* |
| 14 Jul 1899 | *The Attendance has been poor owing to fruit-picking.* |

| 1 Jun 1900 | *Several children are absent fruit-picking.* |

High Days and Holidays

H OLIDAYS AND DAY TRIPS were not accessible to poorer families until the late 19th century, as most working families could neither afford it nor did they have time off. Before the introduction of bank holidays in 1871, Good Friday and Christmas Day were the only two days of leisure which were almost universally granted to working people. The Bank Holidays Act 1871 introduced the concept of holidays with pay and designated four holidays in England: Easter Monday, Whit Monday, the first Monday in August and Boxing Day.

Holidays were granted to the children by the school managers at Christmas, Easter, very occasionally at Whitsun and for the Harvest Vacation in the summer. The date and length of the Harvest Vacation was variable, being determined by the harvest. The pattern of these holidays changed throughout the years covered by this book. Christmas usually lasted a week, or maybe two, if there was inclement weather or sickness in the village. Until 1871 a week was always given at Easter, but then it became more usual to just have Good Friday and Easter Monday. A week's holiday at Whitsun was not always given in the 1860s and 1870s. When the annual inspection started to occur just after Whitsun, the holiday was restricted to just one day on the Spring Bank Holiday. The length of time for the Harvest Vacation varied from three to five weeks in the 1860s and 1870s, to six or seven weeks from the 1880s.

As can be seen from the log book entries, more one-day holidays and half-holidays were given in the 1860s and 1870s. With the passing of Education Acts in 1870 and 1880, schools were more restricted in the amount of occasional days they could take as holidays. As a church school, religious festivals, such as Shrove Tuesday, Ash Wednesday and Ascension Day, were often marked with a holiday, usually after a visit to church. The children were given a half-day holiday on the afternoons of the visits by Her Majesty's Inspector and the Diocesan Inspector, either as a reward, or maybe as a bribe.

Every year, on 24 June, a fair was held at Hadleigh to celebrate Midsummer's Day and this often lasted for two days. *White's Directory* for 1863 recorded that the village *"has a fair for pleasure and pedlery on the 24th of June"*. Fairs were a rare opportunity for the hard working villagers to have fun and socialise, so there was plenty of music, dancing, food, drink and entertainment on offer. As can be seen from the log book entries, when the school managers did not grant a half-holiday, the children simply did not turn up for school. Until 1859, Guy Fawkes Day was a public holiday with parish churches required to hold a service. Celebrations would continue throughout the day with bells ringing and the lighting of bonfires. The children at the National School continued to enjoy a half-holiday on this date for several years.

Log Book Entries

Miss Cecilia Miller had been appointed mistress in 1861

17 Feb 1863	*Holiday in the afternoon being Shrove Tuesday.*
2 Apr 1863	*Holiday tomorrow (Good Friday) and Easter Week.* [One week]
24 Jun 1863	*Half a holiday – Hadleigh Fair Day.*
26 Jun 1863	*The next week to be a holiday. My last day at school. C.M.*

Between 6 July and 27 July 1863, there was no official master or mistress. It is unclear who taught the children

27 Jul 1863	[Last entry in log book for July, so presumably the start of the Harvest Vacation, which lasted nearly six weeks.]

William Batchelor Kingswood appointed master 7 September 1863

5 Nov 1863	*Usual half holiday today.* [Guy Fawkes Night]
17 Dec 1863	*Children are writing letters to take home when the break is for the Xmas Vacation.*
23 Dec 1863	*Broke up according to the wish of the Rev. Godson.* [The curate determined the date of the Christmas Vacation of 11 days.]

9 Feb 1864	*Shrove Tuesday therefore a holiday in the afternoon.*
25 Mar 1864	*Good Friday. No school.*
6 Apr 1864	*Confirmation at Benfleet and a day's holiday in consequence.*
13 May 1864	*Broke up for the Whitsuntide Vacation in the afternoon.* [One week]
29 Jul 1864	*Broke up today for 1 month.* [Harvest vacation]
20 Dec 1864	[Christmas Vacation of nearly two weeks.]

Henry Yeaxlee appointed master 23 January 1865

28 Jan 1865	*Half-holiday.* [Shrove Tuesday]
17 Apr 1865	[Easter Vacation week]
28 Jul 1865	*Visited by Revd. Deacon who dismissed the school.* [Harvest Vacation of six weeks]
6 Nov 1865	*School very thin on account of there being no half holiday given as was customary.* [For Guy Fawkes' night]
22 Dec 1865	*Dismissed the children for the Christmas Vacation.* [One week]

꙾

15 Feb 1866	*Ash Wednesday. Half-holiday.*
2 Apr 1866	[Easter Vacation week]
10 May 1866	*Ascension Day. Gave the children a half-holiday.*
18 Jul 1866	*A whole day* [sic] *holiday, on account of the Rochford Festival.* [Two days before, Henry Yeaxlee had written that a great deal of time had been taken in arranging for this festival, which suggests a level of participation by himself and maybe the choir.]
10 Aug 1866	*Dismissed the children for the Harvest Vacation.* [Four weeks]
12 Oct 1866	*Took about forty of the children to a travelling Circus this afternoon. Gave the rest a half-holiday.*
5 Nov 1866	*Gave a half-holiday.* [Guy Fawkes Night]
21 Dec 1866	*Dismissed the children for their usual Christmas Vacation.* [One week]

꙾

14 Feb 1867	*Gave the children a quarter-holiday this morning. Very few present in the Afternoon.* [The previous day Henry Yeaxlee felt ill.]
6 Mar 1867	*Ash Wednesday. Gave the school a half-holiday as they missed their usual one yesterday.*
22 Mar 1867	*A half-holiday given.*
19 Apr 1867	*Dismissed the school for the usual Easter Vacation.* [One week]
18 Jun 1867	*Gave a half-holiday.*
16 Jul 1867	*Gave a whole holiday in consequence of a festival at Leigh.*
9 Aug 1867	*Dismissed the school this afternoon for the Midsummer Vacation.* [One month]
5 Nov 1867	*Gave a half-holiday; poor attendance in the morning.* [Guy Fawkes Night]
20 Dec 1867	*Dismissed the School for the Christmas Vacation.* [One week]

꙾

26 Feb 1868	*Ash Wednesday – usual half-holiday.*
9 Apr 1868	*Dismissed the School for the Easter Week.*
2 Jun 1868	*Gave a half holiday.*
3 Jun 1868	*Holiday in the afternoon.*
14 Jul 1868	*Closed the school for the Harvest Vacation.* [Four weeks]
5 Nov 1868	*Gave the usual half-holiday.* [Guy Fawkes Night]
18 Dec 1868	[Christmas Vacation of two weeks.]

꙾

10 Feb 1869	*Half-holiday being Ash Wednesday.*
25 Mar 1869	*Dismissed for the Easter Vacation.* [During the week's holiday,

Henry Yeaxlee married Miss Lavinia Harvey of Leigh. The marriage service was conducted by the Rev. Metcalfe on 31 March at St. James the Less.]

6 May 1869   *Holy Thursday. Gave the usual half-holiday.*

17 May 1869   *Whit Monday. Gave a half-holiday at Mr. Metcalfe's permission.*

24 Jun 1869   *Gave the children a half-holiday at Mr. Metcalfe's suggestion, it being Hadleigh Fair-day.*

6 Aug 1869   *Dismissed the children for the Harvest Vacation.* [Five weeks]

5 Nov 1869   *Gave the usual half-holiday.* [Guy Fawkes Night]

23 Dec 1869   *Dismissed the School this morning for the Christmas Vacation.* [One and a half weeks]

2 Mar 1870   *Ash Wednesday. Usual half-holiday.*

15 Apr 1870   *Good Friday. Dismissed the school for the Easter Vacation.* [One week]

24 May 1870   *A whole day* [sic] *holiday in consequence of a Confirmation service at Benfleet.*

26 May 1870   *Ascension Day. Usual half-holiday.*

14 Jun 1870   *Gave the children a half-holiday – as they had none last week.*

24 Jun 1870   *Hadleigh Fair Day. Gave the children a holiday.*

7 Jul 1870   *Gave the children a half-holiday, to see a show in Rayleigh.*

29 Jul 1870   *Dismissed the school for the Harvest Vacation.* [Four weeks]

16 Dec 1870   *Christmas Vacation.* [Two weeks]

22 Feb 1871   *Gave the usual half-holiday.* [Ash Wednesday]

7 Apr 1871   *I do not intend giving the usual holiday next week* [for Easter], *but shall defer it till the season is more advanced.*

19 May 1871   *The children had the usual half-holiday on Ascension Day.*

1 Jun 1871   *I dismissed the School on Thursday for a week.* [The week's vacation was in lieu of Easter week.]

21 Jul 1871   *The School was closed to-day (Friday) because of a Regatta at Leigh, which many children attended.*

8 Aug 1871   *I have closed the school this morning – at Mr. Tyrrell's suggestion, because of the spread of disease in the village.* [The Harvest Vacation lasted for nearly five weeks.]

22 Dec 1871   *I have dismissed the children for their Xmas Vacation.* [Two weeks]

14 Feb 1872   *The school closed for the day.* [Ash Wednesday]

1 Mar 1872   *The school was closed on Tuesday, that being the day appointed for*

the Thanksgiving for the Prince of Wales' recovery. [In 1871 Queen Victoria's eldest son had contracted typhoid fever and his recovery from the illness was widely thought to have resulted from nationwide prayers. A service of national thanksgiving was held at St. Paul's Cathedral on 27 February 1872.]

15 Mar 1872   *I have given a half-holiday to-day by the Revd. W. Metcalfe's permission.*

30 Mar 1872   *As this is Holy Week the school is closed to-day – Good Friday.*

3 Apr 1872   *I have closed the school for Thursday and Friday instead of the usual week, and the school will be dismissed for a week at Whitsuntide. The arrangement is preferable on account of weather, &c.* [Normally the children would have had a week's holiday for Easter.]

17 May 1872   *The school was closed this week in consequence of the Master's illness. This week is reckoned as the Whitsuntide Holiday-week.* [Whitsun was the following week.]

31 May 1872   *The School was closed on Monday and Tuesday Afternoons in consequence of a fair at Rayleigh.*

28 Jun 1872   *Monday being Hadleigh Fair-day, the School was closed in the Afternoon.*

1 Aug 1872   *Dismissed the School for the Vacation to-day – Thursday.* [The intention was for the Harvest Vacation to last a month.]

4 Sep 1872   *Upon reassembling the School, very few children attended. I have therefore only kept the School for two days this week, the Average being 24.*

20 Dec 1872   *I have this afternoon dismissed the school for the Christmas Vacation.* [One week]

10 Apr 1873   *The School was closed on Friday.* [Good Friday]

16 Apr 1873   *This week being Easter-Week, the usual holiday is transferred to Whitsun-Week, and the Whitsun-holiday taken on Thursday & Friday.*

23 May 1873   *Usual half-holiday – it being Ascension Day.*

29 May 1873   *I have dismissed the children to-day for a week, in lieu of Easter-week.*

13 Jun 1873   *The school was closed on Monday and Tuesday there being a fair at Rayleigh, to which the major part of the children went, instead of School.*

27 Jun 1873   *The school was closed on Tuesday Afternoon because of a fair.* [Hadleigh Fair]

15 Aug 1873	*Dismissed the school for the Harvest Vacation, for three weeks. The remaining week to be given after October.* [This extra week was never given.]
7 Nov 1873	*The school was closed on Wednesday afternoon for the usual half holiday.* [Guy Fawkes Night]
19 Dec 1873	*I have dismissed the school this morning for the usual Christmas Vacation.* [Two weeks]

⁕

20 Feb 1874	*The School was closed on Wednesday, it being Ash-Wednesday.*
3 Apr 1874	*The school closed to-day, being Good Friday. I intend to defer the Easter Holiday-week until May, when the weather will probably be finer.*
23 Apr 1874	*I have closed the school to-day to give the school one day Friday and the following week as a substitute for the Easter and Whitsuntide holidays.*
15 May 1874	*The school was closed on Thursday, it being Ascension Day.*
23 Jul 1874	*I have to-day dismissed the School for the Harvest Vacation.* [Three weeks]
6 Nov 1874	*The school was closed in the afternoon yesterday as usual.* [Guy Fawkes Night]
18 Dec 1874	*I have dismissed the school this morning for the Christmas Vacation.* [Two weeks]

⁕

12 Feb 1875	*On Ash-Wednesday Afternoon the children had their usual half-holiday.*

Between 19 March and 17 May 1875, in the absence of a master, the rector ran the school

7 May 1875	*Gave the children a holiday on Thursday being Ascension Day.*

Alfred Hawks appointed master 17 May 1875

25 Jun 1875	*To-day being Hadleigh Fair; I have given the children a half-holliday* [sic].
5 Aug 1875	*Dismissed the School for the Harvest Vacation.* [During the month the school was closed, Alfred Hawks married Miss Sarah Dulton in their home village of Snodland in Kent on 12 August.]
17 Dec 1875	[Christmas Vacation of three weeks.]

〰️

3 Mar 1876	*The usual half-holliday* [sic] *was given on Wednesday.* [Ash Wednesday]
17 Apr 1876	[Easter Vacation of one week.]
26 May 1876	*Yesterday being Ascension-day the School was closed for the usual half-holliday.* [sic]
2 Jun 1876	*The School is to be closed on Monday for the usual Whit-holliday.* [sic]
4 Aug 1876	*I have dismissed the children for the usual Month* [sic] *Vacation.* [Harvest Vacation]
22 Dec 1876	[Christmas Vacation of two weeks.]

〰️

28 Mar 1877	*Dismissed school for usual Easter Vacation.* [Just over one week]
25 May 1877	*The School was closed on Monday this being Whitsun week.* [21 May was the Spring Bank Holiday.]
10 Aug 1877	[Start of one month's Harvest Vacation.]
28 Sep 1877	*The School was closed yesterday afternoon.*
20 Dec 1877	*The School was closed this afternoon (Thursday) for the usual Christmas Vacation.* [Two weeks]

〰️

19 Apr 1878	[No mention in the log book of a holiday for Easter. Good Friday and Easter Monday were bank holidays.]
14 Jun 1878	*A half-holliday* [sic] *was given on Monday.* [Spring Bank Holiday]
28 Jun 1878	*On Monday afternoon there were only seventeen children present, owing probably to the village fair. The School was not opened on Monday Morning, the Managers having given me <u>full</u> permission to close the School.*
2 Aug 1878	*I have dismissed the School this morning for the usual Month's Vacation.* [In fact it lasted five weeks.]
20 Dec 1878	*Closed School for Christmas Vacation.* [Two weeks]

〰️

10 Apr 1879	*The School will be closed tomorrow (Good Friday).*
6 Jun 1879	*A holliday* [sic] *was given on Monday (Whit).* [Spring Bank Holiday]
11 Jul 1879	*A half-holliday* [sic] *was given on Wednesday.*
8 Aug 1879	*A half-holliday* [sic] *was given on Monday being Bank Holliday* [sic].
29 Aug 1879	*Dismiss* [sic] *the children this afternoon for the Harvest Vacation.* [Five weeks]
19 Dec 1879	*Dismissed the Children this Afternoon for the Christmas Vacation.* [One week]

〰️

25 Mar 1880	*Dismissed the School this morning Thursday.* [Good Friday was the following day.]
2 Apr 1880	*Opened School on Monday Morning and gave half-holliday* [sic] *only, as the Exam. is very close.* [Easter Monday]
14 May 1880	*We intend to keep the School open all Whitsun week as the Examination is so close.* [17 May was the Spring Bank Holiday.]
25 Jun 1880	*The School was closed yesterday afternoon on the event of the Village Fair.*
13 Aug 1880	*Dismissed the School for the Harvest Vacation.* [Five weeks]
22 Dec 1880	*Closed School for Christmas Vacation.* [Nearly two weeks]

⁓

15 Apr 1881	*Closed the School this morning and gave half-holliday* [sic], *being Good Friday.*
22 Apr 1881	*A half-holliday* [sic] *was given on Monday (Easter).*
10 Jun 1881	*The School was closed on Monday for the usual holliday* [sic]. [Spring Bank Holiday]
17 Jun 1881	*The School was closed on Wednesday.* [Probably because of the Agricultural Show at Southend.]
29 Jul 1881	[Harvest Vacation lasting six weeks.]
22 Dec 1881	[Christmas Vacation of one week.]

⁓

24 Feb 1882	*The School was closed on Wednesday.* [Ash Wednesday]
6 Apr 1882	*Closed the School this afternoon until Tuesday.* [Easter Weekend]
2 Jun 1882	*The usual holliday* [sic] *was given on Monday.* [Spring Bank Holiday]
4 Aug 1882	*Dismissed the School for Harvest Vacation.* [Five weeks]
22 Dec 1882	*Dismissed the School this afternoon for the Christmas Vacation.* [One and a half weeks]

⁓

23 Mar 1883	*Closed the School to-day Holy Thursday and gave the children Easter Monday.*
11 May 1883	*The Children have the usual holliday* [sic] *on Monday.* [Spring Bank Holiday]
10 Aug 1883	*Dismissed the School this afternoon for the Harvest Vacation.* [Six weeks]
21 Dec 1883	*Break up this afternoon for the usual week's Vacation.* [Christmas]

⁓

11 Apr 1884	*Closed the School this morning Thursday till Tuesday.* [Easter]
28 May 1884	*The School will be closed on Monday.* [Spring Bank Holiday]
4 Jul 1884	*A holliday* [sic] *was given to-day.*

1 Aug 1884	*Dismissed the School for the Harvest Vacation.* [Six weeks]
19 Dec 1884	*Dismissed to-day for Christmas Vacation.* [One week]

✐

3 Apr 1885	[No record of a holiday being given for Easter.]
29 May 1885	*The School was closed on Whit Monday.*
31 Jul 1885	*Dismissed the School this afternoon for the Harvest Vacation.* [Six weeks]
23 Dec 1885	*Dismissed the School on Wednesday for the Christmas Vacation.* [Just over a week]

✐

19 Feb 1886	*A holiday was given on Thursday on the event of a Concert.*
22 Apr 1886	*Dismissed the School this Afternoon till Tuesday morning.* [Easter Weekend]
28 May 1886	*A half holiday was given on Wednesday.*
30 Jul 1886	*The School was closed this Afternoon for the Harvest Vacation.* [Six weeks]
23 Dec 1886	*Dismissed the School for the usual Xmas holiday.* [Just over a week]

✐

25 Feb 1887	*Half holiday on Wednesday.* [Ash Wednesday]
7 Apr 1887	*Dismissed the School this afternoon till Tuesday Morning.* [Easter Weekend]
28 Jul 1887	*Dismissed the School to-day for the Harvest Vacation.* [Six weeks]
21 Dec 1887	*Dismissed the School this morning for the Christmas Vacation.* [Just over a week]

✐

29 Mar 1888	*Closed the School this afternoon till Tuesday.* [Easter Weekend]
25 May 1888	*The School was closed on Monday.* [Spring Bank Holiday]
27 Jul 1888	*A half-holiday was given yesterday.*
3 Aug 1888	*Closed the School for Harvest Vacation.* [Seven weeks]
21 Dec 1888	*Closed School for Xmas week.*

✐

18 Apr 1889	*Close* [sic] *School to-day till Tuesday morning.* [Easter weekend]
7 Jun 1889	*The School will be closed on Monday.* [Spring Bank Holiday]
26 Jul 1889	*The School closed to-day for the Harvest Vacation.* [Seven weeks]
20 Dec 1889	*The School was closed on Thursday for the usual Xmas Vacation – one week.*

✐

11 Apr 1890	*School closed Easter Monday and Friday afternoon.* [Easter Weekend]

1 Aug 1890	*The School was closed to-day Friday, for the Harvest Vacation.* [Seven weeks]
18 Dec 1890	*The School was closed to-day (Thursday) for Xmas Vacation.* [Just over a week]

⁌

26 Mar 1891	*Closed the School to-day till Tuesday for Easter Holiday.* [Easter Weekend]
22 May 1891	*School was closed on Monday.* [Spring Bank Holiday]
3 Jul 1891	*The School was closed on Tuesday afternoon and again on Wednesday and Thursday.*
24 Jul 1891	*The School was closed on Wednesday afternoon.*
7 Aug 1891	*Closed the school this afternoon for the Harvest Vacation.* [Seven weeks]
30 Nov 1891	[The school was closed for six weeks due to a diphtheria epidemic.]

⁌

14 Apr 1892	*Closed school till Tuesday morning.* [Easter Weekend]
10 Jun 1892	*The School was closed on Whit-Monday.*
5 Aug 1892	*Closed the school this afternoon for Harvest Vacation.* [Seven weeks]
21 Dec 1892	*The school was closed to-day for the Christmas week's holiday.*

⁌

17 Feb 1893	*Closed the School on Wednesday Afternoon.* [Ash Wednesday]
30 Mar 1893	*Closed the School to-day @ noon till Tuesday morning.* [Easter Weekend]
19 May 1893	*Closed the School this morning till Tuesday morning.* [Spring Bank Holiday]
4 Aug 1893	*The School was closed to-day for the Summer Vacation.* [Seven weeks]
21 Dec 1893	*The School was closed to-day (Thursday) for the Christmas Vacation.* [One week]

⁌

22 Mar 1894	*The School was closed to-day for the Easter week's Vacation.*
11 May 1894	*Closed the School for Whit Monday.* [Spring Bank Holiday]
2 Aug 1894	*The School was closed to-day for the Harvest Vacation.* [Seven weeks]
21 Dec 1894	*Closed the School for the Christmas Vacation.* [One week]

⁌

11 Apr 1895	*School closed to-day till Tuesday morning.* [Easter Weekend]
24 May 1895	*The School was closed on Thursday afternoon (Ascension Day).*
31 May 1895	*School closed till Tuesday morning.* [Spring Bank Holiday]

26 Jul 1895   *The School is closed to-day for the Summer Vacation when the new Infs-room is to be built and other alterations made.* [Eight weeks]

19 Dec 1895   *Closed the School to-day for Christmas Vacation.* [One and a half weeks]

3 Apr 1896   *The School was closed to-day (Thursday) till Tuesday morning & a half holiday given on Tuesday owing to a Concert in the Evening.* [Easter Weekend]

22 May 1896   *School closed to-day till Wednesday morning.* [Whitsun]

12 Jun 1896   *The School was closed on Tuesday afternoon on the event of a Confirmation in the Parish Church.*

24 Jul 1896   *The School was closed to-day for the Summer Vacation.* [Seven weeks]

23 Dec 1896   *The School was closed to-day for the Christmas Vacation and will re-open on Monday the 4th Jan. 97.* [One and a half weeks]

9 Apr 1897   *The School is closed to-day for the Easter Vacation.*

4 Jun 1897   *The School was closed to-day till Tuesday morning.* [Spring Bank Holiday]

23 Jul 1897   *Closed the School for Vacation (6 weeks).* [Harvest vacation]

22 Dec 1897   *Closed School for Christmas holiday.* [One and a half weeks]

25 Feb 1898   *The School was closed on Ash Wednesday afternoon.*

7 Apr 1898   *The School was closed to-day for the Easter week's holiday.*

29 Apr 1898   *The School was closed on Wednesday on the event of a Confirmation held in the Church by the Bishop of the Diocese.*

27 May 1898   *The School was closed to-day for Whitsuntide holiday.*

19 Aug 1898   *Finding the School could not re-open after the Whitsuntide holiday* [because of an outbreak of measles] *an order was obtained "on the recommendation of the Medical Officer for the District" from the Authorities at Rochford to close the School – at the expiration of the order the summer holidays were given.* [The school was closed for eleven weeks.]

22 Dec 1898   *Closed the School for Christmas Vacation 2 wks.*

30 Mar 1899   *The school was closed to-day for the Easter Vacation.*

14 Apr 1899   *The room not being finished – School did not re-open until Wednesday.* [This meant the Easter Vacation lasted for nearly two weeks.]

12 May 1899	*The School was closed as usual on Thursday afternoon (Ascension).*
22 May 1899	[The school was closed for the Spring Bank Holiday.]
20 Jul 1899	*The school is closed to-day for the Summer Vacation probably five weeks.* [Six weeks]
24 Nov 1899	*The School was closed for Poll yesterday.*
22 Dec 1899	*The School was closed to-day for the usual Christmas Holiday (two weeks).*

12 Apr 1900	*The School is closed to-day for the Easter Vacation and will re-open on Monday 23rd.*
8 Jun 1900	*School was closed on Monday (Whit).* [Spring Bank Holiday]
19 Jul 1900	*The School is closed to-day for the summer holidays.* [Six weeks]
5 Dec 1900	*The School was closed to-day by order of the Medical Officer of the District owing to an outbreak of Diphtheria.* [The school was closed for nearly six weeks.]

Let Us Pray

As the NATIONAL SCHOOL was a Church of England school, the children were expected to attend St James the Less Parish Church on Sundays. Before August 1863, when the Revised Code was introduced, the whole school was able to attend church services to celebrate religious festivals, such as Ash Wednesday, Good Friday and Ascension Day. After this date, church attendance by the whole school was less often. With the masters also expected to be the church organist, William Kingswood and Henry Yeaxlee often attended church services mid-week, either on their own or accompanied by the choir or older children. Although Alfred Hawks was also the church organist at St. James the Less, there is no record in the log book of this practice continuing. The following transcription of the log book only contains entries which are concerned with the children's attendance at church, not the master on his own, or with the choir, which is recorded elsewhere. If the log book is ambiguous and it is unclear whether the children attended, I have omitted the entry.

St. James the Less Church, Hadleigh.

21. St. James the Less Parish Church, Hadleigh

Log Book Entries

Miss Cecilia Miller had been appointed mistress in 1861

2 Jan 1863	*Children went to Church in the morning.*
6 Jan 1863	*Children attended Church.* [Feast of the Epiphany]
30 Jan 1863	*Children went to Church at 10.40 A.M.*
2 Feb 1863	*Children went to Church at 10.40 A.M.* [Candlemas Day]
18 Feb 1863	*Children went to Church in the morning being Ash Wednesday.*
27 Mar 1863	*Children went to Church in the morning.*
14 May 1863	*Ascension Day. Children went to Church at 10 A.M.*
22 May 1863	*Children went to Church at 10.30 A.M.*
26 May 1863	*Children went to Church – Whit Tuesday.*
10 Jul 1863	*Children went to Church in the morning.*
17 Jul 1863	*Children attended Church in the morning.*

William Batchelor Kingswood appointed master 7 September 1863

17 Sep 1863	*Choir & few larger children attended Divine Service in the morning.*
21 Dec 1863	*St. Thomas Day. 1st Class attended Church in morning.*
2 Feb 1864	*Elder children attended Divine Service in the morning.* [Candlemas Day]
1 Dec 1864	*First Class went to Church in the morning.*

Henry Yeaxlee appointed master 23 January 1865

1 Mar 1865	*Took the greater part of the school to Church this morning, being Ash Wednesday.*
14 Apr 1865	*Good Friday. Children attend church.*
15 Feb 1866	*Ash Wednesday. Went to church this morning with all the children in the larger room.*
6 Mar 1867	*Ash Wednesday. Went to Church with children of larger Room.*
30 May 1867	*Ascension Day. Went to Church in the morning with the elder children.*

21 May 1868   *Ascension Day. Went to Church in the morning with the elder children.*

10 Feb 1869   *Went to church in the morning with the Children.* [Ash Wednesday]

15 Apr 1870   *Good Friday. Took the children to church this morning.*
26 May 1870   *Ascension Day. Took the elder children to Church.*

7 Apr 1871   *The children attended church this morning.* [Good Friday]

16 Feb 1872   *Wednesday being Ash-Wednesday the children were taken to the Church Service.*
9 May 1872   *Holy Thursday. The children taken to Church this morning.*

23 May 1873   *On Thursday the elder children attended Church service in the morning.* [Ascension Day]
12 Dec 1873   *The School was closed on Thursday, there being a church service which was attended by the elder children.*

Between 19 March and 17 May 1875, in the absence of a master, the rector ran the school

26 Mar 1875   *Children came to Church this day in morning, being Good Friday.*

Alfred Hawks appointed master 17 May 1875

19 Nov 1897   *During the past week the Children have been to Church at the end of the morning session.*

Fun and Games

L IFE IN A VICTORIAN school was hard, for both the children and the teachers. Occasionally, there were days off to celebrate national events, or a 'treat' or party provided by the rector or the family from the 'Big House' of the district. This was Hadleigh House, one of the largest houses in the area, which stood at what is now Victoria House Corner. It had been the home of Mrs. Martha Lovibond who had provided an endowment in 1820 which helped finance the building of the National School. In 1864 it was bought by Sir Charles Nicholson, who lived there with his wife Sarah following their marriage in 1865. Created a baronet in 1859, Sir Charles Nicholson had been a member of the Legislative Council of the colony of Queensland, Australia. The National School log book records that Lady Nicholson would give cloaks at Christmas to the two girls who produced the best needlework. There is no further mention of the children visiting Hadleigh House after 1873, although the Nicholsons continued their links with the school.

On 23 August 1873 the *Essex Newsman* reported on a School Festival at Hadleigh: *"The children of these schools received a capital day's entertainment on Saturday, in the rectory grounds, where the Rev. W. Metcalfe provided tea with plum cake, bread and butter, and jam in abundance. The amusements were varied and*

22. Hadleigh House, 1828

maintained with vigour. After an address delivered by the rev. gentleman to the children, who then sang some of their school songs in a very creditable manner, hearty cheers were given for Mr. and Mrs. Metcalfe, and the little folks departed in high spirits to their various homes."

Other treats were provided by the Parish Church and by other churches, such as the Methodist Chapel and the Peculiar People Chapel at Daws Heath. Occasionally, the children would be taken for a walk by the school master, presumably for exercise and to study nature.

Log Book Entries

Miss Cecilia Miller had been appointed mistress in 1861

10 Mar 1863   *Children regaled with buns and coffee in honour of the Prince of Wales' marriage.* [Queen Victoria's eldest son married Princess Alexandra of Denmark.]

William Batchelor Kingswood appointed master 7 September 1863

10 Sep 1863   *Holiday in afternoon. Annual School treat and Choral Service at the Church.*

21 Jan 1864   *Most of the Daws Heath Scholars absent to-day, having gone to a treat given by the Minister of that place, at Rayleigh.* [This was probably the Minister of the Peculiar People Chapel which had been built in Daws Heath in 1852.]

28 Mar 1864   *Went to Leigh for a walk in the afternoon with the whole school.* [This would be a distance of about 5 miles.]

20 Jun 1864   *Children went to the Castle Grounds in afternoon with permission of the Managers.*

29 Sep 1864   *Annual School Treat in the afternoon.*

Henry Yeaxlee appointed master 23 January 1865

22 May 1865   *Children took a walk.*

15 Jun 1865   *Children went for a walk this afternoon.*

12 Oct 1866   *Took about forty of the children to a travelling Circus this afternoon.*

Gave the rest a half-holiday.

⁓

11 Feb 1868   *Took the children for a walk this afternoon.*

12 May 1868   *Gave the children an hour's walk.*

10 Sep 1868   *Gave the children a little play-time in accordance with Mr. Tyrrell's wish.* [Mr. James Tyrrell, a local farmer, was one of the managers of the school.]

⁓

24 May 1869   *Poor attendance – took the children for a short walk.*

8 Oct 1869   *No school this afternoon in consequence of there being a feast for the children who attend the Chapel.* [This was either the Methodist Chapel in Chapel Lane or the chapel of the Peculiar People at Daws Heath.]

16 Nov 1869   *Gave the children a short walk this afternoon.*

20 Dec 1869   *Visited this afternoon by Mr. & Mrs. Metcalfe who gave the children notice of a forthcoming treat.*

⁓

4 Oct 1870   *No school this afternoon, in consequence of there being a chapel tea-feast.*

⁓

1 Mar 1871   *Gave the children a walk this afternoon.*

⁓

8 Mar 1872   *On Tuesday afternoon the children were allowed a little play-time.*

⁓

17 Jan 1873   *Mr. Metcalfe gave a half-holiday.* [For Prize Day]

8 Aug 1873   *This evening (Friday) the children are invited to a tea at Hadleigh House, by Sir C. Nicholson's kindness.* [The *Essex Newsman* reported this event as taking place on the Saturday: "The pleasure of the children showed a thorough enjoyment of the bountiful treat, and after songs, and cheers for their host, they separated quite elated."]

15 Aug 1873   *The Average is very low. The small attendance has been kept up principally by the promise of a second school-treat to be given by the Revd. W. Metcalfe tomorrow (Saturday).*

Alfred Hawks appointed master 17 May 1875

13 Sep 1878   *The School was closed on Wednesday Afternoon on the event of a treat in the Village.*

⁓

15 Aug 1879   *The children belonging to the Sunday School were invited to tea by the Rector on Tuesday.*

                  ❧

25 Mar 1880   *Dismissed the School this morning Thursday, and intend taking the Children for a long walk this Afternoon.* [Good Friday the next day]

                  ❧

29 Apr 1881   *We took the children for a walk on Thursday. It was arranged to take them the day before Good Friday, but it being wet on that day we were unable to carry out the arrangement. The Rector and Miss Groomes came with us.*

                  ❧

16 Jan 1885   *A Holliday* [sic] *was given on Thursday.* [Annual school treat]

                  ❧

22 Jan 1886   *A holiday was given this Afternoon on the event of a treat in the School-room.*

                  ❧

14 Jan 1887   *A holiday was given this afternoon for children's Tea.*

24 Jun 1887   [Two days holiday for Queen Victoria's Golden Jubilee.]

                  ❧

20 Jan 1888   *A holiday was given this afternoon and a treat given to the Children in the Evening.*

                  ❧

17 Jan 1890   *A holiday given this afternoon – Annual Xmas treat.* [The Christmas treat had been given in January since 1885.]

                  ❧

16 Jan 1891   *The School was closed to-day Friday on the event of a treat.*

                  ❧

15 Jul 1892   *The School was closed this Afternoon on the event of a treat at the Rectory.* [This may have been to celebrate the marriage of the rector, Dr. Arthur James Skrimshire, to Miss Agnes Maria Groomes. They had married on 10 May at Shalford parish church, the rector's first wife having died the previous year. Miss Groomes' father had been vicar of the parish for twenty-four years before his death. Following the wedding, Dr. and Mrs. Skrimshire spent their honeymoon at Sherborne in Dorset, Mrs. Skrimshire's birthplace. The rector was aged eighty and his bride was fifty.]

                  ❧

6 Jan 1893   *The School was closed this afternoon for the usual Christmas treat.*

7 Jul 1893   *A holiday was given yesterday (Duke of York's wedding.)* [Prince

George, who was later George V, married Princess Victoria Mary of Teck.]

21 Jul 1893   *A holiday was given on Monday and again on Wednesday afternoon on the event of treats.*

5 Jan 1894   *Gave a holiday on Tuesday on the event of a treat in the Village.*

19 Jan 1894   *The School was closed on Friday afternoon on the event of the Annual Treat.*

22 Jun 1894   *The School has the 10 minutes recreation during the Afternoon which will appear on the Time Table for next School year.*

13 Jul 1894   *A holiday was given this afternoon on the event of a School treat.*

18 Jan 1895   *The School was closed on Wednesday Afternoon on the event of a treat.*

17 Jan 1896   *The School has closed this Afternoon on the event of the Annual School treat followed by an Entertainment by the Children. The Average has been good as is usual just before these Events.*

24 Jan 1896   *The School was again closed this afternoon (Sunday School Treat).*

17 Jul 1896   *The School was closed this afternoon on the event of a treat @ the Rectory.*

29 Jan 1897   *The School was closed on Wednesday.* [Annual school treat]

18 Jun 1897   *The School was closed to-day for the Jubilee week.* [This was to celebrate Queen Victoria's Diamond Jubilee.]

22 Dec 1898   *The Rector distributed books for regular Attendance.* [Martha Lovibond's endowment for a Sunday School still produced an income of £21 per annum and, as the Rector was one of the trustees, he may have used some of the money to purchase the books. £21 would be worth nearly £1,200 in today's money.]

26 May 1899   *The school was also closed on Wednesday on the Event of the Queen's birthday.* [Queen Victoria was 80 years old.]

14 Jul 1899   *The School was closed on Monday afternoon on the event of a treat.*

19 Oct 1900   *The School was closed on Wednesday on the event of a Carnival and the regularity of Attendance has been broken in consequence.*

Pleased to Meet You

As A CHURCH SCHOOL, Hadleigh National School was frequently visited by the local rectors and their curates. The rector was also one of the managers of the school. Another visitor in the years 1863 to 1886 was another school manager, Mr. James Tyrrell, who farmed at Blossoms Farm and lived in the farmhouse on the village street. James Tyrrell was a prominent figure in the village, being a churchwarden, an overseer, surveyor and waywarden for the parish. Other prominent members of the village would also visit, including the wives of the rectors and Lady Nicholson of Hadleigh House. From May 1878 Rev. Arthur J. Skrimshire was often accompanied on his visits by 'a lady friend'. This was Miss Agnes Maria Groomes, who lived at the rectory with the rector and his wife. After the death of Mrs. Emily Skrimshire in 1881 after a long illness, the rector married Miss Groomes on 10 May 1892.

Author's Note

To facilitate the reading of this chapter, I have totalled the number of visits by regular visitors such as the curates and Rev. Skrimshire, rather than including each log book entry. These totals are included at the beginning of each year.

Log Book Entries

Miss Cecilia Miller had been appointed mistress in 1861

[Rev. John Godson, the curate at St. James the Less, was a frequent visitor and would often teach Scripture and other subjects to the children. He made forty-nine visits during 1863, visiting at least once each week.]

23 Feb 1863   *The Rector visited the School.* [Rev. Thomas Espinell Espin was the rector at St. James the Less from 1853 until 1868.]

Between 6 July and 27 July 1863, there was no master or mistress. It is unclear who taught the children

7 Jul 1863   *Visited by Mr. Espin.*
9 Jul 1863   *School visited by Mr. Davidson.* [This was probably Rev. Edward Davidson, who had been the curate of Hadleigh about five years earlier.]

William Batchelor Kingswood appointed master 7 September 1863

7 Sep 1863   *W. B. Kingswood acted as Master of the School for the first time. . . Was visited by Mr. Tyrrell, Mr. and Mrs. Espin and Mr. Godson.*

9 Sep 1863   *Mr. and Mrs. Godson looked in in afternoon.* [Rev. John Godson had married Miss Helen Lucy on 1 May 1861 at Holy Trinity Church, Stratford on Avon.]

10 Sep 1863   *Visited by Mr. Espin and friends.* [They visited again on 2 October and on 25 November.]

16 Sep 1863   *Was visited in afternoon by Mr. and Mrs. Espin.* [They visited again on 28 September.]

[Between January and March 1864 Rev. Godson visited nine times. He then left Hadleigh to become the curate at Boyne Hill in Berkshire. His replacement, Rev. Joseph Baines, was also a frequent visitor and taught lessons. Between May and December 1864 he made twenty-three visits, generally visiting once a week.]

5 Jan 1864   *Mrs. Espin with Company visited school in the morning.*

10 Feb 1864	*Mr. Espin visited in the afternoon.*
18 Mar 1864	*Mr. Godson dismissed the Day School in the afternoon.*
1 Apr 1864	*The Rev. Espin and Company visited the school in the afternoon.*
7 Apr 1864	*Mr. Tyrrell visited the school in the morning.*
9 May 1864	*During this interval the school has been visited many times by the Rev. Espin and Company.* [For a month there were no entries in the log book as the key was lost.]
9 May 1864	*The Rev. Joseph Baines first visited the School to-day and assisted in the usual routine thereof.*
27 May 1864	*Miss Tyrrell visited the School in the afternoon.* [This could be any one of James Tyrrell's oldest daughters: Emma, Mary Ann or Alice. Emma Tyrrell became a school mistress so it could possibly be her.]
8 Jun 1864	*We were visited by a Lady.*
3 Nov 1864	*Rev. Espin called in afternoon.*
16 Dec 1864	*Rev. Espin visited School in afternoon.*

Henry Yeaxlee appointed master 23 January 1865

[The curate, Rev. James Walker, made ten visits in 1866 – in February, March, May and July – until he left the district. In October 1866 Rev. Henry Smith, the new curate, visited for the first time. In the three months up to Christmas he made nine further visits, occasionally teaching Scripture. In September Mrs. Espin, the rector's wife, began visiting the school regularly, often accompanied by Mr. David Bellingham, the choirmaster. She made eight further visits before Christmas.]

22 Feb 1866	*Visited by Mr. Tyrrell.*
12 Jul 1866	*Visited by Mr. Tyrrell.*
6 Aug 1866	*Visited by Revd. T. E. Espin who spoke about the attendance, and the Scripture teaching.*
25 Sep 1866	*Visited by Mrs. Espin.*
9 Oct 1866	*Visited by the Revd. Smith.*
16 Oct 1866	*Visited by Lady Nicholson and friend.* [Miss Sarah Elizabeth Keightley had married Sir Charles Nicholson 1st Baronet in 1865.]
18 Oct 1866	*Visited by Mrs. Smith.* [Sarah Adeline Smith had married the curate in 1857 and was the mother of three young children.]
19 Oct 1866	*Visited by Mr. Tyrrell.*

25 Oct 1866	*Visited this afternoon by Lady Nicholson and friend.*
3 Dec 1866	*Visited by Revd. T. E. Espin.*
7 Dec 1866	*Visited by Lady Nicholson with presents for the girls.*
11 Dec 1866	*Visited by Revd. T. E. Espin & certain ladies.*

[In the first six months of 1867 Rev. Smith visited the school on eleven occasions, often teaching Scripture. In September his replacement as curate, Rev. John Yolland, visited for the first time. From 21 October he made thirteen visits. The rector's wife made four weekly visits at the beginning of the year and then did not visit again until May.]

10 Jan 1867	*Visited by Revd. T. Espin who gave away prizes.*
3 Apr 1867	*Visited by Revd. T. E. Espin.* [He made two further visits in April.]
17 May 1867	*Visited by Mrs. Espin.*
3 Jul 1867	*Visited by the Revd. Henderson.* [Rev. Thomas Julius Henderson was the vicar of St. Mary's Church at South Benfleet and a former curate at St. James the Less.]
11 Jul 1867	*Visited by Lady Nicholson and friend.*
17 Sep 1867	*Visited in the afternoon by the Revd. J. Yolland and Mrs. Yolland.*
19 Sep 1867	*Visited by Mr. Tyrell in the morning.*

[Rev. Yolland only made three visits in 1868, as he left the district in January. He accompanied Rev. Espin to Wallasey in Cheshire, where he became his curate. From January 1868 the parish of Hadleigh did not employ a curate. Mrs. Metcalfe, the new rector's wife, visited the school regularly between April and July 1868, generally once a week. She then made three visits in October and November.]

6 Jan 1868	*Mr. Espin paid his farewell visit in the afternoon.* [He left Hadleigh to become the rector of Wallasey in Cheshire.]
12 Feb 1868	*Visited by the Revd. J. Henderson.* [The vicar of South Benfleet probably visited as the parish was without a rector at the time.]
24 Mar 1868	*Visited this morning by Mr. Tyrrell.*
2 Apr 1868	*Visited by a lady.*
2 Apr 1868	*Visited in the morning by Mr. Tyrrell.*
8 Apr 1868	*Visited this morning for the first time by Revd. W. Metcalfe.* [Rev. William Metcalfe was born at Wisbech in Cambridgeshire in about

1831. His previous post had been as curate at St. Mary's church at Brinkley in Cambridgeshire.]

21 Apr 1868   *Visited this afternoon by Mrs. Metcalfe. [Formerly Miss Rosa Sophia Skey, the daughter of a surgeon, she had married William Metcalfe on 5 February 1863.]*

17 Aug 1868   *Visited in the morning by the Revd. W. Metcalfe.*

27 Aug 1868   *Visited by a lady.*

31 Aug 1868   *Visited this morning by a lady.*

7 Sep 1868   *Visited by an unknown lady.*

23 Sep 1868   *Visited by a stranger.*

15 Sep 1868   *Visited this afternoon by the Revd. W. Metcalfe.*

20 Oct 1868   *Visited by Mr. Tyrrell. [He made a further visit on 26 October.]*

16 Nov 1868   *Visited this afternoon by Lady Nicholson and friend.*

16 Dec 1868   *Visited in the morning by a lady.*

[Rev. Metcalfe, the rector, made regular visits to the school, generally once a month. Although he did not visit in February, May or September, there were eleven visits made in 1869.]

28 Apr 1869   *Visited in the Afternoon by Mr. & Mrs. Metcalfe.*

11 Oct 1869   *Visited this afternoon by Lady Nicholson & Mrs. Metcalfe.*

10 Nov 1869   *Visited this afternoon by Lady Nicholson & the Revd. W. Metcalfe.*

19 Nov 1869   *Visited by Mrs. Metcalfe.*

15 Dec 1869   *Visited by Mrs. Metcalfe.*

20 Dec 1869   *Visited this afternoon by Mr. & Mrs. Metcalfe who gave the children notice of a forthcoming treat.*

[There were few visitors to the school in 1870, so all visits have been recorded.]

10 Jan 1870   *Visited by Dr. Byas. [Dr. James Byass, of 'Holly Trees' at Rayleigh Weir, was the local surgeon.]*

15 Mar 1870   *Visited this morning by the Revd. W. Metcalfe. [First recorded visit for nearly three months.]*

16 Mar 1870   *Visited this morning by the Revd. W. & Mrs. Metcalfe who distributed the remaining Christmas prizes.*

4 Apr 1870   *Visited this afternoon by Mrs. Metcalfe.*

19 May 1870   *Visited this afternoon by the Revd. W. Metcalfe, to speak about the Confirmation Day.*

1 Dec 1870   *Visited by Mr. Tyrrell this morning.*

~

[Again there were few visits to the school in 1871. Only two visits by Rev. Metcalfe, the rector, are recorded for the year.]

19 Jan 1871   *Visited by Mr. Tyrrell.*

17 Mar 1871   *This morning (Friday) the Rector and Mrs. Metcalfe visited the School to give the Christmas Prizes.* [This was the rector's first recorded visit since the previous May.]

29 Mar 1871   *Mr. Tyrrell visited the school on Wednesday morning.*

28 Jul 1871   *The Revd. W. Metcalfe visited the School on Monday afternoon.*

22 Sep 1871   *Mr. Tyrrell visited the school on Wednesday.*

~

27 Sep 1872   *The School was visited on Tuesday by Mr. Tyrrell.* [His first recorded visit in a year.]

24 Oct 1872   *Visited by the Revd. W. Metcalfe.* [His first recorded visit for over a year.]

1 Nov 1872   *Mr. J. Tyrrell visited the School.*

~

17 Jan 1873   *On Friday Morning the Rector visited the School to distribute prizes.*

14 Mar 1873   *On Tuesday Mr. Tyrrell visited the school.*

28 Mar 1873   *The School was visited by Mr. Tyrrell.*

3 Apr 1873   *The Revd. W. Metcalfe visited the School on Wednesday.* [The log book records only two visits by the rector in 1873.]

4 Jul 1873   *The school was visited by Mr. Tyrrell on Thursday Morning.*

3 Oct 1873   *The school has been visited by Mr. Tyrrell twice this week.*

~

[Henry Yeaxlee recorded no visits by the rector in 1874, although he may have visited.]

13 Feb 1874   *The school was visited on Thursday morning by Mr. J. Tyrrell.*

13 Nov 1874   *The school was visited on Thursday morning by Mr. Tyrrell*

27 Nov 1874   *The school was visited on Monday by Mr. J. Tyrrell.*

4 Dec 1874   *The school was visited on Monday morning by Mr. J. Tyrrell.*

~

17 Feb 1875   *The school was visited on Wednesday afternoon by Mrs. Metcalfe.* [Her first recorded visit for four years.]

5 Mar 1875   *The school was visited this morning by Mr. Tyrrell.*

Between 19 March and 17 May 1875, in the absence of a master, the rector ran the school

23 Apr 1875   *Mr. Tyrrell visited the School on Thursday afternoon.*

7 May 1875   *Mr. Tyrrell came to the School on Wednesday morning.*

Alfred Hawks appointed master 17 May 1875

21 May 1875   *I, Alfred Hawks, commenced my duties as Master of this School.* [On Monday 17 May.] *Visitors:- Thursday – Mr. Tyrrell, this morning – Mrs. Metcalfe.*

10 Sep 1875   *Visitors:- Tuesday Rev. W. Metcalfe Thursday Mr. Tyrrell.*

24 Sep 1875   *The School and grounds have been visited several times by Mr. Tyrrell.*

22 Oct 1875   *Mr. Tyrrell visited the School on Monday and again to-day.*

12 Nov 1875   *School visited to-day by Mr. Tyrrell.*

26 Nov 1875   *The School was visited by Lady Nicholson on Tuesday who promised some cake to the children on their breaking up for the Christmas Vacation.*

[1876 saw more visits to the school, following the death of the rector, Rev. William Metcalfe, on 17 January. While the village had no clergyman, Mr. James Tyrrell, a local farmer and a school manager, started visiting the school more regularly. Between February and July he visited on ten occasions. The new rector, Dr. Skrimshire, was a qualified doctor who had retrained as a clergyman. From July 1876 he made weekly visits to the school, making thirteen visits altogether.]

25 Feb 1876   *The School was visited by Mr. Tyrrell on Monday.*

16 Jun 1876   *Mr. Tyrrell called yesterday morning and informed me of the new Rector's visit to the village.* [The new rector was Rev. Arthur James Skrimshire, born 15 April 1814 in Peterborough, which was then in Northamptonshire.]

14 Jul 1876   *The School was visited yesterday and to-day by the Rector Revd. Skrimshire.*

4 Aug 1876   *The School was visited by Mr. Tyrrell to-day.*

13 Oct 1876   *Mr. Tyrrell visited the School on Tuesday.*

15 Dec 1876   *The School was visited yesterday by Mr. Tyrrell.*

[In 1877 Rev. Skrimshire continued to make regular visits to the school. In the first six months of the year he made eighteen such visits. From September until the end of the year he only visited once a month.]

16 Feb 1877	*The School has been visited once by Mr. Tyrrell.*
28 Sep 1877	*Visited on Wednesday by the Rector and Mr. Tyrrell.*

[The rector made seventeen visits in 1878. From May he was accompanied on six of these visits by 'a lady friend', who was probably Miss Groomes. Rev. Skrimshire made no visits in June, so these were carried out by Mr. Tyrrell.]

8 Mar 1878	*Visited on Wednesday by Mr. Tyrrell.*
10 May 1878	*The School was visited by the Rector and a lady friend on Wednesday.*
17 May 1878	*On Wednesday the School was visited by a lady from the Rectory.*
7 Jun 1878	*Visited on Tuesday by Mr. Tyrrell.* [This was the day of the annual inspection. He visited twice in the following week.]
5 Jul 1878	*Mr. Tyrrell visited on Tuesday.*
26 Jul 1878	*Visited on Tuesday by Mr. Tyrrell and the Rector.*
27 Sep 1878	*Visited by Mr. Tyrrell this morning.*
4 Oct 1878	*Visited by Mr. Tyrrell on Thursday.* [Mr. Tyrrell visited on three more occasions in October. This was probably due to the measles epidemic which was seriously affecting attendance.]
22 Nov 1878	*Visited by the Rector on Monday and by Mr. Tyrrell on Tuesday.* [This was following the closure of the school for nearly a month due to a measles epidemic.]

[The rector continued to visit regularly, making twenty-four visits in 1879. On four of these occasions he was accompanied by a lady friend. Mr. Tyrrell made more visits in 1879, which are all recorded below.]

21 Feb 1879	*Visited on Tuesday by Mr. Tyrrell.*
15 Mar 1879	*Visited on Tuesday by Mr. Tyrrell.*
25 Apr 1879	*Visited on Wednesday by Mr. Tyrrell.*
9 May 1879	*Visited twice this week by Mr. Tyrrell.* [He also visited on 28 May.]

13 Jun 1879	*Visited on Tuesday and Wednesday by Mr. Tyrrell.* [He made two other visits in June. The annual inspection was held on 20 June.]
29 Aug 1879	*Visited this morning by the Rector and Mr. Tyrrell.*
12 Dec 1879	*Visited by Mr. Tyrrell twice.*

[In the first six months of 1880 the Rev. Skrimshire visited on eighteen occasions, seven of them with Miss Groomes. Between 2 July and 26 October there were no visits from the rector. In November and December he made seven more visits. Mr. Tyrrell made seven visits in the four months from April to July.]

27 Feb 1880	*Mr. Tyrrell called this morning.*
29 Oct 1880	*Visited on Wednesday by Mr. Tyrrell.*
19 Nov 1880	*Visited on Tuesday by Rector and Revd. H. Hayes.* [Rev. Henry Hayes was the vicar of Canvey Island.]
3 Dec 1880	*Visited today by Rector and Revd. H. Hayes.*
26 Nov 1880	*Visited on Wednesday by Mr. Tyrrell.*
10 Dec 1880	*Visited on Wednesday by Mr. Tyrrell.*

[In 1881 Rev. Skrimshire continued to visit each month the school was open, totalling thirty-six visits for the year. On five occasions he was accompanied by Miss Groomes.]

18 Mar 1881	*Visited on Wednesday by the Rector and Rev. Heaton.*
22 Apr 1881	*Visited by Mr. Tyrrell.*
6 May 1881	*Visited by Mr. Tyrrell on Tuesday and today.*
27 May 1881	*Visited by Mr. Tyrrell on Monday.*
3 Jun 1881	*A meeting was held in the School room on Thursday when several fresh gentlemen promised to act as Managers of the School, the Chair was taken by the Rector.*
15 Jul 1881	*Visited by Mr. Tyrrell.*
29 Jul 1881	*Visited this morning by the Rector & lady friend, also by Mr. Tyrrell on Wednesday.*
16 Sep 1881	*Visited by Rector and Miss Groomes this afternoon, also by Mr. Tyrrell, Mr. Gilliat and friend.* [Mr. Alfred Gilliat was living at Hadleigh House at this time.]
30 Sep 1881	*Visited by Mr. Tyrrell on Wednesday.*
4 Nov 1881	*Visited by Mr. Tyrrell on Wednesday morning.*

11 Nov 1881	*Visited to-day by Mr. Tyrrell.*
18 Nov 1881	*Visited on Wednesday by the Revd. Talfourd.* [Rev. William Wordsworth Talfourd was the rector of Thundersley.]
16 Dec 1881	*Visited on Thursday by Mr. Tyrrell.*

[Thirty-five visits were made by Rev. Skrimshire in 1882, although no visits were made by him in April. On twelve of those occasions he was accompanied by Miss Groomes. In fact, in one week in February they visited the school three times.]

6 Jan 1882	*Visited by Mr. Tyrrell.*
15 Sep 1882	*Visited yesterday by Mr. Tyrrell.*
24 Nov 1882	*Miss Groomes called yesterday.*

[In 1883, although Miss Groomes made four visits on her own to the school, she also accompanied the rector on seventeen occasions, mainly in the first five months of the year. Rev. Skrimshire made forty-one visits to the school, including when he was accompanied by Miss Groomes. In August 1883 he started to visit the school to check the registers. This was usually done about twice each month.]

13 Apr 1883	*Visited twice by Miss Groomes.*
25 May 1883	*Visited on Monday by the Rector and Mr. Tyrrell who informed me of the day of Inspection.*
8 Jun 1883	*The Annual Meeting of Managers was held on Monday when the School Account and Registers were thoroughly Examined and found correct.*
13 Jul 1883	*Visited on Monday by Miss Groomes.*
27 Jul 1883	*Miss Groomes called in on Wednesday and Mr. Tyrrell on Friday.*
3 Aug 1883	*Visited on Wednesday by the Rector who checked the Registers and was quite satisfied.*

[In 1884 Rev. Skrimshire visited on thirty occasions, only two of these with Miss Groomes. Mr. James Tyrrell made no further visits to the school after July 1883. He died on 31 August 1886, aged seventy-six.]

| 25 Jan 1884 | *Visited on Tuesday by Miss Groomes.* |
| 22 Feb 1884 | *Visited by Mrs. & Miss Fergusson.* [The wife and daughter of Mr. |

Robert Fergusson currently living at Hadleigh House.]

31 Oct 1884 *Miss Groomes called this morning.*

[Rev. Skrimshire made thirty-four visits to the school in 1885, although over two-thirds of them were made in the first six months of the year. He continued to check the registers, although not so regularly as before. Miss Groomes only accompanied him on two occasions in October and December.]

27 Nov 1885 *Visited on Tuesday by the Rector and the Rev. Henry Hayes, Vicar of Canvey Island.*

[By 1886 Rev. Skrimshire was seventy years old and his visits to the school became less frequent. Only nineteen visits were made during the year, and none with Miss Groomes. This may have been due to the fact that Emily Skrimshire, the rector's wife, was an invalid and needed her husband and Miss Groomes to care for her. The rector generally checked the registers once a month.]

[By 1887 the rector was only visiting the school about once a month, usually to check the registers. He only visited the school on fifteen occasions.]

18 Feb 1887 *Visited on Thursday by the Rector and Miss Groomes.*

[Only six visits are recorded in the log book for 1888, all in the first five months of the year. No visits are recorded after May, although this does not mean that the rector did not visit.]

[Rev. Skrimshire again made only six visits during 1889, usually to check the registers. No visits were made during January, February, March, July, October and December.]

26 Apr 1889 *Visited by the Rector who checked the numbers.* [This was his first visit since 10 May 1888.]

[In 1890 the number of visits by the rector increased to fourteen, although his main reason for visiting was to check the registers.]

21 Nov 1890   *The Rector called with lady friend on Tuesday.*

[Emily Skrimshire, the rector's wife, died on 3 February 1891 after being an invalid for many years. Rev. Skrimshire only visited the school on five recorded occasions during the year.]

16 Jan 1891   *Visited by the Rector.*
13 Mar 1891   *Visited by Rector on Monday.*
16 Oct 1891   *Visited on Thursday by the Rector who checked the Registers.*
30 Oct 1891   *The Rector visited on Tuesday to check the numbers.*
27 Nov 1891   *The Rector checked the Registers.*

[The rector married Miss Groomes on 10 May 1892. He only made three visits during the year.]

24 Jun 1892   *Visited by Rector to check the Registers.*
7 Oct 1892   *The Rector visited on Tuesday to check the Registers.*
25 Nov 1892   *Visited by the Rector on Wednesday.*

[In 1893 Rev. Skrimshire visited on seven occasions to check the registers during the first six months of the year.]

20 Oct 1893   *The Rector visited on Wednesday to check the Registers.*

[Rev. Skrimshire made six visits in 1894, before he left the parish in the summer. Although he was now elderly, he moved, with his wife Agnes, to Bag Enderby in Lincolnshire. Here he worked as the rector until his death on 8 June 1906, aged ninety-two. Agnes Skrimshire, the former Miss Groomes, died on 4 September 1896, aged fifty-five.]

2 Aug 1894   *Visited on Tuesday by the Rector to check the Registers.* [This was Rev. Skrimshire's last recorded visit to the school.
5 Oct 1894   *The Rev. A. G. Metcalfe, the new Rector, arrives to-day.* [Rev. Armine George Metcalfe was a relative of Rev. William Metcalfe, the rector of Hadleigh from 1867 to 1876. Born on 2 August 1868, Armine Metcalfe was the son of a clergyman and had been educated at Selwyn College, Cambridge. Prior to becoming the rector of Hadleigh, he had been the curate of Fressingfield in Suffolk for two years.]

26 Oct 1894	*Visited this afternoon by the Rector Revd. A. Metcalfe who checked the Registers*
2 Nov 1894	*I was absent yesterday afternoon and the Rector came & assisted in the School.* [Two weeks later he gave a Scripture lesson to the children.]
23 Nov 1894	*The Rector called and checked the Registers on Tuesday.*
14 Dec 1894	*Visited on Wednesday by the Rector.*

[Rev. Armine Metcalfe visited the school on fifteen occasions in 1895. He generally visited once or twice a month, although no visits were made in July and October. On four of those occasions he checked the registers. For the first time in twelve years other managers of the school visited.]

15 Nov 1895	*Mr. Stannard, one of the Managers, checked the Registers on Monday Morning, and entered his signature in same.* [Charles Richard Stannard owned *The Stores*, a grocery shop in the village street.]
29 Nov 1895	*Mr. Hart checked Registers on Tuesday.* [Talbot Hart lived in Hadleigh Cottage in Rectory Road.]

[The rector visited the school eleven times in 1896, although on four of those occasions he was in charge of the school. Generally Rev. Metcalfe visited the school once a month, although no visit was made in June.]

21 Feb 1896	*The Rector has taken charge of the School three days this week, owing to indisposition of the Master.*
24 Apr 1896	*School visited Wednesday by Mr. Hart who checked the Registers.*
4 Dec 1896	*The Rector took charge of School on Wednesday Afternoon to allow the Mistress to visit a good School at Southend.*
11 Dec 1896	*Mr. Stannard checked the Registers.*

[In 1897 Rev. Armine Metcalfe generally visited the school once a month, occasionally checking the registers. He made twelve visits in 1897, although no visits were made in July and December.]

[In 1898 the rector made only nine visits to the school, three of them in December. No visits were made by him in February, April, June, and July.]

4 Feb 1898	*Mr. Hart checked the Registers.*
22 Apr 1898	*Mr. Stannard called and checked the Registers on Tuesday.*
22 Dec 1898	*The Rector distributed books for regular Attendance.*

[Rev. Metcalfe only made four visits to the school in 1899 – in February, May, September and December – in order to check the registers.]

[Seven visits were made by the rector in 1900. He made no visits in January, May, June, September and December.]

9 Mar 1900	*The Rector is taking charge of the School this afternoon.*

Bricks and Mortar

ROM THE 1840S THE style of school architecture was deliberately Ecclesiastical Gothic, aiming to promote religion along with education. The National Society for Promoting the Education of the Poor supported the building of National Schools on behalf of the Church of England. The teaching method used influenced the interior layout of the school. George Edmund Street designed the school at Hadleigh in 1855 with one large schoolroom, which could accommodate up to one hundred children, supervised by just one qualified master. His plans show fixed rows of desks facing the master's desk. Traditionally, standards were placed at the end of the rows in this style of school marking the different age groups. This is why the name 'Standard' was later used to describe a class.

It was also in the 1840s that separate classrooms were added to many schools for infants, and the Hadleigh school is built in this style. Street's design includes a gallery, where the desks were arranged on steps, so that the infant mistress could see all the children and they could see the pictures that lessons were based on.

In the winter months in the 1860s and 1870s the school building was used as a

23. Longitudinal section from architect plans, 1855

night school for boys over the age of twelve or thirteen. To earn extra money, the managers of Hadleigh National School would also let the schoolroom in the evening for concerts, as the village had no parish hall. This sometimes necessitated the school closing early, or for a half-holiday, so that the desks could be moved. The National School would not have employed a caretaker so the school was opened by the master or mistress, and the schoolrooms were cleaned by the teaching staff and the children.

From the 1880s the more comprehensive inspection reports received by the school managers, from Her Majesty's Inspectors, commented on the overcrowding in the school. Mr. Arthur E. Bernays, the inspector who visited the school in 1893-5, was critical of the building and suggested improvements to the managers. Following two years of reports criticising the overcrowding in the school, the managers took his advice in 1895 and added a new infant room. In the years 1898-1900, Mr. Frederick Dugard, the school inspector, was more concerned about the state of the outside toilets: *"Special care must be taken to keep the offices in a satisfactory condition."*

24. East and west elevation from architect plans, 1855

Log Book Entries

Miss Cecilia Miller had been appointed mistress in 1861

20 Jan 1863 — *Morning wet and stormy, lower classes thin. Three squares of glass out, attempted to paste them up with brown paper.*

30 Apr 1863 — *Very cold day – unable to open coal house door, consequently could have no fire.* [The school room would be heated by a fireplace, which would give inadequate heat to keep all the children warm.]

11 Jun 1863 — *Mr. Godson* [the curate] *cautioned children against . . . destroying shrubs in School yard.*

William Batchelor Kingswood appointed master 7 September 1863

7 Sep 1863 — *Cautioned children against destroying the fences and laurels in and around the playground.*

11 Sep 1863 — *Was hindered 30 minutes in morning by the removal of chairs etc. after concert.*

4 Jan 1864 — *The coalhouse door was forced open during the Xmas week and the lock injured by someone, but could not discover that anything was missing.*

14 Mar 1864 — *Some of the Boys were engaged in a little industrial exercise in the School Garden at noon and evening.*

15 Mar 1864 — *M. A. Warren was caught actually destroying the Flowers and trees around the School grounds.*

24 Oct 1864 — *Boys rolled the school paths with Rev. Espin's Iron roller.*

31 Oct 1864 — *Reported to Mr. Tyrrell the state of window casements and the arch over door leading into the Infants' room.* [Mr. James Tyrrell, who farmed Blossoms Farm, was a school manager]

Henry Yeaxlee appointed master 23 January 1865

19 Feb 1866 — *Spoke to the managers about the bad state of the windows.*

1 Jan 1867 — *Gave the children a half-holiday to prepare the room for a Concert.*

3 Jan 1867 — *School prepared for a Tea party in the evening.*

12 Apr 1867 — *Dismissed the School a half-hour earlier in consequence of the room*

being let for the evening.

~

25 Nov 1868   *Much inconvenienced in the morning by having to move all the desks &c. back into their places – they having been moved by a conjuror.* [Presumably the school had been let for a magic show!]

~

18 Mar 1869   *Very much hindered this morning by having to rearrange the desks &c., the school having been let last night.*

1 Dec 1869   *Hindered for a few minutes this morning in removing things in the room used at a Choir supper.*

~

13 Jan 1870   *The School Business partly hindered by a concert this afternoon.*

~

3 Feb 1871   *The School was slightly disturbed this afternoon, by arrangements for a Choir Supper.*

4 Feb 1871   *Slightly hindered this morning by the table-moving &c.*

8 Dec 1871   *A present of Fire-wood received this morning from Mr. S. Harvey, for the School.* [Stephen Harvey, a Leigh farmer, was Henry Yeaxlee's father-in-law.]

~

8 Jan 1872   *Upon returning to school I was for some time occupied in re-arranging the desks &c., they having been removed for a concert.*

~

3 Apr 1873   *The Revd. W. Metcalfe visited the School on Wednesday, and inspected the building & walls.*

2 May 1873   *The school premises have been put in thorough order in accordance with the advice contained in the last report.*

31 Oct 1873   *The school was visited on Thursday morning by Mr. Tyrrell, who . . . inspected some bricklayers' repairs to the fire-place &c.*

Alfred Hawks appointed master 17 May 1875

12 Nov 1875   *The School was closed on Tuesday to give the Master a holliday* [sic], *when the windows were mended.*

~

11 Feb 1876   *One of the School desks were* [sic] *mended yesterday.*

19 May 1876   *The School was visited yesterday by Mr. Tyrrell who inspected the playground and back places.* [These were the outside toilets.]

28 Jul 1876   *The fence at the back of the School should be repaired.* [Copy of

HMI Report]

1 Dec 1876   *Yesterday the widows* [sic] *were mended throughout the School.*

15 Dec 1876   *The School was visited yesterday by Mr. Tyrrell who inspected the back-places. I had for some time been endeavouring to find how so many bricks get removed from the top of the closet; but on Wednesday Evening I caught one of the boys on the wall attending to a trap which he had skillfully* [sic] *made, with the aid of four bricks for each trap, which had been pulled off the Closet. I have strong hopes that such proceedings will not continue after the heavy punishment I felt compelled to* . . . [the last word is illegible.]

2 Feb 1877   *A good substantial path has been made from the road to the School-room door which was sadly needed, also drains have been made to carry the water from the playground into a side-ditch. Mr. Tyrrell has given instructions for the water to be carried from the gutters of the School into the ditch. I think, in case we are visited with so much rain again that, both School and premises will be in a much drier state than during the past winter.*

27 Feb 1880   *Mr. Tyrrell called this morning and promised to let us have some new desks if possible. We are also to have a table for the girls' work.*

26 Nov 1880   *Visited on Wednesday by Mr. Tyrrell, who promised to have a new store put in the Infant room.*

14 Jan 1881   *The School was closed on Wednesday afternoon and Thursday morning on the event of a Concert.*

13 May 1881   *The Managers have ordered the fence to be painted, and intend having the School re-coloured and cleaned either before the Inspection or in the Summer Vacation.*

2 Dec 1881   *Closed School on Thursday morning for the rest of the week on account of a Concert.*

26 Jan 1883   *Had half-holliday* [sic] *on Friday on the event of a concert.*

22 Feb 1884   *A half-holiday was given on Friday on the event of a Concert in the evening.*

29 Nov 1889   *The Closets and all the back places have been emptied & thoroughly cleaned.*

⁕

27 Oct 1893	*Most of the Recommendations of H. M. Inspector have already been attended to especially with regard to furniture.*
10 Nov 1893	*Three new desks have arrived and been placed on the Infant gallery which is a great improvement.*

⁕

9 Mar 1894	*The Offices at the back are also being rebuilt, according to the plans approved of by the Ed. Department.* [The offices were the outside toilets.]
22 Mar 1894	*The School was closed to-day for the Easter week's Vacation and the School will be cleaned and painted inside and out.*
1 Jun 1894	*A new Cupboard was placed in the room to-day.*

⁕

5 Jul 1895	*The School was closed on Wednesday on the Event of a Bazaar in aid of the School Building Fund.* [Due to the overcrowding in the school, especially in the infant room, an extension was to be built on the front of the school.]
16 Jul 1895	[Written in the log book and initialled by Mr. Arthur E. Bernays, the HMI.] *Suitable desks shd. be provided for the class-room, when it ceases to be used by the infants, for whom there are not yet enough pictures (none indeed of trees, plants & [word illegible]), and the ball frame ought to be mounted as advised.*
	The offices need more light & ventilation & are at present very offensive.
26 Jul 1895	*The School is closed to-day for the Summer Vacation when the new Infs-room is to be built and other alterations made.*
27 Sep 1895	*The new room for Infants is now in use and the old Inf.-room used as a Class room for Older Scholars. The alterations are of incalculable value & have given Every Satisfaction.*
11 Oct 1895	*The new desks are now fixed for Infants & are very satisfactory. Now that the playground has been made level I hope to have a flower bed or two & thus encourage a love for flowers among the children.*
1 Nov 1895	*Fires have been general throughout the School and each of the rooms have been most comfortable – the tortoise stoves are a great success.* [The tortoise stove originated in Essex in 1830. Charles Portway set up a small foundry to manufacture these slow-burning solid-fuel stoves.]
13 Dec 1895	*A new lamp has been fixed in the Infant room.*

⁕

23 Oct 1896   *The School was closed on Wednesday Afternoon on the event of an Entertainment.*

23 Dec 1897   *A Grant of £25.10.0. has been made under the Voluntary Schools Aid Grant in respect of the current financial year for the purpose of increasing Salaries and effecting repairs.*

3 Mar 1899   *A Grant of £30.10.0. has been made under the Voluntary Schools Aid Grant for . . . equipment & repairs £15.* [The grant of £15 for equipment and repairs would be worth about £855 in today's money.]

26 Jan 1900   *A Grant of £27.0.0. has been made under the Voluntary Schools Aid Grant for equipment & repairs £12.* [The grant of £12 for equipment and repairs would be worth about £684 in today's money.]

The Night School

The managers of the National School ran a night school for boys over the age of thirteen, who wanted to continue their education but had to work during the day. The curriculum was restricted to reading, writing and arithmetic. These classes would have been financed by a small government grant and the pupils' school pence. The Revised Code of 1862 allowed 2/6d (12^1/$_2$p) per night school pupil, based on average attendance, and up to 5/- (25p) per pupil based on the inspector's examination. Usually these night schools were only held during the winter months and there is evidence in the school log book that the night school closed in the spring. There is no further mention of the night school after 1877.

Log Book Entries

William Batchelor Kingswood appointed master 7 September 1863

18 Mar 1864   *The Night School closed this week.*

Henry Yeaxlee appointed master 23 January 1865

31 Oct 1866   [Annual inspection of school by Mr. Nevill Gream, HMI of Schools.]
1 Nov 1866   <u>*Copy of Report*</u>: *No grant will in future be paid for the average number of Evening scholars, unless such of them as have attended 24 times and upwards be also examined. The examination of Evening scholars may be held at any time of the year pursuant to Articles 142-9.*

2 Apr 1867   *The Night School closed.*

24 Feb 1868   *Obliged to be absent from school this morning on night-school business.*

25 Feb 1868   *Examination of Night School by Rev. J. Henderson & Mr. Tyrrell.* [The managers of the school.]

23 Mar 1869   *Night School examined by Mr. Metcalfe and Mr. Tyrrell.* [The managers of the school.]

2 Feb 1871   *Gave the night school their examination last night.*

Alfred Hawks appointed master 17 May 1875

8 Sep 1876   *The Rector* [Rev. Arthur J. Skrimshire] *visited the School on Wednesday and entered into conversation with myself respecting a Night School, which is to become the subject of an Experiment.*

5 Oct 1877   *I have opened a night School this week, with seventeen on the books.*

The Future of the School

I HAVE CHOSEN TO END this book on 1 January 1901 when the 20th century officially began. What did the future hold for the National School in the new century?

When the census was held on 31 March 1901 the population was 1,340, more than double 1891's figure of 520. It was to further increase by the time of the 1911 Census to 1,705.

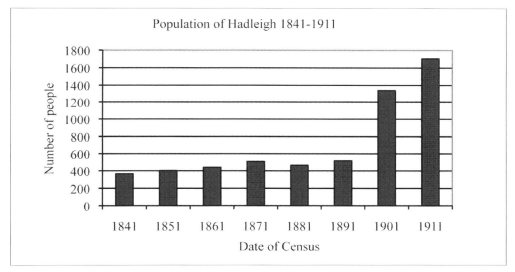

25. Chart of the population of Hadleigh 1841-1911

This massive increase in the population was due to the Salvation Army opening its Farm Colony in 1891. Between June 1891 and the end of the year, the number of colonists increased from 45 to 250. The Salvation Army continued to purchase land and property so that, by 1902, *Kelly's Directory* reported that: *"The Colony now comprises about 3,000 acres of arable and pasture land. . . . At present the Colony numbers some 550 persons."*

This rapid increase in population had an obvious consequence for the National School. In 1895 the school was enlarged to allow it to accommodate 155 pupils. As the last entry in the log book is for 26 February 1909 (unfortunately the next log book is now lost), it is possible to determine how the master, Alfred Hawks, assessed the situation.

In December 1901 he recorded his decision not to admit any more children as the school was full. The average daily attendance, for the week ending 3 October 1902, was 143. A solution was found to the problem in January 1903: *"The School re-opened on Monday and the numbers on books were reduced by 62 leaving only 116. This reduction was owing to a School being opened on the Salvation Army Colony."* The *Chelmsford Chronicle* report of 2 January 1903 gave further details: *"The school buildings in Castle-avenue* [sic], *on the Salvation Army Colony . . . are to be opened on Monday next, with Mr. S. Collins as head master, and Miss Clara C. Abbotts as mistress . . . . The schools are furnished with the most up-to-date desks, books, and general accessories. They are free to children of all ages in the parish of Hadleigh and the neighbourhood."* The main school and the infants school were housed in the Colony citadel and library.

In spite of this, Alfred Hawks continued to admit children to the National School and, by September 1903, there were 148 children 'on the books', with a weekly average attendance of 125. A year later the school was once again overcrowded, with the entry for 28 October 1904 recording: *"This has been a record week the average reaching 161 with 174 on the books."* By May 1905 there were 183 children 'on the books'.

The Inspection Report for 1906 highlighted some of the problems of overcrowding and also the need for refurbishment of the building: *"The premises need cleaning and painting. The cloakroom accommodation for girls and boys is quite inadequate; and there is no lavatory. The class-room is very cramped and ill ventilated. It is not large enough to enable the class to be well organised. The main room is very full. . . . The stove in the main room is nearly worn out. Some of the desks need renewing. There are some bigger children too big for the present desks."*

The Board of Education now intervened to solve the problems in the school. Concerned about the growing population of Hadleigh, which would number 1,705 by April 1911, the Board wrote to the parish council regarding the opening of a new council elementary school in the village. Under the proposal, the Colony school would be closed, with the Board of Education refusing to recognise the school after 30 September 1907. At the Essex County Education Committee meeting on 28 October 1907, it was resolved: *"that formal notice be given re new school to serve the needs of Hadleigh and part of Thundersley (Daws Heath)."*

In response to this resolution, Hadleigh parish council held a meeting on 27 November 1907 to consider the proposed new public elementary school for the village. The meeting was reported in the *Chelmsford Chronicle* of 29 November: *"Mr. H. J. Mitchell, who presided, said they had tried to show the Board of Education that there was no need for the Army Schools to be closed or for a burden to be thrust on the parish which would crush its life. . . . The Chairman said the cost of the school would be £20 per head for the 200 children, and the parish would have to bear two-*

thirds of the cost. Resolutions were carried expressing regret at the intention of the County Education Committee to build a school for Hadleigh and Thundersley protesting against such proposal, and requesting the Chairman to take steps and resist the intention." Incidentally, Alfred Hawks, the master of the National School, had been elected a member of the parish council in March 1907.

The parish council sent a petition in 1907 to the Board of Education and the Essex County Education Committee, which was signed by the ratepayers of Hadleigh, outlining their objections to the proposed school and requesting a Public Enquiry. The Board of Education refused to comply with their requests and, on 10 October 1910, the new Council School, with accommodation for 220 children, was opened in Church Road. The Salvation Army Colony School closed and Major Samuel Collins became the master of the new Council School. The National School, now referred to as the Church School, was enlarged in 1909 to accommodate 162 children, and continued to educate the children of Hadleigh.

School Life 1901-1909

26. The senior pupils with Sarah Hawks, c.1906

The last few pages of the log book show that very little changed in these years. Alfred Hawks still experienced problems with the parents of the children, writing on 13 May 1904: *"There is still a great deal of indifference among the parents with regard to the Education of their children."*

The children were still prone to infectious diseases, with outbreaks of diphtheria in 1901, mumps in 1902, measles in 1903, a five-month epidemic of whooping cough in 1905 and measles in 1907. Fruit picking also led to absenteeism in the summer as it had always done.

National occasions led to holidays from school, which were welcomed by both staff and children. With the ending of the Boer War, the children were given a half-holiday to celebrate the declaration of peace. Although there was no mention of Queen Victoria's death on 22 January 1901 and her funeral on 2 February, Alfred Hawks recorded on 27 June 1902: *"The School was closed on Thursday and Friday owing to the coronation, which however did not take place owing to the King's illness."* Following the king's recovery from appendicitis, the coronation was held on 9 August 1902, during the school's Summer Vacation.

The teaching staff of the school were still overworked with attendances of over 100 children. On 20 June 1901 Mr. F. Dugard, Her Majesty's Inspector, wrote in the log book: *"The number of children in attendance is for the greater part of the year in excess of that for which teaching assistance is provided."* Sarah Hawks, the master's wife, was the infant mistress until October 1901 when she was *"compelled through illness to resign".* The following week her daughter Kate took charge of the infant class. This now meant that three of Alfred and Sarah's daughters were working at the school – Alice, Minnie and Kate. (Edith was working as a pupil teacher at a school in Suffolk.) Alfred was able to concentrate on the children in the upper Standards, as the first Standard was taught by Minnie Hawks and the second Standard by Una Potter. Una was the 15-year-old daughter of George Wayland Potter, a village grocer and had, until recently, been a pupil at the school.

At the 1904 Inspection the teachers at the school were listed as A. Hawks, A. G. Hawks, K. B. Hawks and M. F. Hawks. However, the inspector was concerned that the master's daughters were not engaged under a written agreement. Minnie Hawks left the school on 30 November 1904: *"on the event of her Wedding and was presented with a very pretty silver jam dish".* Minnie married Edward Thorndycraft, a grocer, at Snodland in Kent.

In September 1905 Miss Reeves was appointed Assistant to the infant class. A few months later, in January 1906, Alfred Hawks reported: *"Miss Andrews commenced her duties."* In *Kelly's Directory* for 1906, Miss Ethel Andrews is listed as the infant mistress, and continued to be listed as such until at least 1917. Ethel Andrews was born in Hertfordshire in 1887 and was probably the daughter of William and Ann Andrews of Ashwell in Hertfordshire. In 1911 she was boarding with Alfred and Mary Ridgwell at The Nook in Rectory Road.

Retirement of Alfred Hawks

Alfred Hawks continued to serve as master of the Church School until 1918, ending a career of forty-three years in the village.. The years of the Great War must have been a worrying time for Alfred Hawks as he watched the young men of Hadleigh, whom he had taught, marching off to war. This included his son Arthur Leslie, who volunteered in 1914 and served in France from 6 March 1915 as a private in the East Surrey regiment, and then as a corporal in the Labour Corps. His other sons also served – Gus in the army and Fred in the navy. As chairman of the parish council, he was involved in the erection of the Hadleigh war memorial. At the dedication ceremony on Sunday 15 October 1922, he would sadly have read the names of his former pupils, including brothers Archie, Sidney and Wilfred Staines, brothers James and Sidney Allen, brothers Richard and William Cowell, brothers Ernest and Reuben Mason, Harold Calverley, Stephen Choppen, John McCormick, Sidney Petchey, Arthur Raison, Henry Snow and Philip White.

Following his retirement, Alfred Hawks remained a prominent member of the community, and was chairman of the parish council. He and his wife Sarah spent their retirement at their home, Holboro House, at 40 Chapel Lane, where they celebrated both their golden and diamond wedding anniversaries.

In 1940, concerned about the possibility of German bombing, Alfred and Sarah Hawks decided to return to their birthplace, Snodland in Kent. It was here, at The Cottage in The Grove, that Alfred died on 14 December 1943 aged ninety. Sarah died in January 1948 aged 91.

27. Alfred and Sarah Hawks, 1925

Hadleigh Church School 1918-24

Following the retirement of Alfred Hawks, Cecil Edward Buck was appointed master of the Church School. Cecil Buck was born on 28 April 1893 at Beccles in Suffolk, the son of a journalist and author, Mark Frederick Buck. At the time of the 1911 Census, he was aged seventeen and working as a pupil teacher in his home village. From the limited service records of the Great War, it appears that a Cecil Edward Buck volunteered on the outbreak of war and served in France from 29 March 1915 in the Oxford and Buckinghamshire Light Infantry. He remained at the Church School until at least 1922, when he is recorded in the *Kelly's Directory* entry for Hadleigh. Cecil Buck died in Suffolk in 1981, aged eighty-eight.

In 1923 the managers of Hadleigh Church School sent a notice of closure to Essex Education Committee. At their meeting, in January 1924, the Committee agreed to accept this notice of closure, with the Bishop of Barking commenting that he understood the school was not in financial difficulties, but that the managers were rather discouraged at the small attendance which was about 50, while the annual cost was £500.

After nearly seventy years, the former Hadleigh National School closed and the children transferred to the Council School in Church Road. The old school building became the parish church hall following the closure of the school. After falling into disrepair, the building was purchased and modernised, and reopened as Sandcastles Nursery in September 2000. So, once again, the children of Hadleigh are being educated in this Victorian school building, which was designed for that purpose over a hundred and fifty years ago.

28. Hadleigh Parish Hall, 1980s

Appendix 1

These instructions for the Annual Inspection and Examination of Schools were copied in the log book on the day of Her Majesty's Inspector's visit on 3 July 1893. The transcript below is written exactly as it was in the log book with abbreviations, capitals, punctuation, etc.

1. *Each scholar should be provided with paper (or slate), Reading Books & Copy Books used during the year.*

2. *Examination papers should show distinctly on each side a name of scholar & name of School & Standard in which presented and a Schedule number in Red ink.*

3. *It is desirable that each scholar should wear a small ticket bearing his or her schedule number.*

4. *Before the arrival of the Inspector a red line should be drawn on the Exam. Sch. through the names of all absentees and a numbered list prepared stating the reason of each scholar's absence duly certified. In complying with rules 4 & 5 on the Exam. Schedule the asterisk and the [entry illegible] should be entered in red ink.*

5. *Scholars to be examined for Certificates & proficiency should sit together in their prospective classes.*

6. *The following particulars should be entered in the Log Book a. no. present (boys & girls separately) b. no. absent no. admitted since end of School year, a proposed piece for Recitation & proposed Class Subjects (1 & 2) and course to be taken in each – also maps for V & VII.*

7. *A brief entry should be made in the class Registers stating reason assigned for the removal of each scholar who has left during the year e.g. Left district. Left Attending-Sch. Reached Standard IV, V, VI. NB To reach a Standard is to pass in Reading, Writing & Arithmetic in that or higher Standard. No child can leave a School unless being betw. 10 & 13 he has reached the Standard prescribed by the Bye Laws of district for total exemption. A child is not legally exempt from School Attendance between 13 & 14 years of age unless he has reached Standard IV or since the age of 5 he has made not less than 250 Attendances each year for five previous years whether consecutive or not in not more than two schools in a year.*

8. *Certificates of Proficiency & Attendance must be given on the prescribed form issued by the Educ. Dep. to the Local Authority and supplied by the [entry illegible] free of charge on the application of the Managers. No other form of Certificate is recognised.*

Select Bibliography

Archive Material

Chelmsford Chronicle, The British Newspaper Archive
Hadleigh National School Log Book 1863-1909, Essex Record Office
Hadleigh Parish Registers, Essex Record Office
Hadleigh Vestry Minutes 1835-1922, Essex Record Office
Thundersley Parish Registers, Essex Record Office

Books

Crockford's Clerical Directory
Hancock, M. and Harvey, S., *Hadleigh An Essex Village*, Phillimore (1986)
Horn, Pamela, *The Victorian and Edwardian Schoolchild*, Alan Sutton Publishing Ltd. (1989)
Jenkins, Jane with Evans, Eric, *Victorian Social Life British Social History 1815-1914*, John Murray (2002)
Maclure, J. Stuart, *Educational Documents England and Wales 1816 to the present day*, 5th ed. Methuen (1986)
Parkhill, Gordon and Cook, Graham, *Hadleigh Salvation Army Farm: A Vision Reborn*, Shield Books (2008)
White, William, *History, Gazetteer and Directory of the County of Essex* (1863)
Yearsley, Ian, *Hadleigh Past*, Phillimore (1998)

Websites

Hadleigh and Thundersley Community Archive, *www.hadleighhistory.org.uk*
Institute of London, University of London, *www.ioe.ac.uk*

Index

References which relate to illustrations only are given in **bold**.